American Cinema of the 1930s

SCREEN

 AMERICAN CULTURE / AMERICAN CINEMA

DECADES

Each volume in the Screen Decades: American Culture/American Cinema series presents a group of original essays analyzing the impact of cultural issues on the cinema and the impact of the cinema in American society. Because every chapter explores a spectrum of particularly significant motion pictures and the broad range of historical events in one year, readers will gain a continuing sense of the decade as it came to be depicted on movie screens across the continent. The integration of historical and cultural events with the sprawling progression of American cinema illuminates the pervasive themes and the essential movies that define an era. Our series represents one among many possible ways of confronting the past; we hope that these books will offer a better understanding of the connections between American culture and film history.

LESTER D. FRIEDMAN AND MURRAY POMERANCE
SERIES EDITORS

Ina Rae Hark, editor, *American Cinema of the 1930s: Themes and Variations*

Wheeler Winston Dixon, editor, *American Cinema of the 1940s: Themes and Variations*

Murray Pomerance, editor, *American Cinema of the 1950s: Themes and Variations*

Lester D. Friedman, editor, *American Cinema of the 1970s: Themes and Variations*

Stephen Prince, editor, *American Cinema of the 1980s: Themes and Variations*

American Cinema of the
1930s
Themes and Variations

EDITED BY

INA RAE HARK

RUTGERS UNIVERSITY PRESS

NEW BRUNSWICK, NEW JERSEY AND LONDON

LIBRARY OF CONGRESS CATALOGING-IN-PUBLICATION DATA

American cinema of the 1930s : themes and variations / edited by Ina Rae Hark.
    p.   cm. — (Screen decades)
  Includes bibliographical references and index.
  ISBN–13:   978–0–8135–4081–8   (hbk. : alk. paper)
  ISBN–13:   978–0–8135–4082–5   (pbk. : alk. paper)
  1. Motion pictures—United States—History.   I. Hark, Ina Rae.
  PN1993.5.U6A85735   2007
  791.430973′09043—dc22

                                                              2006032344

A British Cataloging-in-Publication record for this book is available from the British Library.

Visit our Web site: http://rutgerspress.rutgers.edu

Manufactured in the United States of America

To . . . Shirley
Errol and Olivia
Nelson and Jeanette
Cary, Victor, Douglas, and Sam
Judy, Ray, Bert, Jack . . . and Toto, too
Bashful, Doc, Dopey, Grumpy, Happy, Sleepy, and
Sneezy
. . . who inhabit my earliest memories of 1930s cinema

CONTENTS

ACKNOWLEDGMENTS

I suppose my involvement with this book would never have happened had it not been for the program directors of my local television stations in Charleston, West Virginia, in the 1950s who filled up their afternoons and weekends with movie packages consisting mostly of films from the 1930s. My earliest impressions of what real movies looked like started then, so I give a nod of appreciation to WCHS and WSAZ.

The volume itself would not have been possible without the hard work and gifted insights of its contributors: Aaron, Cynthia, Marty, Charlene, Susan, Allen, Sam, and Chuck. I thank you for your cooperation, professionalism, and good humor during all the stages of writing and revision. To the editors for this series, the terrific trio of Murray, Les, and RUP's Leslie Mitchner, thanks for always being engaged, responsive, and supportive from the moment you asked me to edit the volume until its final stages of production. The book would not look as handsome or as professional as it does without the great work of copyeditor Eric Schramm and all the vendors from whom the other authors and I obtained photos. Special thanks to Ron Mandelbaum, Victor Burgos, Cory Plowman, and Doug McKeown at Photofest. Invaluable assistance at the proofreading and indexing phases came from the English Department at the University of South Carolina and graduate student Andy Smith.

As with nearly every scholarly project I have undertaken since graduate school, this book has benefited immensely from the encyclopedic memory, analytical intelligence, and listening ear of Steven Cohan. He has been especially helpful during my work on *American Cinema of the 1930s,* from brainstorming about possible contributors to reading the first draft of my own chapter to lending me a great Astaire-Rogers photo. Most of all, whenever I would get tunnel vision and turn the decade into one endless parade of Warner Bros.' gangsters and swashbucklers, he would always remind me of the centrality of MGM, melodrama, and musicals.

Ina Rae Hark
Columbia, S.C.
15 September 2006

T I M E L I N E
The 1930s

1930

12 MARCH — Mohandas K. Gandhi begins his Salt March to protest British monopoly of and tax on salt in India.

24 MARCH — Pluto, newly discovered and designated as a planet, is given its official name.

31 MAY — The Production Code is drafted by the MPPDA's Hays Office.

14 SEPTEMBER — The Nazis win 107 seats in Germany's *Reichstag* (Parliament).

5 NOVEMBER — The Nobel Prize for literature is awarded to Sinclair Lewis, the first American recipient.

22 NOVEMBER — Elijah Muhammad forms the Nation of Islam in Detroit.

1931

3 MARCH — "The Star-Spangled Banner" becomes the national anthem.

1 MAY — The Empire State Building is completed.

18 SEPTEMBER — Japan invades Manchuria.

17 OCTOBER — Al Capone is convicted of income tax evasion.

20 OCTOBER — *Variety* reports "the end of silent pictures."

1932

1 MARCH — Charles Lindbergh's baby son is kidnapped.

28 JULY — The military is brought in to remove the protesters of the "Bonus Army" from government property in Washington, D.C.

30 JULY — *Flowers and Trees,* the first cartoon to use the new three-color Technicolor process, debuts.

1 OCTOBER — Oswald Mosley forms the British Union of Fascists.

8 NOVEMBER — Franklin Delano Roosevelt is elected the thirty-second president.

27 DECEMBER — Radio City Music Hall opens in New York.

1933

30 JANUARY — Adolf Hitler becomes chancellor of Germany.

3 MARCH — Mount Rushmore is dedicated.

9 MARCH   FDR launches the New Deal by calling Congress into a special
             100-day session.

7 APRIL   Prohibition ends.

6 JUNE   The first drive-in movie theater opens in Camden, New Jersey.

16 JUNE   The National Industrial Recovery Act, which will spawn the
             National Recovery Administration, is authorized.

30 JUNE   The Screen Actors Guild incorporates.

1934

MAY   Great Dustbowl storm.

18 MAY   The Academy Award is first called "Oscar" in print.

23 MAY   Bonnie Parker and Clyde Barrow are killed in a police ambush.

13 JUNE   The Production Code Administration is established.

2 AUGUST   Germany's President Hindenburg dies, paving the way for Hitler
             to become sole Führer of the nation.

16 OCTOBER   Mao Zedong and his communist followers begin their Long
             March to avoid defeat by the armies of Chiang Kai-shek.

1 DECEMBER   S. M. Kirov is assassinated in Leningrad; Stalin uses the event as
             an excuse to begin two years of purges and show trials of
             political rivals.

1935

27 MAY   The Supreme Court declares the NRA unconstitutional.

31 MAY   Twentieth Century Pictures merges with Fox Film Corporation,
             creating Twentieth Century Fox.

13 JUNE   *Becky Sharp,* the first feature-length film using an improved
             three-strip Technicolor process, premieres.

15 AUGUST   Record-setting aviator Wiley Post and his friend Will Rogers die
             in a plane crash in Alaska.

15 SEPTEMBER The Nuremberg Laws deprive German Jews of citizenship and
             the swastika becomes the official symbol of Nazi Germany.

3 OCTOBER   Italy invades Abyssinia (Ethiopia).

1936

30 JUNE   Margaret Mitchell's novel *Gone with the Wind* is published.

18 JULY   The Spanish Civil War begins.

1–16 AUGUST The Berlin Olympics are dominated by African American track
             star Jesse Owens.

14 SEPTEMBER   MGM's boy wonder producer Irving Thalberg dies at age thirty-seven.

3 NOVEMBER   FDR wins a landslide reelection victory over Alfred M. Landon.

10 DECEMBER   King Edward VIII of Great Britain abdicates to marry American divorcée Wallis Warfield Simpson, "the woman I love."

1937

6 MAY   The *Hindenburg* explodes over New Jersey before live newsreel cameras and radio microphones.

9 MAY   The Screen Actors Guild is recognized by studios as the official union for performers in films and is allowed to enter into labor negotiations on their behalf.

28 MAY   The Golden Gate Bridge opens.

2 JULY   Amelia Earhart disappears over the Pacific Ocean.

13 AUGUST   The Japanese attack Shanghai, starting war with China.

21 DECEMBER   The first feature-length animated film, Disney's *Snow White and the Seven Dwarfs*, opens.

1938

12 MARCH   Hitler annexes Austria.

22 JUNE   Joe Louis KOs Max Schmeling.

30 SEPTEMBER   The Munich Pact cedes Sudetenland to Germany.

30 OCTOBER   Radio broadcast of Orson Welles's "The War of the Worlds" causes panic.

1 NOVEMBER   Seabiscuit beats War Admiral in a match race at Pimlico.

9 NOVEMBER   The Night of Broken Glass (*Kristallnacht*): Nazis attack homes and businesses of German Jews.

1939

9 APRIL   Marian Anderson sings before 75,000 at the Lincoln Memorial.

30 APRIL   Television in the United States makes its formal debut at the World's Fair in New York City.

4 JULY   Lou Gehrig delivers his famous retirement speech in Yankee Stadium.

23 AUGUST   The German-Soviet Non-Aggression Pact is signed.

1 SEPTEMBER   Germany invades Poland; World War II begins.

5 SEPTEMBER   FDR declares U.S. neutrality.

American Cinema of the 1930s

Irene Dunne gets the upper hand on a usually-not-so-rumpled Cary Grant in this publicity still for one of the decade's signature screwball comedies, *The Awful Truth* (Leo McCarey, Columbia, 1937). Collection Ina Rae Hark.

INTRODUCTION

Movies and the 1930s

INA RAE HARK

■■■■■■■■ **A Decade of Dislocations and Transformations**

In perhaps no other decade did the Hollywood film industry and its product look so different at its conclusion as compared to its beginning. In 1930, the industry had not totally solved the problems that came along with the transition to talking pictures. Hollywood was still negotiating content standards that would appease critics in the heartland and yet enable the production of movies that sold in the big cities. Whether the industry could survive the economic effects of the stock market crash was up in the air. By the end of the decade, however, in what has been called "Hollywood's Greatest Year," spectacular films that used both color and sound had established themselves as American icons. The major studios had consolidated their power as a mature oligopoly—a term economists use to describe an alliance of certain businesses in the same field who grant each other reciprocal benefits in order to monopolize trade—vertically integrating production, distribution, and exhibition of films. They had weathered the Depression, the establishment and enforcement of the Production Code, and labor actions and unionization among the creative ranks to become a well-oiled industrial powerhouse.

The chapters in this volume are linked by several common threads. First, the availability of sound and the voices of performers drove many changes. The musical became an important genre for the first time. Many of the stars to emerge during the decade had very distinctive voices: comedians like Mae West and W. C. Fields with their peculiar comic inflections; the foreign-accented exoticism of everyone from Greta Garbo to Bela Lugosi; the instantly imitable vocal rhythms of Katharine Hepburn, Cary Grant, James Stewart, or James Cagney.

Secondly, the reality of film audiences was characterized particularly by sudden and unexpected shifts of fortune. An American head of household could be a plutocrat one day, a pauper the next. A comfortably bourgeois

German Jewish family could suddenly have to flee for its very survival. Governments changed from democracies to dictatorships overnight. Independent nations found themselves "annexed" by invaders. It is no surprise, then, that such radical transformations into a totally altered existence became a common theme during the decade. Among the characters we meet in films discussed in this book are a midwestern farm girl who, having survived a cyclone, opens her front door onto a brightly colored landscape full of strange, magical beings; a seventeenth-century Irish physician who finds himself convicted of treason and sold into slavery; and an heiress who ends up among the *hoi poloi,* riding a bus, then hitchhiking and sleeping in a field.

However, the films of the era confronted these transformations obliquely, so that the concerns fueled by the rise of fascism or fears of economic dislocation were transported to other climes and other eras more often than anchored in a contemporary setting. The thirties were years of considerable fear and uncertainty, which Hollywood displaced but did not ignore. There was an equal measure of transgressive desire and normative pressure, sympathy for the marginalized and respect for hegemonic authority, all of which affected film narratives, characterization, and genre construction. Viewing thirties films provides a sense of hybridity, sepia-toned Kansas in a parallel universe with Technicolor Oz.

The World beyond the Screen

The decade commenced a little more than two months after Black Tuesday, the stock market crash of 29 October 1929, and concluded four months after the initial declaration of hostilities in World War II. From the start it occupied two complementary historical movements. On the one hand was the struggle for nations to emerge from crippling economic chaos. In the United States the collapse of the stock market and the failure of many banks and the businesses they financed were accompanied by severe droughts in a heartland that had been farmed recklessly, the eroded soil turning cropland into nothing but swirling windstorms full of desiccated earth—the Dust Bowl. A turning point came when the ineffective efforts of the Hoover administration to stabilize the economy and relieve the suffering of those suddenly thrust into poverty were rejected at the polls in November 1932. A particularly dark moment had occurred in the summer of that year when the president sent federal troops to disperse the "Bonus Army" camped around Washington, D.C. These were veterans of World War I who were demanding that a stipend due to be issued to them in 1945 be disbursed earlier in order to relieve their present dire financial straits. (Ironically, several officers who would be heroes in the next war led the charge against their fellow soldiers: Douglas MacArthur, Dwight Eisenhower, and George Patton.)

The election of Franklin Delano Roosevelt revived the nation's hopes, changing their tune from "Brother, Can You Spare a Dime?" to "Happy Days Are Here Again." During the first years of his administration, FDR implemented the famed programs of his New Deal. Some, like the Civilian Conservation Corps and the Federal Theater Project, did not continue once conditions improved. The National Recovery Administration (NRA), a "voluntary" system of standards negotiated with the federal government to which businesses were to adhere, was ruled unconstitutional two years after its creation. Yet other New Deal programs that were designed to improve federal regulation of the economy and support citizens in time of need are still with us: Social Security, the Securities and Exchange Commission, the Federal Deposit Insurance Commission, the Federal Communications Commission, the minimum wage, food stamps, and unemployment insurance.

As the world waited for the Depression to end, people wondered when the next global war would begin. Treaties and alliances were being made and broken constantly; governments formed and fell apart with the same regularity. Attempts at democratizing former autocratic European monarchies had not been very successful, and two more extreme political models were competing for power given the openings provided by the international economic meltdown. On the right was the idea of centralized state control, even at the expense of individual rights. In Italy, Mussolini's fascists had "made the trains run on time," and this efficiency would appeal to great numbers of distressed populations. The most ominous fascist success came with the ascendancy of Adolf Hitler and his Nazi Party in Germany during 1933 and 1934. On the left was the example of the Bolshevik Revolution in Russia, whose promises of a Communist workers paradise still appealed to many despite the increasing authoritarian brutality of the Soviet regime under Josef Stalin. In the established democracies, fears of labor unrest and socialist takeover tended to dominate, making them unwilling to confront the fascist threat as it grew; in several countries, distrust of leftist political groups led to right-wing regimes being established in response. Protected by two oceans, American leaders were much more wary of the importation of communist ideology than the imposition of fascist rule from overseas. It would take events that occurred beyond the thirties finally to shake the United States from its isolationist position.

The Spanish Civil War of 1936–1939 played out this conflict, with a leftist "Popular Front" elected government (the Republicans) challenged and eventually overthrown by a Nationalist Coalition led by right-wing general Francisco Franco, despite the influx of International Brigades of eager socialists from throughout the world to fight on the Republican side. Widely viewed as a rehearsal for the international conflict that was destined to follow, the war in Spain continued the impression that this conflict would be between left and right. When Hitler and Stalin signed a non-aggression pact on 23 August 1939, one that announced their intention to partition Europe between them, a stunned world learned that the real conflict would be between democracy and totalitarianism, as Germany soon demonstrated when it invaded Poland eight days later. The democracies had not forcefully opposed previous territorial incursions throughout the decade—Italy's annexation of Abyssinia, Japan's occupation of Manchuria, Hitler's grab of Sudetenland from Czechoslovakia and the *Anschluss* into Austria—but now they realized that they were not safe within their borders. For the second time in two decades the world was at war.

For all the grimness that characterized the thirties, popular culture flourished: not only Hollywood films, but everything from swing music to sports to popular fiction to the comics. *Billboard* established its "hit parade" and baseball opened its Hall of Fame in Cooperstown, New York. Nancy Drew and Dick Tracy began fighting crime in very different neighborhoods. Technological innovations were evident as well. Of particular relevance to the movie business was the invention of air conditioning: motion picture theaters were among the first businesses to invest in the new cooling systems, an added enticement to audiences during the summer months. Television made a splash when RCA produced a broadcast from the grounds of the New York World's Fair in 1939. By that time there were already several local stations on the air, but the new medium would not begin to flourish until after the war. This was also the case with another visual innovation, the drive-in theater; the first began operating in Camden, New Jersey, in 1933.

The repeal of Prohibition in that very same year paved the way for more widespread imbibing, but the establishment of Alcoholics Anonymous and the invention of Alka Seltzer in subsequent years may have been necessitated by the increase in tippling. Other American fixtures first invented or established in the decade include ball point pens, laundromats, Scotch Tape, Scrabble, Monopoly, instant coffee, Zippo lighters, night baseball, Teflon, nylon, red and green traffic lights, Hostess Twinkies, cheeseburgers, nudist colonies, parking meters, and paperback books; each of these could have been declared "the best thing since sliced bread," which was first sold in 1930.

Because of the trying times that were never totally out of mind, however, many significant aspects of 1930s American culture were freighted with metaphorical meaning beyond winning, losing, and entertaining. People needed heroes, which motivated Jerry Siegel and Joe Schuster to spend four years creating and developing the first great comic book fighter for "truth, justice, and the American way"; Superman debuted in DC Comics' June 1938 issue. Sports also was prominent in offering messages of hope. The scrawny, underdog racehorse everyone had given up on, Seabiscuit, became a symbol for every forgotten man or woman felled by the Depression. His defeat of elite thoroughbred War Admiral on 1 November 1938 was seen as one of the populist triumphs of the decade (see Hillenbrand). That same year, Joe Louis's defeat of German heavyweight Max Schmeling was taken as a harbinger for the eventual defeat of Hitler's racist and expansionist goals. The first chapter in that story had been told two years earlier at the Olympic Games in Berlin, when the Nazis' intention to demonstrate Aryan athletic supremacy was derailed by the multiple medals earned by African American competitors, particularly the five golds won by Jesse Owens, whose hand Hitler petulantly refused to shake.

That heroism could be clouded by tragedy as well as triumph was also a strong lesson of the decade's events. It was the greatest era for stretching the bounds of aviation via individual heroics, with new feats and new records occurring every year. Amelia Earhart became the first woman to fly the Atlantic in the very same year in which her male predecessor, Charles Lindbergh, lost his young son to kidnapping and murder. Earhart herself would vanish over the South Pacific in 1937, her fate still a mystery. Record-setting pilot Wiley Post also died while flying, going down in 1935 with the beloved humorist and star of stage, radio, and film, Will Rogers, as his passenger. Probably no tragedy resonated with Americans more than that of New York Yankees' slugger Lou Gehrig. Baseball's original "Iron Man" (for having played in over 2,000 consecutive games) and a member of the legendary "Bronx Bombers" that dominated the sport from the late twenties through the late thirties, Gehrig was struck out by amyotrophic lateral sclerosis, whose popular designation still bears his name. His gracious and heart-breaking farewell to a packed Yankee Stadium on Independence Day in 1939 seemed to sum up for the country its own feelings of steadfastness in enduring hardship and suffering; each American could identify with Gehrig's ironic self-characterization as "the luckiest man on the face of the earth."

■■■■■■■■■ **The Studios: From Years of Turmoil**
to Hollywood's Greatest Year

The Depression snuck up on the American movie business. The year following the crash, 1930, saw theater ticket sales at an all-time high. But the three years that followed reversed that trend. Admissions and profits plummeted, theaters closed, and RKO, Paramount, Fox, and Universal studios ended up in receivership by 1933. As Tino Balio explains, the boom to build more and bigger movie palaces in the late twenties turned "the so-called deluxe theaters, built in flush times and at recklessly extravagant costs [into] white elephants, at least for the duration of the Depression. In short, the major companies could not meet their fixed cost obligations, which simply meant they did not have the cash to pay their mortgage commitments, short-term obligations, and the heavy charges on their funded debts" (16). Financial control and management of the studios as a result reverted to financiers and moneymen in the East, but creative decisions would remain with the studio executives in Hollywood, among them legendary names like Jack L. Warner, Darryl F. Zanuck, Louis B. Mayer, Irving Thalberg, David O. Selznick, Harry Cohn, and Walt Disney.

Movie attendance revenues did not keep spiraling down for long, however. The box office slump bottomed out in 1933, but the exhibition sector of the industry had to make a few adjustments along the way. Ticket prices were reduced, and various stratagems adopted to entice audiences with the prospect of getting more for their money: double features, giveaways, and contests such as "Dish Night," "Screeno," and "Bank Night." The A-picture or feature film became just one part of a comprehensive entertainment package. Various short subjects were added to the program, inspiring more and better newsreel coverage and a boom in animated sound films. Such cartoon icons as Betty Boop, Bugs Bunny, Popeye the Sailor Man, Donald Duck, and Daffy Duck made their debuts during the decade. The need for second features on double-bills gave opportunities for small studios like Republic and Monogram to find their niche in churning out inexpensive serials, since even the busy B-film units of the majors could not keep up with the demand for product. Film series also became useful with the double-billing strategy. The majors gave audiences long-running adventures of sleuths like Philo Vance and Charlie Chan, the medical crises of Dr. Kildare, and, rising to the A-picture level, the Thin Man series, featuring socialite sleuths Nick and Nora Charles (William Powell and Myrna Loy) and their terrier Asta, as well as the Andy Hardy series, starring Mickey Rooney as Andy and Lewis Stone as his wise patriarch, Judge Hardy.

Concession sales also became a vital component of keeping theaters afloat. As Robert Sklar points out, "In hard times they discovered that candy machines returned a 45 percent profit on gross sales and that popcorn, which had heretofore been synonymous with a cheap show, could earn profits three or four times its cost. Food and drink sales became for many theaters the difference between making money or closing their doors" (*Movie-Made* 169).

In addition to the economic crisis, Hollywood had to deal with two other long-running problems. The first concerned the increasing public outcry against what were perceived to be the moral deficiencies of motion picture content. The second concerned labor-management issues between the studios and their employees, and the federal government's attempts to regulate industry salaries and business practices.

From the movies' inception, certain guardians of morality had viewed them with suspicion. Studies had been commissioned to document scientifically their baleful influence, especially on the young. Scandals involving the offscreen behavior of actors and other creative personnel reinforced distrust of cosmopolitan urbanism by those living in the nation's heartland, some of it having ugly origins in nativist Protestant bigotry against the primarily Jewish immigrants who dominated the industry's leadership. (One organization favoring strict movie censorship identified its membership as "Patriotic Gentile Americans" [Sklar, *Movie-Made* 124].) Always fearful of government restrictions, the industry itself, through the Motion Picture Producers and Distributors of America (MPPDA), set up a self-censorship mechanism presided over by former postmaster Will Hays. In 1930, the Hays Office drew up a recipe for ensuring moral content in Hollywood films, called the Production Code. The studios signed on to this document, but they were likely to pay only lip service to it if more violence and sexual innuendo were found to be the antidote to declining revenues. After several years of conflict over film content that the adoption of the Code had not resolved, the Hays Office in 1934 created a mechanism for actually enforcing Code provisions, the Production Code Administration (PCA) under the direction of Joseph Breen (see Maltby, "Production Code"). This enforcement created enough of a change in what Hollywood movies could represent that it has become a commonplace to refer to films of the thirties as pre-Code or post-Code. In fact, violence and sex were not so much displaced as disguised: the Code inspired narrative tactics that soon became legible to most audiences, such as a fade-out after two lovers kiss indicating an unrepresented sexual encounter.

Just as it preferred to handle censorship and content regulation in-house, so Hollywood believed in rewriting labor-management conflicts into disagreements between over-indulged serfs and their benevolent feudal lords, the studio bosses. The standard seven-year studio contract robbed talent of any rights or control over their own careers, requiring them to work on whatever projects the studio dictated, including being "loaned out" to other studios. If they refused, they were suspended without pay and without any ability to find work elsewhere. When the Roosevelt administration implemented the National Recovery Act, it intruded upon these private fiefdoms. As Danae Clark writes in her case study of actors' labor in 1933:

> Will Hays's assertion that Hollywood provided the best wages and working conditions in the world was challenged by nearly every industrial labor group during the NRA period. Thousands of discontented workers staged or threatened strikes, and studio executives were confronted with numerous demands for union recognition under the collective bargaining provisions of the NRA Code. . . . Though the Roosevelt administration had sided with the major producers on issues of trade, its decisions regarding employment practices sided with labor. The open-shop policy was condemned, better working conditions were outlined in specific detail, and, on the eve of the Code's ratification, special allowances were awarded to the industry's creative workers. (69)

Unfortunately for those workers, the NRA Code was declared unconstitutional in 1935. Despite the formation of the Writers Guild of America and the Screen Actors Guild in 1933 and the Screen Directors' Guild (now Directors Guild of America) in 1936, real labor reform in Hollywood would have to wait for court decisions in the next decade. As for federal concerns, an antitrust suit filed against the studios in 1938 would lead a decade later to a fundamental restructuring of the vertically integrated industry.

Given the turbulent times, Hollywood could not ignore stark socioeconomic and political realities, but given its own peculiar concerns as an industry, it rarely tackled them head on. Nick Roddick borrowed the term "Burbanking" from critic Abel Greene to describe the way that even the supposedly more socially conscious films produced in Warner Bros.' Burbank studios inevitably pulled their punches. To "Burbank" was to use melodramatized narratives to turn "an examination of a social problem into an affirmation of the values which had produced it" (252). Probably no better summation of the relationship of 1930s films to 1930s history has ever been given than this one written more than thirty years ago by Andrew Bergman, who proved his industry savvy by going on to become a successful Hollywood screenwriter and director:

What happens in depression movies is that traditional beliefs in the possibilities of individual success are kept alive in the early thirties under various guises, that scapegoats for social dislocation are found and that federal benevolence becomes an implicit and ultimately dead-ended premise by the end of the decade. Hollywood would help the nation's fundamental institutions escape unscathed by attempting to keep alive the myth and wonderful fantasy of a mobile and classless society, by focusing on the endless possibilities for individual success, by turning social evil into personal evil and making the New Deal into a veritable leading man. (xvi)

Nevertheless, if the American film industry pulled a lot of punches in confronting the multiple ills of the thirties, it also redefined the cinema with sound and color and produced polished entertainments that still compare favorably with the output of decades far more technologically advanced.

Indeed, as an indication of the depth and quality of films of the thirties, the contributors to this volume closely examine sixty works of lasting importance and still have no room for such classics as *All Quiet on the Western Front* (1930), *Hell's Angels* (1930), *Min and Bill* (1930), *The Champ* (1931), *Little Caesar* (1931), *Grand Hotel* (1932), *Back Street* (1932), *Red Dust* (1932), *I Am a Fugitive from a Chain Gang* (1932), *Dinner at Eight* (1933), *Of Human Bondage* (1934), *The Thin Man* (1934), *The Scarlet Empress* (1934), *The Informer* (1935), *Top Hat* (1935), *David Copperfield* (1935), *The Bride of Frankenstein* (1935), *San Francisco* (1936), *The Great Ziegfeld* (1936), *Mr. Deeds Goes to Town* (1936), *The Life of Emile Zola* (1937), *Captains Courageous* (1937), *Snow White and the Seven Dwarfs* (1937), *The Awful Truth* (1937), *The Good Earth* (1937), *The Prisoner of Zenda* (1937), *Boys Town* (1938), *Dark Victory* (1939), *The Women* (1939), *Gunga Din* (1939), and *Wuthering Heights* (1939), just to name a few.

During the decade itself, the film industry staked its reputation, if not the entirety of its profits, on a class of films called "prestige pictures." Usually based on works of literature or history and biography, these films inhabited other places and other times, had lavish production values, and attempted to establish an aura of films as fine art and conveyers of moral uplift. They dominated the offerings at the big, urban, first-run picture palaces that each of the majors owned. Often winning the trifecta of industry awards, critical praise, and healthy box office, many of these films, like *Anna Karenina* (1935) or *The Story of Louis Pasteur* (1935), seem stuffy and overwrought years later. Still maintaining their vast entertainment value, however, are the best of the genres that the thirties created or innovated.

▬▬▬▬▬▬ Singing and Dancing, Laughing and Crying

Although some of the genres that predominated in this decade were not new, the remaking of silents into talkies resulted in a sort of *de novo* creation. Musicals could not exist without music and silent comedy could not make use of witty dialogue, dialect humor, or sound effects. The first sound feature, *The Jazz Singer* (1927), had been a musical, and a plethora of other musicals poured out of studios converting to the new technology. This initial glut caused the production of musicals to taper off in the early thirties, but the genre had a huge revival in 1933, driven mostly by three backstage musicals from Warner Bros. (*42nd Street, Footlight Parade,* and *Gold Diggers of 1933*) with dazzling ensemble choreography by Busby Berkeley. *Gold Diggers* would become an annual franchise for Warner. MGM countered with its own backstage musical franchise, the *Broadway Melody* films of 1936 and 1938. Paramount came up with the idea of using radio performers for a different kind of backstage musical with *The Big Broadcast* in 1932, and then revived the franchise for other *Big Broadcasts* of 1936, 1937, and 1938.

When one thinks of musical stars of the decade, two famous pairings particularly come to mind. First and foremost, of course, were the ineffable dance and song romances of Fred Astaire and Ginger Rogers, inaugurated by *Flying Down to Rio* in 1933. Less remembered now are the series of European operettas produced at MGM, directed by W. S. Van Dyke, and starring Jeanette MacDonald and Nelson Eddy. This was a territory often featured in musicals starring Maurice Chevalier. Hollywood also used the genre to feature its young performers: many of Shirley Temple's early films at Fox have song and dance numbers, MGM made *Babes in Arms* (1939) with Judy Garland and Mickey Rooney putting on a show, and Universal in 1936 began a series of films built around teenager Deanna Durbin's impressive singing voice. Finally, music and song played an integral part in the animated films of the decade.

Charlie Chaplin maintained his silent career throughout the decade, adding in music and sound effects to *City Lights* (1931) and *Modern Times* (1936) but not speaking a word of intelligible dialogue himself until *The Great Dictator* in 1940. No other comedian had the international appeal to carry this off, however, and the new film comics of the sound era, while continuing to deploy kinetic and supple bodies in physical comedy, added jokes, fractured logic, and notable inflections to their comic arsenals. No one had more of these weapons than the Marx Brothers. Harpo retained the best of the silent tradition with his antics, Groucho spat out wordplay and non-sequitur with the staccato bursts of a gangster's tommy gun, and Chico fractured both sense and pronunciation with his dialect humor. Joining them in showing up absurd social conventions and overturning traditional pieties were Mae West, Eddie Cantor, W. C. Fields, and the duo of Stan Laurel and Oliver Hardy.

Post-Code and post-New Deal, these "Anarcho-nihilist laff riots," as Bergman calls them, lost touch with the times and were superseded by the other main thirties innovation of the genre, screwball comedy. Notable titles include *It Happened One Night* (1934), *My Man Godfrey* (1936), *The Awful Truth, Easy Living,* and *Topper* (all 1937), *Bringing Up Baby* (1938), and *Midnight* (1939). Sklar declares that they

> were the last refuge of the satire, self-mockery and sexual candor of early 1930s filmmaking, but their iconoclasm was used, overtly at least, to support the status quo. They belonged firmly to the tradition of romantic comedies whose purpose was to show how imagination, curiosity and cleverness— those dangerous levers of social change—could be channeled into support of things as they are. The screwball comedies by and large celebrated the sanctity of marriage, class distinction and the domination of women by men.
> (*Movie-Made* 188)

In these films, there were still zany, madcap people who didn't play by the rules—indeed, they insisted "how attractive it was to be a person who liked to have fun" (Sklar, *Movie-Made* 188)—but the films' narratives sutured social schisms rather than creating them. Bergman notes, "Their 'whackiness' cemented social classes and broken marriages; personal relations were smoothed and social discontent quieted. If early thirties comedy was explosive, screwball comedy was implosive: it worked to pull things together" (133–34).

The silent genre that required the least manipulation to adapt to sound was the melodrama, from whose nineteenth-century stage tradition so many of the narratives of early cinema sprang. In the thirties, melodrama was embraced particularly in conjunction with the studios' belief that women were the decision makers when it came to movie attendance. Their belief must also have been that women were drawn to sagas of renunciation and suffering, since popular forms of the women's picture involved the degradation of "fallen women," mistresses who give up their man rather than shatter even the most hollow of loveless marriages (usually for the sake of the children), and "maternal melodramas" in which women give up everything for the sake of their own (often illegitimate) children. From *Back Street* (1932) to *Imitation of Life* (1934) to *Camille* (1936) to *Stella Dallas* (1937) to *The Old Maid* (1939), female stars as formidable in other genres as

Irene Dunne, Claudette Colbert, Greta Garbo, Barbara Stanwyck, and Bette Davis had to take their obligatory turns through the wringer of masochistically enjoyed self-abnegation.

Gangsters, Shysters, and Monsters—Oh My!

Other notable thirties genres owed their innovations to the instability of the times. Three of these predominated, especially in the pre-Code and pre–New Deal years. The failure of honest hard work and prudent investment to guarantee financial security resulted in the explosion onto the scene of gangster films. Already well established in 1930, the genre produced three major classics in 1931 and 1932. Warner Bros.' *Little Caesar* and *The Public Enemy* (1931) made screen icons of Edward G. Robinson and James Cagney, while director Howard Hawks used future Warner star Paul Muni in a dark psychological portrayal of a fictionalized Al Capone in *Scarface* (1932) from maverick independent producer Howard Hughes. The gangster was a violent individualist who liberated the Horatio Alger dream from its moral underpinnings. Although the gangster's inevitable fall and violent death were meant to remind audiences of those underpinnings, the charismatic attraction of this bad man was hardly obliterated by the belated return to traditional pieties. At most, his fate would strengthen the identification audiences had with those who, like themselves, had worked hard to achieve something only to have it capriciously ripped away by the Depression. Because of the obvious appeal of Rico Bandello, Tom Powers, and Tony Camonte, the forces of moral uplift were especially vociferous about the necessity of reining in the production of further films in this vein, and the Code pretty much killed the genre in its raw, classical form. Eventually crime films came back with a shift to the perspective of either those fighting the criminals (*G-Men* [1935], *Bullets or Ballots* [1936]), or criminals seeking to reform or redeem themselves by sacrificing for the greater good (*Manhattan Melodrama* [1934], *A Slight Case of Murder* [1938], *Angels with Dirty Faces* [1938]).

A more transient genre comprised movies "that concerned themselves with corrupt and racy people who lived and worked in the city. These 'shyster' films—centering around the activities of lawyers, politicians, and newspapermen—were similar to the gang films in that they also assigned a feckless role to the law. Unlike the gang films, their protagonists were given no tragic dimensions" (Bergman 18). With *The Front Page* (1931) as its best remembered example, the shyster film did share another aspect with the gangster movie: the protagonists who were ostensibly being condemned

The Dead End Kids (left to right: Bernard Punsly, Bobby Jordan, Billy Halop, Leo Gorcey, Huntz Hall, and Gabriel Dell) are in danger of following Rocky Sullivan (James Cagney, center) into a dark life of crime until he agrees to play "yellow" when going to the electric chair. Lobby card from *Angels with Dirty Faces* (Michael Curtiz, Warner Bros., 1938). Photofest New York.

proved most appealing to audiences well prepared to see someone slick and clever enough to beat the system.

The early thirties were of course a time of uncertainty and fear, the "fear itself" that FDR identified as the main obstacle to dealing with the Depression in his first inaugural address. The Big Bad Wolf knocking at the door of the Three Little Pigs in the 1933 Disney cartoon was immediately seen as a metaphor of Depression hardships. If the terror of the times could easily become the monster at the door, it is no surprise that another genre that flourished at the beginning of the decade was the horror film. A genre perfected in the silent era in Germany, it would benefit from the experience with expressionist techniques brought over by those many German artists who would flee the Nazis—though its initial Hollywood classics appeared prior to Hitler's ascendancy.

Released the same year (1931) as Paramount's version of *Dr. Jekyll and Mr. Hyde, Dracula,* directed by Tod Browning, and *Frankenstein*, directed by James Whale, established franchises for Universal Pictures, which had produced two of the more memorable movie grotesques in the silent era, Lon Chaney's *Phantom of the Opera* and *Hunchback of Notre Dame*. What Warner was to gangsters, Universal was to monsters. Having made indelible icons of Bela Lugosi and Boris Karloff, Browning and Whale would add to their horror resumes with *Freaks* (1932) and *The Invisible Man* and *The Bride of Frankenstein* (1933 and 1935). Other Universal directors would add to its monster roster *The Mummy* (Karloff) and *The Wolf Man* (Lon Chaney Jr.). Probably the most iconic thirties monster of all, however, came to life at RKO: 1933's *King Kong*. The giant ape who fought off warplanes high above Manhattan but succumbed to his love for an unattainable beauty most clearly epitomizes the monster as both menace and victim, attracting audience sympathy for what is supposed to embody their fears, just as was the case with the gangster. Even the Universal ghouls often had good cause for the damage they wreaked on hapless innocents.

Stars and Directors

If sound and color necessitated the reinvention of film genres, they also necessitated the re-creation of the movie star. Very different talents and attributes were required of the actor who spoke and moved through more naturalistic mises en scènes. The thirties were still to some extent an experiment on what constituted star quality, and probably no decade produced more diverse leading men and women. The most star-studded studio, MGM (with its motto "more stars than there are in the heavens"), made features headlined by Wallace Beery, Mickey Rooney, Clark Gable, Norma Shearer, Marie Dressler, Greta Garbo, and Jean Harlow. The studio contract system also allowed for repeated pairings of players who "clicked," as well as the ability to try performers out in a wide variety of roles and genres in order to find their niche.

In the thirties, more than in any subsequent decade, being singular and eccentric rather than adhering to a normative standard was no barrier to success. There were of course many a classic beauty and handsome hero to be seen, but lots of the memorable stars of the era had some distinctive quality that made them stand out. As noted above, instantly recognizable speech patterns and inflections characterized stars from Stewart and Cagney to Fields and West to Hepburn and Harlow. Nor were foreign accents necessarily considered drawbacks. Performers whose first language was not English had illustrious careers: Marlene Dietrich, Charles Boyer, Garbo, Chevalier, Lugosi. Children and young people often starred in films aimed at adults. In addition to Temple, Rooney, Garland, and Durbin, child actors such as Jackie Cooper, Freddie Bartholomew, the Dead End Kids, and the Our Gang ensemble made memorable contributions.

On the other hand, because many actors who came to prominence in the thirties remained stars for another thirty or forty years, the decade can also be seen as one that defined what it took to be a star. Because it is more difficult for women to maintain careers that long, the lasting thirties icons tend to overrepresent men, when in fact female stars never dominated more than in this decade. Still, sheer talent and force of personality—not to mention longevity—made Bette Davis, Joan Crawford, Katharine Hepburn, and Barbara Stanwyck forces to be reckoned with for decades just as much as James Stewart, Henry Fonda, Spencer Tracy, Cary Grant, Fred Astaire, James Cagney, and John Wayne.

There is no formula that allows one to predict long-term box office success—although an untimely death, like Jean Harlow's, can assure an immortal star image unconnected to actual performances in films. Nevertheless, there are certain trends that divide those whose stardom was anchored in the thirties from those who would become stars for the ages. For the women, there was a necessity for indomitability and independence, a sense that even if they wept for loss of a man, they would do quite well without him, thank you very much. At the least, one could imagine them as the senior partners in relationships, and they often also conveyed a sense that if crossed they could be dangerous, an adjective used as the title of a Bette Davis film in 1935.

For male stars there were three paths to possible iconicity and one that usually detoured away from it. Nearly every studio developed an attractive and agile leading man who could star in action-adventure films. MGM had Clark Gable, Paramount had Gary Cooper, Warner had Errol Flynn, and Fox, rather late in the game, assigned this role to Tyrone Power. Each of them had a subsidiary specialty as well. Gable was the romantic leading man, comfortable in both drama and comedy, known for his pairings with Harlow and Crawford. Flynn avoided contemporary settings more than Gable did but also was part of a well-known screen couple because of his many films with Olivia de Havilland. Cooper was paired with a number of big female stars, from Dietrich to Jean Arthur to Claudette Colbert, but his image was always separate from any romance plot. The star of the early talkie western *The Virginian* (1929), he had in reserve the persona of a homespun, taciturn hero, which worked for him in Frank Capra's *Mr. Deeds Goes to Town* (1936) and fitted him well for the return of the "A" Western, one of the first of which, *The Plainsman* (1936), featured Cooper as Wild Bill Hickok. Power fit easily into any historical era and could be counted on to support but not overshadow female stars like Norma Shearer (*Marie Antoinette* [1938]) or Alice Faye (*In Old Chicago* [1936], *Alexander's Ragtime Band* [1938]).

A second type of male star produced by thirties cinema can be defined as the man of integrity who stands up for his principles. Spencer Tracy seems to have been born to play such parts and always did so with the utmost confidence in his moral position and stubbornness in carrying it through. (We see a rare dark side to these qualities of the Tracy persona in the lynching victim out for revenge in Fritz Lang's *Fury* [1936].) After a number of films in which MGM showed that it had no clue what to do with him, James Stewart joined this group after Frank Capra cast him as the idealistic, small-town newspaperman discovering the corruption of Congress in *Mr. Smith Goes to Washington* (1939). With the help of another strong director, John Ford, Henry Fonda found his persona as the reluctant hero in *Young Mr. Lincoln* (1939).

A more limited category, essentially produced by one studio, Warner Bros., comprised the urban tough guy on either side of the law. Cagney, Robinson, and Humphrey Bogart belong to this group, although Bogart's full stardom would not really come until the 1940s. A fourth potential member of this group, *Scarface* star Paul Muni, instead was given by the studio one of the most singular careers in American cinema as "Mr. Social Problem," starring most often as a social victim, usually ethnically marked (*I Am a Fugitive from a Chain Gang, Bordertown* [1935], and *Black Fury* [1935]) or as a heroic historical figure, usually also of non-Anglo extraction (*The Story of Louis Pasteur, The Life of Emile Zola, Juarez* [1939]). Virtually all his major films were films of the thirties.

Although Muni's career was *sui generis,* there were certain thirties types that also were less likely to lead to decades-long stardom. The suave, pomaded, often Continental sophisticate did not embody the masculinity of the future. If they sang and danced, like Chevalier or Astaire, such male romantic leads could still achieve iconic stature, but for the Charles Boyers, Adolphe Menjous, Herbert Marshalls, and William Powells, top billing as romantic leads would not last. Among the women, neither the gifted comediennes who made screwball comedy work—like Claudette Colbert, Jean Arthur, or Kay Francis (Carole Lombard's early death canceled the possibility she might prove the exception)—nor the ethereal beauties who suffered through the trials of many a melodramatic women's picture like Norma Shearer and Janet Gaynor were able to continue being stars past that certain age.

Nevertheless, how a star rose in the thirties is no guarantee of how—or when—it set. This can be demonstrated by looking at the careers of Irene

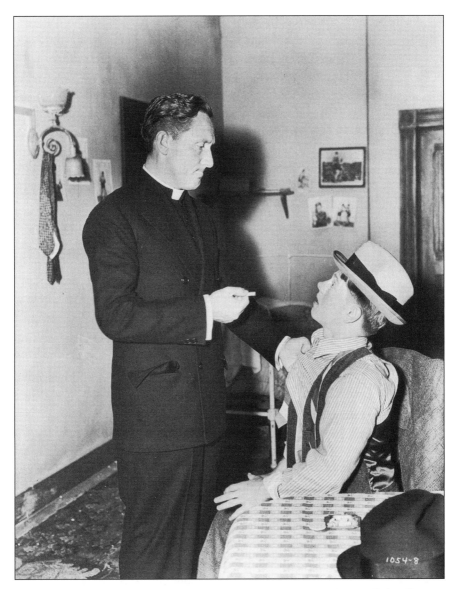

Typical of his stubborn, tough, but principled star persona, Spencer Tracy as Father Flanagan straightens out young aspiring hoodlum Whitey Marsh (Mickey Rooney) in *Boys Town* (Norman Taurog, MGM, 1938). Collection Ina Rae Hark.

Dunne and Cary Grant, the two leads in one of the decade's most celebrated screwball comedies, Leo McCarey's *The Awful Truth*. Primarily trained as a singer, Dunne caught the attention of Hollywood when she was starring on the stage in the Jerome Kern musical *Show Boat*; she would appear in the film version in 1936, after making two other Kern musicals, *Sweet Adeline* in

1934 and *Roberta* (with Astaire and Rogers) in 1935. Her second film role and first to earn her notice, however, was in a nonsinging western, *Cimarron* (1931), in which she played a strong-willed pioneer woman who becomes a crusading newspaper owner and politician. For the first part of the decade, however, Dunne's signature roles were in women's melodramas like *Back Street* (1932), *Ann Vickers* (1933), and *Magnificent Obsession* (1935). Great success in the comedy *Theodora Goes Wild* in 1936 led her to try out other screwball farces, *The Awful Truth* being the only other one in the thirties. Yet she never abandoned her earlier genres, making a musical western, *High, Wide and Handsome,* that same year and her ultimate romantic melodrama, the sublimely weepy *Love Affair,* in 1939.

Stack up Dunne's thirties roles against those of Katharine Hepburn—who would also have notable screwball successes with Grant (*Holiday* and *Bringing Up Baby* [both 1938])—factor in another triumphant decade of playing iconic mothers, especially in *I Remember Mama* (1948), and one does wonder why Dunne—who lived until 1990—is nearly forgotten by twenty-first-century audiences. Is it because she never found a director like George Cukor who completely understood what to do with her on the screen? Is it because she had a long, happy marriage to someone not in the business and saw no need to continue into playing grandmothers? Did her chameleon-like talents disguise the utter distinctiveness that makes a Hepburn inimitable?

In retrospect, Grant too is inimitable, but he also had an odd thirties career that might have rendered him more a peer of Robert Taylor than the peerless icon he became. Perhaps Grant's greatest achievement of the decade was to have spent it more or less in tow of various strong female stars without ever losing his self-possession, good humor, or masculinity. Early roles cast him as boy-toy to Mae West and Marlene Dietrich, and as he coupled with everyone from Hepburn to Constance Bennett to Dunne and Lombard, he inevitably got second billing. (It is regrettable that he never played opposite Bette Davis, as a refreshing change from the George Brents and Leslie Howards she bowled over like ninepins.) It was probably crucial that Howard Hawks saw the traditional heroic leading man in Grant for *Only Angels Have Wings* (1939) even after, in *Bringing Up Baby,* he had helped him unleash the completely zany comedian that few handsome leading men ever risked. Nor did it hurt that, of all the male romantic leads of the thirties, Grant actually became more handsome as he aged.

As the preceding discussion shows, directors and stars were not more or less interchangeable despite the studio contract system. If there is one director who both tapped into the concerns of the thirties and whose films of the decade most specifically define his career, it would have to be Frank Capra, whose screwball populism animated critical and popular successes such as *It Happened One Night, Mr. Deeds Goes to Town, You Can't Take It with You* (1938), and *Mr. Smith Goes to Washington.* Of the two other giants of cinema history who came into their own in the thirties, John Ford really only found the register in which he would establish his distinctive voice in the last year of the decade, when he worked with John Wayne as the archetypal western hero in *Stagecoach* and Henry Fonda as the diffident man of the people in *Young Mr. Lincoln.* The eclectic Howard Hawks, on the other hand, had perfected his dual focus on men as comrades in crisis and on the battle of the sexes as madcap farce before mid-decade.

George Cukor's deft touch in directing actresses and making films about and for women also revealed itself at once. From *The Royal Family of Broadway* (1930) to *Little Women* (1933) to *The Women,* Cukor showed himself an expert at translating the works of female authors to the screen. Continental sophistication resided reliably in the hands of Ernst Lubitsch, Rouben Mamoulian, and Josef von Sternberg, who plied their trades freely at Paramount. The latter filmmaker, in his films with Dietrich, demonstrated that director-performer synergy could result in the performer becoming, in a sense, the subject of the director's art. William Wyler, over a three-year span, directed a group of remarkably polished films from very different genres: *Dodsworth* (1936), *These Three* (1936), *Dead End* (1937), *Jezebel* (1938), and *Wuthering Heights.* William Wellman, working for most of his career in Hawks tough guy territory, with 1931's *The Public Enemy* and 1939's *Beau Geste* as suitable bookends for the decade, surprisingly pulled off two classic women's pictures in 1937: *A Star Is Born,* where male and female melodrama get equal time, and the screwball romance *Nothing Sacred.* The female stars—Janet Gaynor and Carole Lombard—were emblematic of their genres, while Fredric March, whom one might consider the male Irene Dunne, provided perfect support in both.

Other directorial names of distinction from the decade include Berkeley, Whale, McCarey, and Browning, Frank Lloyd, Norman Taurog, Dorothy Arzner, Mervyn LeRoy, Lewis Milestone, Clarence Brown, Mitchell Leisen, Frank Borzage, Gregory LaCava, Tay Garnett, Edmund Goulding, Raoul Walsh, King Vidor, John Stahl, Henry Hathaway, Henry King, George Stevens, and Michael Curtiz. Other distinguished filmmakers from outside the studio system included the master of the "race" film, Oscar Micheaux, documentarians Pare Lorentz, Jay Leyda, and Joris Ivens, and avant garde experimenters such as James Sibley Watson, Ralph Steiner, and Lewis Jacobs. But good films do not have to be made by great directors: we should not forget that the two most enduring films of the decade, *The Wizard of Oz* (1939) and *Gone with the Wind* (1939), are credited to Victor Fleming, of whom the kindest overall career assessment would have to be "serviceable contract director."

Oblique Approaches and Disavowals of Desperation

In the chapters that follow, the contributors to this volume focus on how the decade unfolded year by year in regard to its films. They emphasize such themes as portrayals of class, ethnicity, and race; representations of gender and sexuality; the deployment of the actor's voice and of his or her body, and the discourses of stardom more generally; the resistance to tyranny in the past and the attempt to ignore its ascendancy in the present; the influence of the New Deal and of the industry's decision to foreground its own achievements in a consciously promoted "greatest year" to end the decade.

In his chapter on 1930, Aaron Baker examines how the period of the adaptation to synchonized sound "promoted the development of certain genres that benefited from the new technology," while at the same time this broader array of cinematic technologies enabled these genres to interrogate previously dominant Hollywood fantasies that the Depression called into question. He develops his thesis through the examination of two prison films (*The Big House* and *Up the River*), two female melodramas (*Anna Christie* and *Morocco*) and two comic musicals starring Jewish vaudevillians (*Animal Crackers* and *Whoopee!*). A key element was the additional attention that speech brought to ethnic and national differences, whether it showed them as indicators of a tendency toward crime, as subversive liberators of stuffy WASP society, or, in the accents of a Garbo or a Dietrich, how they stressed the performative aspects of gender in stories of the fallen woman.

Cynthia Erb continues to scrutinize the centrality of the voice to films in the early years of the decade. Her examination of 1931 considers the distinctive vocal styles of Bela Lugosi as Dracula and James Cagney as gangster Tom Powers, but she is especially interested in the larger evolution of a silent film aesthetic—dual silent/sound versions were still being released in this year—into one increasingly dependent on dialogue and vocal characterizations. Factoring into this change, as her analyses of *Cimarron* and *The Front Page* stress, are the ideological implications of dialogue, which in turn ties into the presence of many New York–based writers who flocked to the movie business with the coming of sound, often bringing with them more left-leaning political ideas than films of the silent era had expressed. Yet the transition in sound aesthetic had not yet been completed, and even during 1931 itself the "talkie" style was vying with the "modulated sound track," which would win out in the end: "By mid-year, *Variety* was announcing a 'reduction of chatter in pictures,' one of many signs that the talkie style was finally receding in favor of the modulated sound track. . . . The difference between pre-classical and classical sound styles can be detected in the contrast between the hybrid style of *Dracula* and the balanced classicism of *Frankenstein*."

David Lugowski sees 1932 as a year in which everything and its opposite occurred simultaneously: "Experimentation in genre and technique, overcoming the static qualities of earlier talkies; spectacle ranging from the uniquely exotic to the vaudevillian and the sweetly sentimental; controversy in matters sexual, criminal, and political; a pushing of the envelope alongside outcries about both film content and Hollywood's often conservative, middle-class escapism—all these mark the year in American cinema." Focusing on the more transgressive discourses concerning sexuality, Lugowski considers the pansexual comedy-horror of openly gay director James Whale's *The Old Dark House,* the meditation on normality and abnormality in Tod Browning's *Freaks,* the various erotic kinks of Clara Bow in *Call Her Savage* and Marlene Dietrich in *Blonde Venus,* the Lubitsch touch on an implied *ménage a trois* in *Trouble in Paradise,* Paul Muni's incestuous gangster in Howard Hawks's atypically stylized and symbol-laden direction of *Scarface,* and the sentimental and patriotic love story *Smilin' Through*—which, however, earns its happy ending after two generations of jealousy, murder, and renunciation. Even the avant garde, leftist documentary by Jay Leyda, *A Bronx Morning,* is "an exercise in abstract modernism and a rich commentary on the emptiness and emasculation created by unemployment."

Martin Rubin views 1933 as a key moment of transition for Hollywood and the nation, as the films released in this year bridge FDR's election, inauguration, and the famous first 100 days of his New Deal, that special session of Congress convened to jump-start his legislative remedies for the Depression. Rubin points out that they illustrate "the shift from early 1930s 'turbulence' to mid-1930s 'order,' the upswing in morale inspired by the FDR administration, the battles over screen censorship, and the debate over the function of entertainment. As always, fluctuations in movie genres and gender roles provide important indicators of major trends in a pivotal period." Using a chronological approach, he leads the reader from *Cavalcade* to *Little Women* by way of the three highly topical Warner Bros./Busby

Berkeley musicals which revived that genre, stopping also to note the Depression metaphors audiences found in *Three Little Pigs*, the ambivalence about entertainment in a Depression setting of *King Kong*, and "risen woman" Mae West's joyful assertion of female sexuality and female empowerment in *She Done Him Wrong* amid the wreckage of other films' "fallen woman" comeuppances.

The political and economic dislocations of the decade are treated through discourses of marginalization and Otherness in a group of films Charlene Regester focuses on in her study of 1934. We see a young urban worker forced to make a go of it with other similarly disenfranchised citizens on a cooperative farm in *Our Daily Bread* and a spoiled and rebellious rich woman learning to live like regular folks in the year's surprise biggest hit, *It Happened One Night*. That film's star, Claudette Colbert, finds herself, in *Imitation of Life*, both a woman in the business world of men and a white widow deeply involved in the lives of her black servant (but also business partner) and that woman's troubled, light-skinned daughter. In *Manhattan Melodrama* two orphaned friends grow up to be a clever crook and a crusading attorney/politician, but at crucial points in their lives their moral positions look equivalent or even reversed. And in *Judge Priest*, the title character identifies less with the people that his white race and position of judicial authority grant him than with Blacks and social outcasts. The last three films, especially, stress "the interdependency of Blacks and whites" and the tendency of white characters to appropriate "blackvoice" in a variety of surprising ways.

In my essay, I view 1935 through the lens of films that dealt with tyrants and how to oppose them, although usually in non-American locales and pre-twentieth-century settings. Looking at *Captain Blood, Mutiny on the Bounty*, and *The Lives of a Bengal Lancer*, I conclude, "Corrupt regimes or venal imperialism are represented less as political problems than as problems of businesses with poor management philosophies. A few labor reforms, and all is well. The films all disregard the fact that although corrupt individuals may be replaced or censured, the systems that facilitated tyranny remain in place, ready to oppress again should oppressive men inhabit them." I then move on to Shirley Temple's Civil War film, *The Littlest Rebel*, to examine further the paradox of a nation founded in rebellion being so hesitant in its popular culture to endorse rebellion of any kind a mere seventy years later.

Susan Ohmer finds that the films of 1936 offer an object lesson on the ability of the medium of cinema to achieve transcendence of the material world: "In them, we see how formal devices such as music, sound, camerawork, set design, and costumes incorporate elements of the material world but lift us beyond it into another realm." She concentrates on five films that "demonstrate that the idea of 'escape' is too simple. In *Show Boat, Swing Time, Modern Times,* and Disney's *The Country Cousin* and *Thru the Mirror,* we see characters who strive to move beyond their worlds, and appreciate how the medium of cinema conveys their struggles and aspirations."

Allen Larson selects four of the many films from 1937 that showcased female stars in order to reveal how the discourses surrounding them relate to changes in industry strategies brought about by political pressures: "In varying ways, each of the four films examined in this chapter—*A Star Is Born, Stage Door, Saratoga,* and *Nothing Sacred*—directly engages the peculiar fact of female stardom's entanglement in efforts to gauge, define, and control 'the moral climate of America,' further illuminating the cultural and industrial pressures that molded the manufacture of female stardom, and thus classical Hollywood cinema as a whole, in the second half of the decade." Writing stardom into the country's pioneer myth and setting it up in a symbiotic relationship with death are two of the strategies he uncovers.

Sam B. Girgus broadly classifies the films of 1938 into three categories that define Hollywood's response to the growing fascist threat: "melodramas of history and romance that reveal fear of change and the concomitant desire for maintaining social order through social and class hierarchy; comedies that in turn can be divided between films of comic containment, in which detachment through humor establishes distance from economic and social conditions, and insanity comedies that include the traditional screwball form but that also imply deep, underlying incoherence and uncertainty regarding the meaning, significance, and organization of life and events; and finally, films of entrapment and oppression." Yet all eight films he analyzes—*The Adventures of Robin Hood, Marie Antoinette, A Slight Case of Murder, The Mad Miss Manton, You Can't Take It with You, Bringing Up Baby, Jezebel,* and *Algiers*—finally end up "whistling in the dark" rather than confronting social problems directly.

Charles Maland maintains that in 1939 the industry began to turn on the lights and stop whistling: "The year was one of achievement and crisis, both in the movie industry and the broader culture, and the sense of crisis shook the industry loose, however tentatively, from its public position that the industry's sole commitment was to entertain moviegoers by suggesting that movies might also serve a larger social purpose." It is instructive to note, however, that three of the six films Maland sees as exemplary— *Juarez, Stagecoach,* and *Gone with the Wind*—are set in the nineteenth century. Only *Mr. Smith Goes to Washington* and, especially, *Confessions of a Nazi Spy* take on problems of the present day. *The Wizard of Oz* has its contemporary Kansas farm story but takes place primarily in a fantasy dreamworld.

This is one reason it is a signature film of the decade. "Burbanked" movies on topical issues usually veer off in some other narrative direction before the end. Prestige pictures transport social problems beyond America's oceans and into its past. And most 1930s films do not even start out in the direction of a problem. They disavow it for a trip to a fantasy place where the "magic of cinema" simply transcends the urgent realities confronting offscreen America in the 1930s.

1930

Movies and Social Difference

AARON BAKER

In the year in which Sergei Eisenstein arrived in Hollywood and left six months later without making a film, it is fitting that three of the biggest inventions in the United States were products that would become corporate mainstays. In March frozen foods packaged by Clarence Birdseye went on sale. Birdseye had developed a method for quick-freezing food products in convenient packages without any loss of taste. Another food high on taste but low on nutritional value, the Twinkie snack cake, was also introduced by the Interstate Bakeries Corporation. At a time when many people had to repair broken possessions rather than replace them, an engineer working for the 3M Company invented the first transparent cellophane tape. Scotch Tape, as it was called, sold so well that it became a generic name for any kind of adhesive tape.

The music of Paul Whiteman & His Orchestra, Guy Lombardo and the Royal Canadians, Paul Robeson, Rudy Vallee, and Fred Astaire dominated the pop charts. One of Astaire's hits was his recording of Irving Berlin's *Puttin' on the Ritz* that was inspired by the fad of wealthy New Yorkers dressing up to visit jazz clubs in Harlem. This year also marked the debut of the radio program "The Shadow" in which the furtive crime solver would know what evil lurked in the hearts of men for a quarter of a century. On the stage Eugene O'Neill's *Strange Interlude,* about a loveless marriage, and for which he had won a Pulitzer Prize, continued its long run. Noel Coward added to his string of hits with *Private Lives,* in which he also starred. The literary world saw the publication of three important novels: William Faulkner came out with *As I Lay Dying*, a stream-of-consciousness story—with fifteen narrators—about a poor Mississippi farm family; recently returned from a trip to Russia to study socialism, John Dos Passos published the first of his *USA Trilogy, The 42nd Parallel*; and Knopf released Dashiell Hammett's hard-boiled detective novel *The Maltese Falcon*. Its story of a coolly detached detective with his own sense of justice fit perfectly into the Hollywood ideology of self-reliance and would be adapted three times for the cinema.

This was a year of growing economic and social crisis in the United States. During the five months from the October 1929 stock market crash until March, unemployment more than doubled, from 1.5 million to at least 3.2 million people. President Herbert Hoover announced in a 7 March speech that "the worst effects of the crash upon unemployment will have passed during the next sixty days" (Watkins 50). Instead, joblessness continued to rise rapidly, and in another six months hit 7.5 million (Watkins 54).

Bank failures also created economic instability and a lack of consumer confidence. More than 1,300 U.S. banks, with $852 million in deposits, failed. Business failure reached its highest rate ever recorded up to that time (Watkins 55). Drought, especially in the Midwest, Great Plains, and South, hit agricultural production hard. Late summer rainfall in those regions dropped 40 percent below normal, resulting in food shortages and hardship for many of the eleven million Americans who lived in rural areas (Watkins 64).

Despite such severe economic problems, box office for Hollywood films stayed strong. While national income dropped sharply, attendance at motion pictures reached an all-time high of eighty million per week (Balio 13). There were notable films of all types. World War I was refought in *Hell's Angels, Journey's End,* and *The Dawn Patrol.* A documentary team was *With Byrd at the South Pole.* Detective Philo Vance solved *The Bishop Murder Case* while jewel thief *Raffles* baffled police. The women referenced in the titles of *Charley's Aunt, Ladies of Leisure,* and *Mammy* couldn't have been more different from one another. Fantasy and the uncanny reigned in *Outward Bound, The Cat Creeps, Just Imagine,* and the sound version of *The Unholy Three.* The latter film was Lon Chaney's last; D.W. Griffith made his next-to-last feature, *Abraham Lincoln.* There were also some great beginnings. John Wayne starred in his first western, *The Big Trail* (shot in 55 mm, an early widescreen process), and James Cagney made his screen debut in *Sinners' Holiday.* The terrific onscreen chemistry between Marie Dressler and Wallace Beery characterized their most famous pairing as *Min and Bill.* As a sign of Hollywood's confidence, prestige productions led the way. In the words of Tino Balio, "nearly all the titles on Film Daily's Ten Best in 1930 were prestige pictures. . . . Pathé's *Holiday* . . . MGM's *Anna Christie* . . . Universal's *All Quiet on the Western Front*" (181). Balio describes such films as "injected with plenty of star power, [and] glamorous and elegant trappings" (180). Perhaps their appeal came from how such extravagance pushed aside the scarcity so many Americans faced. The trailer for another of the year's prestige productions, *Morocco,* described it as "a super picture with Gary Cooper, Marlene Dietrich . . . and a cast of thousands."

During this year the adoption of and ongoing adaptation to synchronized sound promoted the development of certain genres that benefited from the new technology. Noting that this occurred during a period of grave economic crisis, Andrew Bergman points out that Hollywood responded to the effects of the Depression on American society in that its movies "depicted things lost or things desired" (xii). Jonathan Munby is more specific in describing this connection between Hollywood and the effects of the Depression: "Such circumstances enhanced the appeal of stories and characters that debunked older Hollywood fantasies and gestured toward a grittier truth" (*Public Enemies* 43).

The box office success of sound films supported the production of genres that took advantage of the new technology: over seventy musicals were made in this year, including *Paramount on Parade, The King of Jazz, The Rogue Song, The Vagabond King,* and *Whoopee!* Although the coming of talkies had banished from U.S. pictures those foreign performers who couldn't speak English fluently, a non-American accent in and of itself was no hindrance. Among other Europeans, Greta Garbo, Marlene Dietrich, and Maurice Chevalier appeared in American films this year. Gangster films, although already popular in the silent era, were significantly enhanced by sound; it was no coincidence that the first all-talkie was *Lights of New York* (1928), about bootlegging. Gangster films used sound to present the audio from the nightclubs, cars, and guns that energized their stories, and, along with prison films such as *The Big House* and *Up the River,* employed it to re-create the colloquial speech of criminal characters.

The heavily marked language of crime pictures, in which slang, non-standard English, and ethnic, regional, and class dialects were emphasized, foregrounds one major change that talking pictures brought to audiences. In silent films, all the subtle clues gleaned from a character's origins and personality according to the way he or she speaks are lost. While visual signals or intertitles may provide spectators with such information, being able to hear differences in accent or fluency gives them far more weight. Moreover, some rural movie-goers might never before have heard the distinctive speech patterns of the urban-immigrant working class; similarly, those urban audiences might have had no conception of the way a midwestern farmer or southern cotton mill worker sounded.

Because sound gave the cinema new ways to emphasize differences in class, gender, and ethnicity, it proved a valuable tool for filmmakers to stress the social distinctions among members of these categories and the societal inequities often inherent in them. Seven genre films considered here—the gangster movie *The Doorway to Hell*; prison movies *The Big House* and *Up the River*; women's films *Morocco* and *Anna Christie*; and musical comedies *Animal Crackers* and *Whoopee!*—represent social conflicts exacerbated by the Depression, and their use of language impacts what these films say about those issues and about the diversity of the American populace.

■ Criminal Talk

Since the mid-1920s American media had focused on the exploits of famous criminals, and by the end of the decade, according to *Variety*, every major studio "had taken a crack at one or more gangland films" (Balio 283). Gangster films of the year included *Night Ride, Ladies Love Brutes, Outside the Law, Born Reckless,* and *The Doorway to Hell,* in which Lou Ayres played a character modeled on Al Capone.

One of the most prominent characteristics of these early sound crime films was their emphasis on ethnicity. Ayres's Louie Ricarno, Edward G. Robinson's Tony Garotta in *Night Ride,* and even John Ford's Irish American comic criminals in *Up the River* are what Munby calls "hyphenated Americans . . . living in two worlds and yet not belonging to either" (*Public Enemies* 20). Such "ethnic as gangster" characters in the media had contributed to the anti-immigrant, anti-urban sentiments of the 1920s as evidenced by legislation to limit immigration in 1921 and 1924, the rise of the KKK, and Prohibition (21). Yet the social authenticity of these crime films, how they "played out ethnic lower class resentments about being subject to nativist ideals of 'naturalization' and 'Americanization,'" rejected the idea of ethnicity as an inferior other in relation to "true" American identity (26). Furthermore, the dire economic conditions brought on by the Wall Street crash and the Depression undercut the legitimacy of the ethnic status quo (34).

As evidence of the increasing acceptance of films about ethnic criminals, *The Doorway to Hell* found a significant audience. Nick Roddick considers the film to be a straightforward morality tale about the rise and fall of a gangster, told with "the strongly hectoring tone of a silent melodrama" (99). Ricarno succeeds in organizing his gangland activities along a business model and then tries to retire, but he must return to wage a war against the competing criminals who killed his younger brother, and this leads to his own death. However, Colonel Jason Joy, the chief supervisor of the Production Code, objected to the end of the film in which an Irish American cop, O'Grady (Robert Elliott), sets up Ricarno for execution by a rival gangster, because the police know they can't make a case against him themselves (Munby, *Public Enemies* 101). The script was altered to absolve the law officer of conniving in Louie's murder by having O'Grady warn him of the threat on his life; yet other than that the picture was released, with Hays Office approval, unchanged, and it had a successful run. According to Carleton Simon, crime consultant to the Code authorities, "As long as the public craves underworld pictures, that demand must be met" (102).

The way sound conveys the gangster's distinctive language defines his world as separate from the larger society. Sarah Kozloff notes that the colloquial directness of his speech indicates his working-class status, and its often aggressive tone, full of bragging, intimidation, and threat functions as an important part of his masculine self-assertion. Louie states the following to put himself in charge:

> Now we're all in one racket or another and lately there's been a lot of double crossing—one mob crashing into another mob's territory. We're in big business. The only thing wrong with it is that it needs organizing and it needs a boss. I'm taking over both jobs. I'm gonna lay this town out in zones—I'll give each mob what I think is comin' to 'em and not one inch more. Get that! Each gang'll kick into me and I'll take care of everything. . . ." (Rosow 146)

The new sound film gangster used language frequently as well as forcefully. As Kozloff puts it, "As the gangster is unrestrained in his approach to violence, so is he promiscuous in his approach to words" (212). However, as his language defines the gangster culture as different, talking must remain within that separate world. Speaking outside it risks the betrayal of *talking,* squealing, providing evidence to the police or a competitor (Kozloff 217).

Kozloff speculates that, besides his challenge to the class status quo, perhaps the gangster is punished for how he clouds the distinction—both through language and concern with appearance—between normative gender roles, what she calls "the strictures of masculinity" (213). That the cinematic gangster speaks to assert himself yet violently reacts to the misuse of language reveals his ambivalence toward it. As Fred Gardaphe points out in his book on cultural representations of the Italian American gangster, "Italian masculinity is typically expected to be displayed through actions rather than words: 'Le parole sono femmine' (Words are feminine) goes an Italian saying; but 'i fatti sono maschi' (actions are masculine)" (16).

A similar pattern of gender transgression through language and its punishment occurs in *The Big House.* The film takes an almost documentary-style approach to the particulars of life in a large penitentiary. Broadly defined criminal types constitute the central characters, with the spotlight on the brutal, uneducated Butch Schmidt (Wallace Beery), the spoiled and weak-willed rich boy Kent Marlowe (Robert Montgomery), and the decent guy from a deprived background, John Morgan (Chester Morris). Prominent in the dialogue is the inmates' use of the tough prison argot: "screws," "bulls," "the hole," "rat," and "squeal," a sub-language that for most earlier viewers of silent film would have been relatively unfamiliar. But we also witness a quietly emotional scene between two hardened cons as John reads to his illiterate cellmate a letter informing him of his mother's death. The latter convict, Butch, is the most conventionally masculine of all the men in the story: physically strong and quick to violence. When we first meet him, he brags about how many men he has killed in his career. Yet he is also a storyteller, entertaining the other men in the yard with colorful tales of his criminal and sexual exploits. At the end of the film, he is killed, ostensibly for his role in leading an attempted breakout; but if we accept Kozloff's theory that the punishment of film criminals also has something to do with the unconventional masculinity their excessive relation to language signals, then his love of talking may also be a factor in his demise. Not coincidentally, the craven Kent, who likewise dies in the violence created by the attempted escape, engages in the inappropriate use of language as well, in his case telling the warden about plans for the breakout. In contrast to Butch and Kent, John defines himself in a more conventionally masculine manner through action rather than words. It is he whom the film recuperates as capable of rehabilitation and redemption.

His reformation through "good" actions rather than "wasteful" words enables *The Big House* to endorse conservative ideas of class as well as gender. The film reinforces the utopian view that exercising individual initiative and following the rules will allow a man access to a better life. While the working-class urban milieu of the gangster film posits an environment of disadvantage as a cause for criminality, our view of the world outside the prison is limited to Kent's middle-class but compassionate family. Their son has gone to jail because of a tragic accident in which he was driving drunk and killed another person. Kent is therefore offered as proof of the view that crime results from individual mistakes rather than social environment. When John escapes and visits the Marlowe family, Kent's sister Anne (Leila Hyams) demonstrates her compassion by helping him elude capture and falling in love with him. This motivates the convict to act in a more ethical manner when, even after being captured and returned to prison, he protects guards caught in the crossfire during the confusion of the break, and is rewarded with a pardon that allows him to begin a new life on the outside with Anne. The violent breakout, which prompts an equally violent response from the warden and then hostage-taking and murder by Butch, is the big event the film is leading up to, and the choices made by each of the three featured convicts determine their fates. Rather than a critique of the widening gap of class difference created by the Depression, *The Big*

House affirms the idea that the right actions can overcome that difference, even for a working-class convict.

Up the River also uses a prison setting to comment upon class differences. Fox had planned to produce a film about life behind bars but dropped the idea after MGM released *The Big House*. Director John Ford got the studio to revive the project by redefining it as a "comedy drama" about a prison where life is so good that two escapees break back in so that they can play in a big baseball game against the inmates from another facility (McBride, *Ford* 174). "Bensonatta, a penitentiary in the Middle West," seems more like a coed college than a prison: besides baseball, the inmates spend their time practicing in their brass band, gossiping about romantic involvements, and putting on a vaudeville show. The warden's young daughter, Jean (Joan Marie Lawes), wanders unguarded among the inmate population and seems to view them as so many uncles and aunts. Indeed, Bensonatta comes to resemble a utopian fantasy of the American melting pot, where people of all classes, races, and regions mingle harmoniously as if belonging to one big happy family, with the warden (Robert Emmett O'Connor) as father and the well-meaning but naive prison welfare worker Mrs. Massey (Louise Mackintosh) as mother.

The plot centers on four cellmates whose speech precisely marks their class and ethnic identities. Saint Louis (Spencer Tracy) and Dannemora Dan (Warren Hymer) are career criminals from New York, veterans of many correctional institutions all over the country. (The film opens with them escaping a state prison in the South.) Dan speaks the stereotypical patois of the "mug" from Brooklyn. He has poor grammar and his pronunciation is full of "dese," "dem," and "dose" as well as phrases like "woid for woid." Branded a "moron" by a psychological evaluation administered at the prison, he is a convenient stooge for Saint Louis, with whom he has an on-again, off-again criminal partnership and a contentious but ultimately loyal homosocial relationship. Saint Louis's speech bears traces of the urban working class as well, but he is a glib and effective talker whose powers of persuasion are as forceful as his valued pitching arm. Significantly, language is the locus of his integrity. He constantly asserts the sanctity of his word.

He and Dan join two other convicts already incarcerated at Bensonatta. Pops (William Collier Sr.), a lifer with an Irish American brogue, lives to win the prison league baseball championship, a goal that is constantly blocked by his best players either escaping, being released, or getting executed. The trusty Steve Jordan (Humphrey Bogart) has parallels with *The Big House*'s Kent in regard to his privileged social background and with John in his basic decency and redemption through love of someone outside his class. The son of a well-to-do New England family, whose speech is standard and refined, he was about to embark on a boat to China when he accidentally killed a man in a fight. Now about to be paroled, he has managed to convince his family that he is still in Asia and to conceal his crime from them. However, his life becomes complicated when he meets Judy (Claire Luce), who was arrested for working as a shill for a stock swindler, Frosby (Morgan Wallace). Steve promises to wait for her release and asks her to marry him. Although Judy believes that rich boy/poor girl romances only work in story books, he points out that they are now both equal as ex-convicts, free to rebuild their lives together. When Frosby tries to use their relationship to blackmail Steve and defraud his mother, unlikely Cupids Dan and Saint Louis break out to save the day, then return in time to give Pops's team a fighting chance in the big game.

Fox had made $9 million in 1929, but the balance sheet this year was headed in the other direction (the studio would go on to lose $3 million), which probably motivated Ford's fast and efficient work in making the film. He shot the ninety-two-minute movie in less than three weeks, mostly using medium or medium-long shots of extended duration, and printing the first take of every shot unless an actor muffed a line of dialogue (Sklar, *City Boys* 25). While such a shooting style may have been prompted by the need for economy, as David Cook points out, the limitations of early sound technology made it necessary for many filmmakers to conceive of their movies as "a series of talking photographs taken from the same angle at medium range and varied only when the talking stopped" (223). The majority of conversations in *Up the River* are shot just this way. Microphones that had limited range, but were very sensitive within that range, forced actors not to move too much, and also limited the movement of the camera because it had to be encased in a booth to reduce motor noise (Cook 223). Ford does make use of longer shots and a moving camera in scenes where there is no dialogue, such as the atmospheric first sequence in which Dan and Saint Louis escape, running atop the prison's fog-shrouded outer wall.

However, as David Bordwell points out, some filmmakers during this transitional period used several cameras and longer lenses to allow closer framings, helping them to generate multiple views of a scene which they could intercut without moving the camera too close, generating noise, or altering the synchronization of the sound track recorded during shooting, since post-synchronized sound was not yet technologically feasible. Such procedures made it possible to retain the classical mode of editing with its "ability to cut from place to place . . . to play upon the imagination of the audience to the point where they are almost in the scenes depicted before them on the screen" (Bordwell 305). Retaining the ability to cut within scenes served as a corrective to the slower pacing made necessary by dialogue, which could render films too static.

In a scene in which Steve proclaims his love for Judy in the prison yard, Ford makes use of multi-camera set-ups for both of these reasons, to retain the viewer access of classical editing and to energize the pacing of his narrative. Since the men and women are segregated in the prison, the couple talk through a gate of steel bars. Much of the conversation is shown in a medium long two-shot, and the take needs to be fairly long (forty-six seconds) to give Steve a chance to explain his feelings. Yet to break up the slow pacing of this scene, Ford at one point cuts to a close-up from another camera position of Judy's reaction to Steve telling her he loves her, and he also cross-cuts to another part of the yard where Saint Louis and Dannemora Dan engage in comic banter with Jean.

Up the River was the Hollywood debut for Spencer Tracy. Ford had seen him in a New York play entitled *The Last Mile* in which he also played a convict, and, as Joseph McBride tells us, "the two Irish Catholics, who shared similar guilt feelings over their heavy drinking and womanizing, proved a good creative match" (*Ford* 175). Both Tracy and Bogart, here in his second film, were part of a wave of actors with New York stage experience who were hired by Hollywood studios in the early sound period because film directors could no longer call out instructions while filming and therefore wanted actors used to playing long pieces of dialogue (Cook 224). (Of course, such young performers were also attractive to studio heads because they could pay them a fraction of what silent stars earned [Sklar, *City Boys* 23].) Tracy proves his skill in this regard when he uses the following monologue to persuade Steve not to kill Frosby because of the swindle:

> Forget it, forget it, Steve. Nobody but chumps uses guns. Steve, did you ever see a guy go to the chair, huh? Well, I did. I spent eight months in that condemned row, watched them go, one by one, pals of mine, guys that you'd say good morning to in the morning and you'd say good night at night. And then they'd go. And I'd wait day after day, week after week, month after month, wondering if I was going to be the next one to go. And that's no picnic, kid. Listening to the drone of that lousy motor and watching those lights go dim!

The ease with which Ford changed a serious prison film into a comedy reveals a lack of concern with a realistic portrayal of the harsh treatment and violence of life behind bars. His focus instead is more on the humor in his script, and what McBride calls its "'grace notes' . . . directorial touches, often nonverbal, that reveal character or capture emotion" (*Ford* 175). One example is Ford's use of a tracking shot to show the men in close-up reacting in emotional unison to a song about motherly love during the variety show; another is a pan across the crowd at the baseball game when the inmates sing the title song to affirm their unified support ("You can depend on a pal . . .") for the home team. Still another occurs in a scene in which Saint Louis and Dan help Steve's mother recover bonds that she has been swindled out of by Frosby. These mobile shots, which show the men as a community and the escapees' heroic action, foreground Ford's concern with the camaraderie and moral fiber of working-class men, important themes in a number of his films.

But that's not to say that Ford's film doesn't at times comment on issues tied to its Depression-era context. In the same year he made *Up the River,* Ford started a working relationship with screenwriter Dudley Nichols, a former New York newspaper reporter who first gained notoriety for his coverage of the Sacco and Vanzetti trial. McBride claims that Nichols was "an outspoken liberal," the kind of "intellectual person that Ford disdained," but nonetheless his "strongly held beliefs deeply influenced Ford during the depression era," perhaps because "he was also a navy veteran of World War I and had some Irish ancestry"; just as important, the director's "growing need to be taken seriously and to be granted more stature by both Hollywood and the critics was enhanced by his association with Nichols" (*Ford* 174–75).

Although McBride sees *Up the River*—which Ford co-wrote with William Collier Sr.—as a deviation from the social engagement and aesthetic seriousness that marked his collaboration with Nichols, nonetheless there is an early scene that makes pointed comments on social injustice as Dan and Saint Louis rate the southern prison quite low on their list of penal favorites:

Saint Louis: I hope I never see that place again.
Dan: Yeah, the food was bad.

The griping is presented as comic, but it also references the terrible conditions in state prisons at the time, especially in the South. As historian Edgardo Rotman points out, southern penitentiaries often were characterized by "ruthless exploitation with total disregard for prisoners' dignity and lives. The states leased prisoners to entrepreneurs who, having no ownership interest in them, exploited them even worse than slaves" (176). According to Rotman, most attempts at reforming prison life to make conditions for prisoners more humane with the intention of rehabilitating them and preparing them for a productive life on the outside were in federal penitentiaries. The term "big house," from which the MGM film got its name, referred to federal efforts during the Progressive Era to create large model prisons like San Quentin and Sing Sing "designed to eliminate the abusive forms of corporal punishment and prison labor prevailing at . . . state prisons that maintained late nineteenth century practice" (185). It is therefore no coincidence that Bensonatta, where the convicts receive such gentle treatment and develop a sense of community, is a federal facility in the Midwest.

A second instance of Ford's combining comedy and social commentary occurs in the film's next scene. After driving off without him, Saint Louis later finds Dan in Kansas City, preaching on the street for a religious group called the Brotherhood of Hope. As Dan moralizes that "crime doesn't pay," Saint Louis arrives in a new car, well dressed and accompanied by two young women. He loudly honks the horn, as if giving Dan the raspberry; his prosperous appearance offers ironic refutation of the street corner sermon. Ford further critiques the kind of simplistic moralizing central to the new Production Code later in the film when he introduces Frosby, dressed in elegant clothes, speaking with mellifluous diction, and approximating a look of legitimacy that we learn has been made possible by selling phony stocks to unknowing investors. The combination of the Frosby character and the story's response to his swindles betrays Ford's view of the Depression from the perspective of a populist ideology: crooked capitalists like Frosby may be to blame, but the best response is to retain the self-reliance demonstrated by Saint Louis when he sneaks into the conman's office and retrieves the bonds that Steve's mother has given Frosby in return for some of his worthless securities. Such populist thinking had developed originally in the nineteenth century to articulate the support of middle-class rural Americans for the rights of the individual in the face of the Industrial Revolution and growing corporate control of the American economy. In its later incarnation, populism influenced not only Ford but many films in Depression-era Hollywood because it appealed to both sides of the political fence: its attacks on the excesses of capitalism in defense of the common man appealed to the Left, while the solution based in self-reliance that it offered also fit the conservative agenda. Ford's encapsulation of the economic hard times in *Up the River* through Frosby's attempts to swindle good people out of their savings and Saint Louis's heroic actions to stop him offered a populist combination of Depression cynicism and the self-reliance central to the American Dream (Roffman and Purdy 64).

■■■■■■■■■ **Fallen Women Complain about a Raw Deal**

In addition to musicals and movies about criminals, Hollywood also emphasized the women's film, seeing it as an important genre for appealing to female viewers. Movies such as *Anna Christie* and *Romance,* both starring Greta Garbo; *Morocco,* featuring Marlene Dietrich; and *The Divorcée* with Norma Shearer involved their heroines in conflicts related to relationships, and led to resolutions that required the woman's sacrifice or loss (Balio 235). MGM alone produced six such films.

Like many women's films, *Anna Christie* and *Morocco* present "fallen" main characters who have experienced limited choices and whose economic situation leaves them with "nothing to sell but sex" (Bergman 50–51). Despite their similar circumstances of being forced to prostitute themselves to men, both Garbo's and Dietrich's characters voice a critique of their social and economic situation, describing its unfairness and questioning the assumptions about gender that underlie the inequality. In *Morocco* Dietrich's Amy Jolly demonstrates her rejection of conventional gender roles during her first nightclub performance, dressing in a tuxedo, spurning the advances of men in the audience, and kissing a female spectator on the lips as a parody of their aggressive come-ons. By the laughter of the audience in the club in response to this kiss, the film suggests our receptive reaction to its parody of male behavior. As if to assert her right to the same degree of self-interest shown by the main male character, French Legionnaire Tom Brown (Gary Cooper), Amy later asks him, "Nothing like independence, is there?" She continues, "There's a Foreign Legion of women . . . no uniforms, no medals, but we're brave."

In *Anna Christie,* Garbo's character has access to Eugene O'Neill's dialogue to speak with equal candor about the injustice of having had to sell herself to survive. She finds her aged father after fifteen years of separation and confronts him about how, by not supporting her, he has forced her into prostitution. Although Garbo "admitted being insecure about her ability to speak or understand English well, especially O'Neill's slang," she rejected the idea of any language coaching (Swenson 217). Dietrich, on the other hand, accepted director Josef von Sternberg's insistence that she work with a voice coach to remove the "Teutonic traces" from her English (Bach 130). Both performers had a star image that stemmed from visual allure, whether the mask-like mystery of a Garbo close-up or the fetishizing lighting and cinematography Sternberg lavished on Dietrich. That they were not Americans added to this appeal: they were both erotic and exotic. Nevertheless, when the exotic origins were accompanied by heavily accented awkward-

Lit and costumed as only Josef von Sternberg's fetishizing direction could achieve, Marlene Dietrich becomes a glittering erotic spectacle in this publicity still from *Morocco* (Paramount). Collection Ina Rae Hark.

ness in handling spoken dialogue, the wholeness of the screen persona threatened to fracture.

Robert Ray argues that the coming of sound transformed acting in American films, forcing performers "to shed the Victorian trappings . . . of Griffith . . . a style that was declamatory, grandiose and abstract to give way to one that was intimate, vernacular, and specific" (29). With this change, a performer's broken English could easily become jarring to an audience. Dietrich adjusted better than Garbo to the colloquial diction this new style required, what Maria DiBattista calls the "often rude speech of the everyday . . . the modern idiom," while the basis of Garbo's stardom was an intense, stately self-possession that involved speaking in a more formal kind of language. This perhaps explains why Garbo waited so long to do her first talkie (DiBattista 240). DiBattista sums up the relationship between Garbo's elegant style and her use of language in the movies: "She [Garbo] utters words as if they are too full of meaning . . . to be so casually tossed off" (240).

Unfortunately, in *Anna Christie* Garbo plays a character who, because of her difficult experience as a prostitute, uses the hardboiled speech that she has difficulty delivering as an actress. When she speaks her famous first line to a bartender, "Gimme a whisky . . . and don't be stingy, baby," it is slightly garbled and unconvincing, as if she is reluctant to assume the tough dame affect it is meant to establish. Another instance of how Garbo fails to deliver naturalistic language effectively comes when she confronts the two men in her life, her father (George F. Marion) and her boyfriend, Matt Burke (Charles Bickford), for their arrogance in trying to turn her into a respectable married woman despite her desire for independence:

> You can go to blazes, both of you. You're all wrong, see . . . I've been meaning to turn it loose on you . . . nobody owns me, excepting myself . . . so put that in your pipe and smoke it.

Garbo's attempt to use vivid slang ("go to blazes," "put that in your pipe and smoke it") sounds more rehearsed than forceful. Her speech patterns were not generally delivered at the quick pace typical of characters who are coded as working class in films of this period. In general, the faster a character talked, the humbler was his or her background. The elite and mon-eyed segments of society considered rapid-fire patter a mark of vulgarity; various protocols of refinement and politeness made their speech more measured. As she tries here to emulate such rapid speech to communicate her anger, her diction breaks down ("nobody owns me, excepting myself"). Conversely, a few minutes later in the scene, she speaks to her father in language that is less stylized and rapid fire, but more effectively describes the nature of their conflict:

> Didn't I write you? You just didn't want to be bothered with me . . . But one thing I never wrote you . . . fellas looking for a chance to marry me . . . they weren't looking for marrying . . . and who's to blame for it? Me or you?

Greta Garbo's dialogue delivery style did not quite match the character of the lower-class, hard-drinking, fast-talking protagonist of *Anna Christie* (Clarence Brown, MGM). Collection Ina Rae Hark.

While Garbo's limitations with the colloquial English required for O'Neill's dialogue undercut the feminist assertion of her character, both *Anna Christie* and *Morocco* also soften the force of their critique of gender roles in American society through the foreignness of these stories. The two films rely on European actresses turned Hollywood stars, and the idea for the latter came from the novel *Amy Jolly* by Benno Vigny. The film version of *Anna Christie* was based on O'Neill's 1922 play about a Swedish barge captain and his daughter that premiered in New York, yet MGM underscored the European quality of the movie not only by casting Garbo, but by making a German-language version with a different cast except for its female star. While Dietrich is more comfortable with the casual exchanges in English with Cooper's character and the other male lead, Adolphe Menjou, her performance in *Morocco* stresses the non-American roots of the character, for instance when she sings her first song in French. Paramount advertised the film with what Balio calls "a huge publicity campaign that emphasized a rivalry with Garbo, and *Variety* in its review of *Morocco* underlined their European origins—and association with the women's film genre—when making a comparison between the two stars: 'The Dietrich girl has the Continental acting tricks like Garbo. One is the tragic face, always tragic'" (242–43).

The foreign elements in these two films and the foreign accents of their leading ladies function therefore to displace onto other cultures their critique of the unfairness experienced by their heroines as a result of their gender and economic conditions. As such, the disadvantage for Dietrich's character and Garbo's appears as less the fault of American society and more the result of alien cultural influences. Indirectly, American culture even comes off as enlightened and modern by virtue of Hollywood's willingness to expose the problem.

In addition to the displacement of this critique of gender roles onto a foreign culture, both movies eventually push it aside in the end in favor of the power of the two women's desires for their men. Despite the fact that both male romantic leads have shown themselves overbearing and selfish, their strong self-assertion seems only to fuel the women's love; as testament to the power of that attraction, both films conclude with the couples reuniting, as if to say what the women really want isn't fair treatment, but self-denial. The absurdity of this narrative logic is demonstrated in their conclusions, in which Dietrich's Amy marches barefoot into the desert after Brown when he deploys with his regiment of legionnaires, and Anna suddenly gives up her strong feelings of resentment, makes peace with her father, and decides to marry Matt. While the new sound technology allowed the female leads in *Morocco* and *Anna Christie* to denounce normative gender roles, that critique falls silent in the face of Hollywood's insistence on happy endings built around romantic couples.

Ethnic Talk, Crazy Talk

Dialogue is also important to how Victor Heerman's *Animal Crackers* and Thornton Freeland's *Whoopee!* fit the main characteristics of early sound comedy. One of these characteristics is the tendency to foreground the performance of star comics, whose dialogue is less about characterization and development of the narrative than comedic gags that form what Henry Jenkins calls a "self-conscious spectacle" (129). Such presentational performance by the headlining comics involving frontal staging, direct address to the audience, muttered asides, and self-reflexive gags creates more "audience consciousness," as opposed to the absorption within the narrative encouraged by the invisible formal style of Classic Hollywood movies (Jenkins 132). This critical distance becomes significant for *Animal*

Crackers and *Whoopee!* as the comic leads question the conservative ideas of race and ethnicity promoted by characters representing WASP authority, generally performed in a more naturalistic style. The WASP characters appear self-absorbed as a sign of their sense of superiority but also distracted, to open up space for the comic barbs of the ethnic comedians. Beyond their focus on race and ethnicity, these two films also exemplify the tendency in early sound comedy toward what Jenkins describes as anarchy or social disorder. This usually involves a story with a "natural," uninhibited protagonist such as the Eddie Cantor character Henry Williams in *Whoopee!*, or several such free thinkers in the Marx Brothers film, resisting the repressive forces of social order that attempt to restrict freedom with conformity and limits on expressive pleasure (Jenkins 221).

The Marx Brothers in *Animal Crackers* and Eddie Cantor in *Whoopee!* all play characters who at first appear to be part of WASP society, but wind up subverting it. In *Animal Crackers* Groucho is introduced as an African explorer named Captain Jeffrey T. Spaulding, who has been invited by Mrs. Rittenhouse (Margaret Dumont), a wealthy Long Island socialite, to her estate as part of an event celebrating the display of an expensive painting by Beaugard, *After the Hunt,* owned by Roscoe W. Chandler (Louis Sorin). It is quickly apparent, however, that Groucho's respectable name and profession are just a pretext for him to engage in extended comic routines that have nothing to do with exploring, but rather aim to entertain by undercutting the social pretensions of Mrs. Rittenhouse and her guests. Consider the following exchange between Spaulding, Mrs. Rittenhouse, and another socialite, Mrs. Whitehead (Margaret Irving):

> *Spaulding* (to Mrs. Rittenhouse): Ever since I met you I've swept you off my feet. . . . Something I must ask you . . . would you wash out a pair of my socks? (Mrs. Rittenhouse stares at him dumbfounded.) You have got money, don't you, 'cause if you haven't we can stop right now.
>
> (Mrs. Whitehead joins them.)
>
> *Spaulding:* Will you marry me?
>
> *Mrs. Rittenhouse:* Which one of us?
>
> *Spaulding:* Both of you.
>
> *Mrs. Whitehead:* That's bigamy.
>
> *Spaulding:* Yes, it is big of me. . . .
>
> *Mrs. Rittenhouse:* I think marriage is really a noble institution.
>
> (Spaulding whinnies like a horse.)
>
> *Spaulding:* It [marriage] was put over on the American people while our boys were over there.

During this comic exchange, Groucho disrespects the social position of the two women that the event at Mrs. Rittenhouse's estate functions to maintain. He also pokes fun at the institution of marriage that is a central value of her respectability—the pretext of their conversation is her interest in his proposal—and that is also the controlling desire of the young couple, John Parker (Hal Thompson) and Mrs. Rittenhouse's daughter, Arabella (Lillian Roth), who demonstrate their earnest love elsewhere in the film through a more realistic performance style.

Groucho adopts the presentational performance style typical of early film comedy by interrupting his exchange with the two women to move in and out of a direct-address parody of playwright Eugene O'Neill. The choice of O'Neill's play *Anna Christie* as the basis for Garbo's sound debut demonstrated the cultural prestige and appeal of the American playwright's work. At the time when *Animal Crackers* opened in August, another O'Neill play, *Strange Interlude*—viewed by critics as distinctive for its spoken asides and soliloquies to express a character's thoughts—had been running for forty weeks in New York. After excusing himself with "Pardon me while I have a strange interlude," Groucho steps forward, and, in a solemn tone appropriate to O'Neill's emphasis on tragic human failure, speaks the following aside:

> What makes you think I'd marry either one of you . . . How happy I could be with either of these two, if both of them just went away . . . The gods look down and laugh.

While the effect of Groucho's direct address soliloquy may have been satiric absurdity rather than tragic seriousness, the discontinuity it produces is just as appropriate for his comedy as it was in O'Neill's play.

Gerald Mast has written that the Marx Brothers dealt with the challenge of the new sound technology by each adopting a particular mode of establishing "individual relationships to talk" (*Comic Mind* 292). While for Chico this involved humor based on his misuse of English, and for Harpo his comedy retained the physical emphasis of silent slapstick, in the case of Groucho this meant a fast-paced delivery that "shoots word bullets" at his interlocutors within the narrative, leaving them, and the audience, disarmed. Furthermore, before anyone can reorient themselves to reply, Groucho has already moved on to his next verbal assault (282). When he invokes O'Neill in the scene described above, both women give Groucho a puzzled look or smile stupidly as if they don't understand his insults—or at least have never seen an O'Neill play. Nonetheless he continues without waiting for them to catch up. As Groucho steps forward for his O'Neill interludes, the women stand frozen in the background, their faces out of focus as an image of their incomprehension.

Like Groucho, Chico and Harpo are also introduced at first as affecting the pretense of belonging in the upper-class WASP milieu of Mrs. Rittenhouse's party. Both receive formal introductions, Chico as Señor Emanuel Rivelli, a highly paid musician engaged to perform at the social event, and Harpo as the Professor, arriving in tuxedo, top hat, and cape. As with Groucho, their masquerade is immediately revealed, and in a subsequent scene in which they substitute John Parker's copy of *After the Hunt* for Beaugard's original, their working-class ethnicity is emphasized through a misuse of English and allegiance with the unknown young painter. Charles Musser points out that Leonard Marx developed the Italian immigrant character that would become Chico growing up "on the tough streets of polyglot New York," an experience from which he "learned to assume different identities as a way of escaping different situations" (69). In the scene in which they switch the painting, Chico and Harpo make comedy from the "confusion, frustration, and wacky wordplay that they probably heard growing up on the Lower East Side," where "first generation Jews and Italians constantly struggled to communicate with each other in a language that neither had yet mastered" (Musser 66). When Chico asks Harpo for "a flash" in order to see in the darkened room where the painting is stored, the latter pulls on the flesh of his cheek, and takes from his pocket a fish, a flask, cards in a flush, and a flute before finally understanding and removing a flashlight from under his coat. Not only does this scene make fun of their English, but by helping John Parker get his painting seen, Chico and Harpo also deflate the prestige of Mrs. Rittenhouse's presentation of the Beaugard, showing instead that the work of a young unknown, with neither money nor prestige, may warrant as much attention.

In another scene that foregrounds the constructedness of social identity as well as again emphasizing his ethnicity, Chico unmasks Chandler as really Abie the fish peddler:

> *Chico:* How did you get to be Roscoe W. Chandler?
> *Chandler:* Say, how did you get to be an Italian?
> *Chico:* Never mind, whose confession is this?

The exchange hints at the fact that "Chico" the Italian and "Roscoe" the WASP are in reality two Jews, Leonard Marx the comic and Abie the fish peddler. By pointing out the need for Jews to masquerade, to hide their ethnicity, the film comments on a lack of Jewish access to opportunity. Musser sums up this critical dimension of the Marx Brothers' resistance to the social hierarchy represented by the Rittenhouse party when he describes

The Marx Brothers (left to right: Groucho, Harpo, Zeppo, and Chico) disrupt a staid WASP society gathering with their ethnic and sartorial nonconformity in *Animal Crackers* (Victor Heerman, Paramount). Collection Ina Rae Hark.

them in *Animal Crackers* as "Jewish hustlers insinuating themselves into WASP high society. . . . This comic premise is an aggressive assault on the exclusionary policies being applied to Jews by WASP-dominated universities, country clubs, and other public and private institutions" (63).

But despite the critiques of class privilege and exclusion of Jews to which he contributes in *Animal Crackers*, Chico's character also fits the pattern of Italian American representation that Fred Gardaphe describes as a kind of minstrelsy, developed further by other Jewish actors such as Edward G. Robinson and Paul Muni in classic gangster films that would soon follow. These characters stereotyped Italians as intellectually inferior through their misuse of broken English—made more glaring in *Animal Crackers* by contrast to Groucho's verbal dexterity (even if ethnically inflected)—and in the case of the gangster characters, through their criminality and violence. As Musser points out, the linguistic patterns of these characterizations may have had some basis in historical fact; nonetheless they endorsed essentialist ideas about Italian immigrant identity and offered Anglo-American viewers reassurance of their superiority (14).

Like *Animal Crackers, Whoopee!* originated as a hit Broadway play. Before making the movie version, Samuel Goldwyn signed Cantor to a five-year, five-picture deal, promising him $100,000 per film and 10 percent of the profits (Jenkins 171). Such a lucrative contract was motivated by his success on Broadway, where *Whoopee!* was the top earning musical in 1928–29, averaging over $40,000 in ticket sales per week (Jenkins 155). As with John Ford's use of Tracy and Bogart in *Up the River,* this signing was part of an established pattern since the adoption of synchronized sound, whereby Hollywood studios lured away "top talent from the eastern stage for talking pictures" (Jenkins 153).

In *Whoopee!* Cantor plays a hypochondriac who travels to the Southwest for a rest cure, but instead gets mixed up in the family conflict between Sally Morgan (Eleanor Hunt) and her rich father. She wants to marry a young man named Wanenis (Paul Gregory), but since he is half Indian, her father forbids it, insisting that she wed Sheriff Bob Wells (Jack Rutherford) instead.

Again like the Marx Brothers in *Animal Crackers,* Cantor in *Whoopee!* has an Anglo name, but is also an ethnic outsider who creates social disorder by contributing to a comic critique of WASP privilege. Cantor's use of Yiddish inflections, puns, double entendre, and his subtle references to the experience of Jews becoming white, along with his masquerading as both Native American and in blackface, all undermine the idea of social difference that structures the film's romance narrative. However, while Jenkins is correct that Henry's ability to assume different racial and ethnic identities at will "undercuts the rigid racial categories and strict boundaries of the romance plot," the prerogative to present such racial and ethnic masquerade, along with his romantic relationships with his blond nurse, Mary (Ethel Shutta), also demonstrate Cantor's ability to present his character as white (173). An example of this dual positioning occurs as Henry listens to Wanenis bemoan how race prevents him from marrying Sally:

> *Wanenis:* But I'm only a small part Indian . . . my great grandfather married a white girl.
>
> *Henry:* So did mine. What is that. . . . Did you know I'm a half-breed?
>
> *Wanenis:* Are you a half-breed?
>
> *Henry:* Sure, I "breed" through one side of my nose.

This exchange between Henry's character and Wanenis exemplifies Cantor's skill with the humor based on homonyms and puns that the Marx Brothers also manipulated so effectively. Furthermore, it refers to the immigrant experience whereby Jews were often regarded as less than white, what Karen Brodkin describes when she states that "the United States has a

history of anti-Semitism and of beliefs that Jews were members of an inferior race" (116). Yet while the narrative in *Whoopee!* doesn't allow Wanenis
to marry the white girl until it is shown that he never was Indian after all,
Henry, because of his ability to pass as white, never faces such a barrier with
the blond Mary. In describing this exchange between Henry and Wanenis,
Michael Rogin comments on the Cantor character's ability to occupy both
sides of this racial divide: "He [Henry] is speaking as a white man, but since
Jews were 'Oriental,' racially stigmatized . . . the [half-breed] joke has a
double edge" (151).

Whoopee! found its audience mainly in northern cities (Jenkins 166).
Because small-town theaters had been slower to convert to sound, the
numerous musicals made in the early years of talkies were aimed more at
urban audiences, with their large numbers of immigrants, many of them
Jewish immigrants. Excitement over the considerable returns from their
urban-based strategy caused studios to deemphasize the "westerns and
other film genres favored by small town exhibitors. . . . Only about a third
of the films planned for the 1929–30 season would be available as silent pictures" (Jenkins 162). Small-town theaters were therefore forced to either
add the sound equipment or go under, but studios also realized they could
reach a larger audience by providing a product that would appeal to audience tastes outside the big northern cities (Jenkins 162). Therefore
Whoopee!'s mixing of genres—comedy with the western and the musical—
was also an example of a broader strategy of combining genres with proven
appeal in cities with comedy to form a hybridized kind of film "that might
attract both urban and rural audiences" (Jenkins 167).

Cantor and the Marx Brothers were attractive to Hollywood precisely
because they had the versatility to mix comedy with musical performance.
The varied structure of *Whoopee!* and *Animal Crackers,* moving from romance
to comic performance to musical number, allowed them to combine the different genre elements in a way that moved quickly enough to avoid boring
audience members of diverse tastes. Similarly, the humor of these New York
comics could play both to those viewers who understood its commentary
about ethnicity and race and to audiences who liked it simply for the zany,
anarchistic world it created.

Richard Maltby has written that most analyses of American films of the
early 1930s—before the restrictions of the Production Code were fully in
force—have foregrounded how they subverted dominant ideology, but
often by taking too few films as representative and ignoring the economic
factors that, in his view, were more determinative of Hollywood movies in
this period:

The dominant critical paradigm has accepted and inverted the perspective of contemporary moral reformers, valorizing as subversive, for instance, what reviewers at the time denounced as "the fashion for romanticizing gangsters." In many accounts, such assumptions are confirmed by a critical interpretation of around twenty-five movies—roughly one percent of Hollywood's total output of feature films during the period 1930–1934—taken to be representative of Hollywood's output. . . ."Pre-Code" Hollywood is represented by "Some Anarcho-Nihilist Laff Riots" featuring the Marx Brothers, the subversion of dominant sexual ideology by Mae West and Marlene Dietrich . . . and a trio of gangster movies.   ("Production Code" 39–40)

The seven films analyzed here as representative of genres that were prominent in this year do not typify Hollywood production for the year as a whole. Rather, they used the new technology of sound, and worked within the demands of genre, to present insightful critiques of inequality within American society made worse by the Depression. In that sense they place the social issues of the time within a broader context of materialist cinema history, a history that now included spoken dialogue in all its diverse forms.

1931

Movies and the Voice

CYNTHIA ERB

The Depression Deepens

As the economic crisis stretched into its second year, any sense that Hollywood and the nation at large might be pulling out of the Depression was vanishing. At the end of the year Walter Lippmann wrote, "It is no longer open to serious question that we are in the midst, not of an ordinary trade depression, but of one of the great upheavals and readjustments of modern history" (5). Motor vehicle sales plummeted, causing the Detroit auto factories to lay off 100,000 workers. Almost three thousand banks failed.

One person whose financial fortunes had not been harmed by the Depression, gangster Al Capone, was finally brought to justice this year. While the government could never convict him of the many murders he had authorized, they managed to prove him guilty of failing to pay taxes on his ill-gotten gains. Also on the justice front was the beginning of what would become a protracted case of race and prejudice. In Alabama, two groups of unemployed young people, one black and one white, were riding the rails looking for work and got into an altercation. By the time the train arrived at its destination, nine black men, the "Scottsboro Boys," had been arrested and accused of gang rape. It would take many years and many trials for the charges to be proved baseless and the crime to have been fabricated.

Meanwhile, aspiration and innovation did not cease in the face of the crushing economic collapse. Many responded by reaching for the sky. French balloonist Auguste Piccard ascended to the stratosphere, and aviator Wiley Post flew around the world in the fastest time ever recorded. The famous statue of Christ was erected on a mountaintop overlooking Rio de Janeiro, Brazil. In New York two landmark skyscrapers, the Chrysler Building and the city's tallest, the Empire State Building, were completed.

Artists created Felix the Cat and Dick Tracy in the comics, *Night Flight, The Waves, Tropic of Cancer,* and *The Glass Key* were added to bookshelves, the curtain rose on *Cavalcade* and *Mourning Becomes Electra,* and the *Grand Canyon Suite* and *Mood Indigo* appeared in record stores. Women had their first opportunities to dye their hair with Clairol, feed their babies Beech-Nut foods, and make breakfast pancakes with Bisquick. And the United States officially embraced "The Star-Spangled Banner" as its national anthem.

The film industry continued to slash production budgets, lay off personnel, and adopt more conservative operating methods. The introduction of sound had delayed the Depression's impact on Hollywood, but this year Warner Bros. and Twentieth Century Fox went into the red (Balio 15). Already in debt from 1930, Universal shut down in February for a brief production recess. After having temporarily abandoned production of spectaculars such as *All Quiet on the Western Front* the previous year, the studio shifted to less expensive A-class films such as its horror hits, *Dracula* and *Frankenstein*. RKO, which had entered into reorganization, produced the epic western *Cimarron,* which ended up on the list of the year's top box office attractions, yet was so expensive it still failed to turn a profit. The mixed success of this and other westerns may account for the studios' abandonment of A-westerns for much of the decade.

It was the closing year in the transition to sound, which had begun in 1926. By the end of this year, the studios had adopted what Donald Crafton calls the "modulated sound track"—an approach to sound based on harmonious mixing of voice, music, and sound effects, as well as restraint and narrative motivation of sound elements (443). We have become so accustomed to films employing the modulated sound track that films made during the transition-to-sound period may seem creaky by comparison. The early years of sound were actually a time of experimentation with the sound track. Some films showed an interesting play with voice and sound design that would not be possible later on, as principles of the modulated sound track took hold.

Four films released early in the year, *Dracula, The Front Page, The Public Enemy,* and *Cimarron,* occupy this brief moment between the end of silent cinema and the full adoption of classical sound style. Their sound aesthetics are based on the rich vocal performances of such actors as Bela Lugosi and James Cagney. During this period, the film industry had been recruiting novelists and playwrights to provide dialogue for the talkies. Some of these writers had prior experiences with leftist politics, as well as modernist artistic movements. Studying the writers who created dialogue for the early talkies can enrich our understanding of the varied political and stylistic possibilities of this period.

The studios' drive to economize may have supported the push toward full standardization of the sound track. At the beginning of the year, release patterns were still characterized by the three transitional "versions" of the transition-to-sound period—dual versions, foreign language versions, and synchronized versions. Dual versions were films released simultaneously as both silent and sound productions. *Dracula* was a late dual version. Foreign language versions (or multilinguals) were made for international markets, usually in German, French, or Spanish. A Spanish version of *Dracula* was made by a different cast and crew, who shot after hours on the same sets used for the original production.

Charles Chaplin called his hit *City Lights* a non-dialogue film, but it was essentially a synchronized version with music and sound effects. *Tabu*, a romance in Tahiti with a synchronized score, was released only days after the untimely death of director F. W. Murnau in an automobile accident at the age of forty-three. Throughout the transition-to-sound period, studios had been in the habit of creating "new" synchronized versions by adding music and sound effects to their old silent films. Early in the year, a synchronized version of *The Birth of a Nation* (1915) created turmoil in numerous release markets such as Detroit, where the mayor ordered the film's withdrawal two days after it opened to forestall protests and rioting.

At the beginning of the year, then, the last remnants of the silent cinema could still be detected in release patterns. By mid-year, the studios were pushing hard for total conversion to the talkies. They abandoned production of foreign language versions, citing their expense, as well as a belief that foreign audiences were favoring the stars of the original films (Crafton 436). Instead, they turned to recently improved techniques in dubbing and subtitling. *Variety* reported that not a single dual or synchronized version had been announced for the 1931–32 season. At the beginning of the year, about 5,000 "silent" theaters still existed (either unwired or still using sound-on-disc). By October, that number had dropped to about 1,500, which would have to convert or no longer function as film theaters ("End of Silent Films" 62).

This year's films were the first to exhibit the impact of the 1930 Production Code. The studios never really flouted the Code, but initially their adherence to its strictures was uneven. As ticket sales sagged, the studios seemed more open to risqué material. The popular fallen woman genre was a case in point. Fallen woman films, such as *A Free Soul* with Norma Shearer and *Dance, Fools, Dance* with Joan Crawford, illustrated the industry's belief that women made an enormous impact on filmgoing—comprising well more than half the film audience, and influencing the filmgoing choices of a percentage of male customers. Greta Garbo had a hit with *Susan Lenox, Her Fall and Rise,* the title of which refers to the sexual "fall" and class rise characteristic of the genre. A montage sequence shows Susan sleeping her way to the top (literally), ending up in a skyscraper penthouse. As this image of the ascent of the tall building symbolizes, fallen woman films accorded the free sexuality of their protagonists a "phallic" presence, which eventually attracted the wrath of censors.

Two genres that received new life this year were the newspaper film and the gangster film. Though both had existed in the 1920s, they seemed to epitomize the way the silent genres were being reconstituted for sound. Along with comedy hits such as the Marx Brothers' *Monkey Business,* the newspaper and gangster films established an early sound aesthetic based on speed, wit, topical references, and urbanity. Critics were becoming sensitive to how quickly sound was transforming screenwriting practices. One critic chided Frances Marion, a famous screenwriter from the silent period, for not realizing that the type of "old silent" story found in *The Champ* did not play anymore (Hall 29).

If the rapid changes brought by sound were celebrated, the writers who helped make the revolution possible were not. In the late 1920s and 1930s, Hollywood had recruited new writers from Broadway and the publishing world to specialize in dialogue for the talkies. During the year, *Variety* published a series of backlash articles charging that these overpaid screenwriters from the East were too often being bailed out by old stalwarts from the silent days (see "Breaks Again" and "Waste in Story Preparation"). The agenda fueling this backlash remains unclear. Perhaps it was a conservative reassertion of the authority of industry insiders; perhaps it represented a reaction against labor unrest among writers. Whatever the case, the new writers were perceived as a group of outsiders who were inspiring unease.

Historians Paul Buhle and Dave Wagner, who study the Blacklist, have challenged film historians to pay more heed to the leftist political backgrounds of many of the writers who came to Hollywood at this time—such as John Bright, one of the writers for *The Public Enemy* (7–9). Actually, the writers from the East represented a wide range of political perspectives, but their work was key to a new set of political impulses in early sound cinema. Moreover, a self-consciousness about voicing and sound found in some of these films may have been related to the writers' previous experiences in literary movements of the 1910s and 1920s. Strictly speaking, the films were not modernist, but they often exhibited the rhythms and themes favored by the American moderns.

Therefore, a consideration of the "voice" in the films of this year has to take into account the last remnants of the silent tradition; scripting and dialogue; vocal performance; and language as a theme.

Dracula Talks

A popular discourse still found on the DVD for *Dracula* asserts that Tod Browning was an experienced silent filmmaker who was intimidated by sound, even to the point of yielding some of the direction to cinematographer Karl Freund. This critical stance finds the film lacking, particularly against its successor at Universal, James Whale's brilliant *Frankenstein*. While *Dracula*'s unevenness can be traced to its sound track, and particularly to an unease surrounding the voice of the vampire, Judith Halberstam reminds us that Bram Stoker's epistolary novel *Dracula* accords the vampire few lines (91). Murnau's *Nosferatu* (1922) was silent. And the stage play by Hamilton Deane and John Baldeston, which featured Bela Lugosi and became the basis for the Browning version, kept the vampire offstage most of the time and gave him few lines. The Browning version thus marked the first time it could really be said, "Dracula Talks!" As it turned out, this was a problem.

Dracula's release in dual versions complicated its relationship to dialogue. In addition, using the play as a source presented the production team with a dilemma, as it was set entirely in England, and it emphasized vampire-hunter Van Helsing (Edward Van Sloan) and estate agent-turned-vampire's lackey Renfield (Dwight Frye) more than Dracula. At the time of production, Murnau's *Nosferatu* was out of circulation, due to litigation from the Stoker estate. Universal reportedly secured a print, which was consulted by the crew (Lennig 91). The reason for *Dracula*'s hybrid style pertains in part to the nature of Browning's assignment—that the film should work in both silent (titled) and sound (talkie) forms. This produces a schizophrenic effect, in which part one, set in Transylvania, seems strongly inspired by *Nosferatu,* while part two, set in England, has the drawing room effects of the play.

Although *Dracula* does not seem frightening now, it was the first major horror film in sound. We must consider the possibility that its sound track made a great impact on its audiences. The lingering impact of its sound elements may help to account for a surprising decision to censor Dracula's dying groans (heard offscreen as he is being staked by Van Helsing) for a reissue of the film in the late 1930s (Lennig 120). This censorship of Dracula's voice is related to a larger pattern for representing the vampire's voice in the film:

sometimes the authority of Dracula's voice is exploited; other times long passages of his silence are emphasized. Although Lugosi had gained a reputation for Dracula by playing the part for years onstage, Universal almost refused to consider him, believing he was "too foreign" for the part (Lennig 95). The accented voice is of course the key signifier of foreignness; this early sound film tended to approach it in contradictory terms of both foregrounding and censorship. In part one, sections that stress the vampire's silence reinforce his hypnotic command over humans and creatures; similar passages of silence contribute to the marginalization of the character in part two. And whereas Dracula's thickly accented voice supports the poetic, atmospheric effects of the Transylvania scenes, his foreign voice becomes a source of mockery and exoticization in the British scenes of part two.

The revelation of the monster in any horror film requires build-up, but it is surprising that the build-up to Dracula's meeting with Renfield should make such heavy use of silence. The sense that there is too much silence in the Transylvania section has inspired the legend that Browning did not know what he was doing. Following talkie scenes that establish the time and locale comes a long section, occasionally punctuated by atmospheric sound effects, comprised of mostly silent scenes of the emergence of Dracula and his wives from their coffins and Dracula's night ride by stagecoach to fetch Renfield to his castle. The sense of a silent aesthetic dominating this section derives from its tendency to quote *Nosferatu* almost directly. Murnau's vampire had been a rat-like creature, associated with primitivism and pestilence. To a limited extent, *Dracula* sustains this conceit. Parts of the castle are in ruins and have dirt floors. When the hands of Dracula and his wives raise the coffin lids, they are match cut with shots of a rat and an insect—associating the vampires' touch with contamination.

For the most part, however, this version is known for dispensing with the idea of Dracula as a grotesque creature. Browning's version cleans him up and turns him into a well-dressed count, exhibiting the charm and sex appeal of Erich von Stroheim's decadent aristocrats. Browning thus established what we still think of as the "definitive" version of the vampire—a stylish, seductive figure. If the film *Dracula* is uneven, there is nothing missing in Lugosi's performance. He possessed the features that made him the definitive Dracula: he was tall, with large, graceful hands used extensively in the film. In his youth, his arresting good looks had led to Romeo-type roles on the Hungarian stage; he was not afraid to play Dracula with the excessive sexual self-confidence the role requires. And Lugosi had the right ancestry: born in Hungary, not far from Transylvania, he had the right voice. The stories that Lugosi's English was not good are not borne out by the film.

After the long stretch of silence, Renfield enters the castle and encounters Dracula, a commanding figure at the top of a grand staircase. Many lines in this scene have become famous. When the wolves outside begin to howl, Dracula pauses to express appreciation: "*Lis*-ten to them . . . *chil*-dren of the night! *What* mu-sic they make!" These are quotable lines, partly because they are well written, but also because Lugosi's intonation makes them unforgettable. Lugosi's accented speech worked both dramatically and poetically. He broke sentences in unexpected places. Sometimes he spoke rhythmically, in cadence; other times he slowed down and overenunciated for effect. When Renfield and Dracula begin to discuss the Carfax Abbey real estate deal that will take Dracula to England, the quality of their voices marks out a difference between East and West that will recur throughout the film. In a crisp, perfect articulation of English, Renfield says, "I followed your instructions implicitly." Dracula replies that he has already chartered a ship for England. He leans over Renfield and speaks slowly, "We will be *lee*-ving . . . to-*mor*-row . . . *ee*-ve-ning."

The first half of the film ends with another silent scene. Having been drugged by Dracula, Renfield faints and Dracula's three wives appear, moving in to attack him. Reappearing, Dracula waves them back, then bends down himself, hands reaching out for attack. The way this scene is shot silent establishes a pattern continued in the later attacks on Lucy Weston (Frances Dade) and Mina Harker (Helen Chandler). There is a story that when Universal head Carl Laemmle Jr. read this scene, he wrote, "Dracula should go only for women" (Lennig 94). Whether true or not, this is but one of a number of indications that the producers understood not just the eroticism of the vampire story, but the transgression implied by Dracula's sexual presence. Against critiques of Browning's hesitation with sound, it could be argued that he deliberately invoked the silent aesthetic to get around censorship. Original audiences were still accustomed to the silent tradition. The film uses speech and the sound aesthetic to suggest clarity and authority, while the silent aesthetic encourages the audience to understand images as ambiguous and to look for encrypted meanings. Shot silent, the last scene in Transylvania suggests a transgressive fluidity of sexuality in the exchange of looks and silent communication between Dracula and his three wives, and in Dracula's attack on Renfield (followed by a fade-out).

Part one establishes a relationship between scenes exhibiting a persistent silent aesthetic and scenes foregrounding the power of Dracula's voice. In part two, which is set in England, this pattern falters, since it uses the talkie format of the play, which originally gave Dracula few lines. A hypnosis plotline is introduced, possibly to give Dracula more visual presence

in scenes showing his hypnotic control over characters. And yet, in a curious reversal of part one, this is a talkie section in which Dracula is much too silent. It is as if Lugosi's thickly accented voice needs containment in the England sections.

Critics who study the vampire have come to stress his foreignness as much as his sexual power: Halberstam and Thomas Elsaesser note that the Stoker and Murnau versions stress the vampire's roots in Central and Eastern Europe, then home to Slavic and Jewish peoples (Halberstam 90). The 1920s had been marked by extreme turmoil around the issue of immigration in the United States, as exhibited in the 1924 passage of the National Origins Act, which severely limited the number of immigrants and effectively ended the great era of immigration (Boyle 8). There was, however, lingering anxiety about Eastern Europe as breeding ground for communism and socialism. Every version of the Dracula story attributes new meanings to the blood motif. Renfield's speech about Dracula's power over him, cemented by the offer of blood-rich vermin to slake his hunger, almost certainly signaled the threat of the "red menace" to original audiences: "A red mist spread over the lawn, coming on like a flame of fire. . . . And I could see that there were thousands of rats with eyes blazing red, like his only smaller. . . . He seemed to be saying, 'Rats, rats, rats. Thousands, millions of them! All red blood, all these I will give you if you obey me.'"[1]

The idea of containing Dracula's force in the England section appears in a small but revealing bit of business involving his first meeting with Dr. Seward and his daughter, Mina. (Character names and relationships from Stoker's novel were changed for the film.) Dracula has traced the Sewards and their companions, John Harker and Lucy Weston, to a concert hall, where the vampire hypnotizes an usher, forcing her to introduce him to the group during intermission. The usher throws open the curtains of the theater box to reveal Dracula, who stands in the aisle behind the theater box. The staging is such that, throughout their conversation, Dr. Seward stands higher on a step than the count. This deliberately reverses the earlier staging of Dracula and Renfield on the staircase at the castle: now, the Western European character stands high on the stair. The entire section works this way: in Transylvania, the power of the vampire emanated with little trouble; in England this power is insistently contained.

In the subsequent scene, one of the first things Mina does is mimic Dracula's (Lugosi's) voice: "It re-*minds* me of the *bro*-ken battlements in my *own* castle . . . in *Tran*-sylvania!" The vampire's voice that was poetic and fascinating in part one has become a joke. Unlike Mina, Lucy has immediately been drawn by Dracula's exoticism. She jokes with Mina, "You prefer

Van Helsing (Edward Van Sloan) confronts Dracula (Bela Lugosi) with a cigarette case containing a mirror in *Dracula* (Tod Browning, Universal). Collection Cynthia Erb.

someone normal, then, like John?" As if to confirm a certain anxiety about the foreign voice in this section, Dracula has little conversational contact with the women; mostly, his voice is used for verbal jousts with the other foreign-accented character, the Dutch Van Helsing. The ideological force of the film is particularly apparent in this antagonist: though he should be the enemy of the vampire, Van Helsing's foreignness continually binds him to Dracula. In one scene, the audience learns that Dracula's image is not reflected in the mirror of a cigarette case. As the two face one another, Van Helsing holds the case up between them, so that the staging makes it clear they are doubles.

At the end of the film, while Van Helsing goes off to stake Dracula, Mina and John Harker march up a long flight of stairs to exit Carfax Abbey—a move associated with life and the future. The couple leaves behind in the dark vault the vampire and his slayer, the two foreign caretakers of death. The original ending of *Dracula* was an epilogue taken from the stage play, in which Van Helsing stepped out onto a theater stage and directly addressed the outgoing audience: "When you get home tonight and the lights have been turned out and you are afraid to look behind the curtains . . . just pull yourself together and remember that after all, *there are such things*" (Deane and Balderston 58). The original finale's juxtaposition of the gruesome sound effect of Dracula's dying groans with the extra-diegetic effect of Van Helsing's comic speech reinforced the film's overall tone, which combined horror with moments of knowing wit. Though Van Helsing and Dracula were intended to be the last to be heard in the film, their foreign voices were eventually cut.

The Front Page: Speech as Noise

The Front Page exemplifies a topical realism common to early sound films—a fascination with what was then the recent historical past. Nearly every character in *The Front Page* was based on a real person from Chicago in the 1910s and 1920s, the period during which Ben Hecht and Charles MacArthur, who wrote the stage version of *The Front Page,* worked in the city as reporters. Walter Burns and Hildy Johnson were based on a famous editor and reporter at the *Chicago Herald-Examiner*. And there was a Chicago murderer who escaped from prison days before his execution (like Earl Williams) (Hilton 2–3). And yet, in creating a play about an editor and reporter in pursuit of the perfect story, Hecht and MacArthur were less interested in topical references than in celebrating the type of criminal reporting both had done in Chicago. In addition, Hecht, who would become one of Hollywood's most important screenwriters, brought to the project a rich and varied literary background that combined journalism with work on modernist literary magazines (such as Chicago's *Little Review*), as well as participation in literary salons (such as New York's celebrated Algonquin Round Table) (Martin 12–13). Critics and playwrights have singled out *The Front Page* as one of the most important American stage comedies of the twentieth century, and this has something to do with the play's distinctive approach to speech—a quality sustained in the film adaptation (Hilton 1). For *The Front Page*, Hecht adopted a highly self-conscious approach to dramatic speech—an approach that would in turn influence the speed and percussive sound of speech in American film comedies of the 1930s. Lines in *The Front Page* communicate, but are not limited to communication in their effects. Sometimes they work poetically, existing merely to create rhythm and noise. Through vocal foregrounding, the film idealizes the language of journalism, suggesting that—in a paradoxical fashion—even when it is deceitful and manipulative, it is still the only kind of language that can be "true."

The film opens as prison employees are running a test of the gallows for the execution of Williams (George E. Stone). The test involves hanging a burlap sack of flour emblazoned with the slogan "Sunshine Flour Insures Domestic Happiness." The image of the flour sack condenses two of the film's targets: domesticity and advertising. This same day, reporter Hildy Johnson (Pat O'Brien) plans to leave for New York, where he will be married and will begin a new career in advertising. Hecht may have been using advertising to satirize other forms of commercial writing, such as Broadway and Hollywood (since he had left journalism for both). In a larger sense, this image points to what Ann Douglas has called the "terrible honesty" of American modern writing—an aggressive, unblinking use of language designed to reject a Victorian sentimentality that was itself figured as feminine (Douglas 33).[2] The film constantly disparages domesticity in favor of the bracing life of the criminal reporter. It rejects the fake, sentimental language of advertising in favor of the singular mix of action, speech, and writing found in newspaper reporting.

The reporter watching the test heads back to the pressroom, where reporters talk and play cards, periodically interrupted by ringing phones. (Walter Burns [Adolphe Menjou] repeatedly calls the pressroom, looking for Hildy.) The reporter picks up a banjo, tunes it, and begins to play "By the Light of the Silvery Moon." Background music was possible at this time, but rarely used. Transition-to-sound films created their texture largely through voices, which functioned in the absence of music scoring (though diegetic or source music was common). As if to comment on this, the tuning and start-up of banjo music, interwoven with the reporters' voices, cues us to the fact that voices and sound effects will be orchestrated like music in this film.

Technical developments in sound filmmaking had made fluid camera movement and quick cutting much easier. Director Lewis Milestone employed a range of visual and sound devices to open up the play. The entrance of Burns offers a dramatic example. In a long tracking shot, Burns storms across the newsroom yelling, "I'm after that bunch of . . . lily-livered politicians who think they're running this town! We've got to have Johnson!" This is a succinct summary of the film's goals—to expose the corruption around the Williams case and to bring Hildy back into reporting. Burns continues onto a loading dock; a low camera angle accents his imposing figure. The blasting of the machinery forces Burns to yell even louder. The mingling of voice and machine sounds recurs in the film, often as voices interact with sounds of phones and typewriters. Like the gangster film, the newspaper film exhibited the fascination of all things modern. Throughout the film, Hildy insists he wants to get married and go to New York, but his behavior around Burns indicates otherwise. Tracking Hildy to his neighborhood, Burns throws a fire alarm switch to create an apparent emergency and draw Hildy outside. Hildy has been talking with his fiancée, Peggy (Mary Brian), in clear standard English. When the alarm goes off, Hildy races toward the door, speaking so fast it is hard to make out what he is saying (something like "If only I had a camera with me"); there are times when the words themselves are of less significance than the conveyance of pure speed. Later in the pressroom, Hildy announces his impending marriage, provoking a reporter to remark, "Why, you'll be like a fire horse tied to a milkwagon." The line obviously pits the high-speed newspaper world against the dullness of domesticity. As the film progresses, it becomes restricted to the single set of the pressroom. The fast speech of Hildy and Burns becomes the film's main form of action.

The cost of creating this hard, fast world is that the film is constantly cruel to those who cannot keep up—women being a case in point. The film's tough modernism pits it against all things feminine, such as Peggy's mother (who is kidnapped in a slapstick stunt) and the prostitute Mollie Molloy (Mae Clarke). Ironically, Mollie's excessive, hysterical voice serves great purpose in the film. In keeping with Douglas's comments, *The Front Page* despises sentimentality, yet it needs Mollie to voice a critique of the heartlessness of the press in its handling of the Williams case. Her attacks on the callous press encourage us to consider the reporters' conduct, but this does not elevate her standing in the film, nor does it lessen the film's attacks on domesticity.

When Burns and Hildy finally get together, it becomes clear they are made for each other. Their bond is defined by the speed and modern devices preferred by the film. Phones delineate their relationship: in one scene, Hildy "breaks up" with Burns yet again, then throws the phone out the pressroom window. In another, Hildy grabs the phone to tell Burns he has gotten the Williams story: "Yes, yes, yes. Don't worry, I'm on the job." Burns and Hildy form an ideal, balanced partnership when they dominate the empty pressroom, one talking on the phone, the other typing. Their work together saves Williams, but inadvertently. This sense of saving Williams as a byproduct is crucial to the film's tone (which differs from that of the remake *His Girl Friday* [1940]). To address directly the victimization of Williams would be to give in to sentimentality. Instead, the film consistently prioritizes a pure, tough commitment to reporting—the quest for the perfect story. The fulfillment of this quest creates as byproduct the heroism that saves Williams and brings down a corrupt political machine.

In later years, the Code would forbid using sound effects to mask obscene language. The film's final line (spoken by Burns), "The son of a ____ stole my watch," is interrupted at the right moment by the slam of a typewriter carriage. This is one of those cases in which censorship actually improved the text (Burns's line had been spoken with the profanity on Broadway). The film, which has promoted the punctuation of dialogue by modern machine sounds, ends on the same note.

Speech and Orality in *The Public Enemy*

Perhaps because *The Public Enemy* exhibits a topical realist style, critics usually discuss it in historical or sociological terms (see Maltby "Why Boys," for example). And yet the psychological dimensions of the film may have influenced later gangster films even more than did *Little Caesar* or *Scarface* (1932). It most clearly demonstrates that the gangster film's conventions refer back to orality—the earliest, most primeval of the stages of infant development. *The Public Enemy* is strongly structured by food and drink motifs. The space of orality predates differentiation: the infant relates to the breast alone, as object of comfort and nourishment; libidinal pleasure (stimulation of the mouth); and even aggression (biting the nipple). This sense of moods layered over the same undifferentiated topography seems useful for considering the entanglements and repetitions of *Public Enemy*'s screenplay. Tom Powers's worlds are constantly entangled: his domestic life is continually ruptured by aspects of mob violence. More striking is the way his mob life keeps echoing his familial conflicts, evident in the replication of parental figures (Putty Nose [Murray Kinnell], Paddy Ryan [Robert O'Connor], Jane [Mia Marvin]), and in the way best friend Matt's (Edward Woods) name and physical features resemble those of Tom's brother, Mike (Donald Cook).

The mingling of pleasure and aggression in orality may account for its traditional association with the mood disorders (depression, bipolar disorder). This in turn is useful for considering James Cagney's pathbreaking performance as the young Tom Powers.[3] Trained as both vaudeville dancer and actor in the naturalist theater, Cagney was equally at ease in comedy and drama. In *The Public Enemy,* he displayed a singular ability to shift rapidly and fluidly through the mood registers, playing one moment with comedic charm, the next with teeth-baring rage. His signature tendency to show his teeth while speaking is but one detail suggesting that his voice should be viewed against the film's overall system of orality. Cagney did not use more slang or ethnic accenting in his lines than the other actors, but his vocal delivery—characterized by nasal intonation and lightning speed—established a mark of difference, such that Tom Powers is the only one in the film who seems to speak "from the street."

The dynamics of voice and orality are most apparent in the "beer and blood" scene and the grapefruit scene, which work to illustrate the entanglement of Tom's private and public worlds. Both scenes are strongly structured by motifs of food and drink. Most significant is beer, which becomes an overcoded symbol signifying both the gangster world and Irish American ethnicity. Indeed, the film overlays domestic and violent uses of beer in a fashion that strikingly resembles the double role of the breast in the oral stage. The "beer and blood" scene depicts Mike's homecoming from World War I. Tom and Matt have placed a large beer keg in the center of the Powers family's dinner table. A sign of Tom's success in bootlegging, the keg literally disrupts family relations, as characters struggle to see around it during the meal. Domestic scenes like this one showcase Cagney's style, as they stage Tom's rebellious outbursts. Donald Cook performs the part of Mike in a fashion that is stiff and formal even by 1930s standards. Apparently struggling with war trauma, Mike sits upright and motionless, staring at the keg in stony silence. Mike's silence and his military uniform echo the film's opening scene, in which Tom's father, wearing a police uniform, had also been completely silent. The silence of Mike and the father establishes both as figures of severity and the law. This silence, of course, contrasts with Tom's tendency to rebel through outpouring of raging speech.

As the family begins a toast to Mike, he jumps up and screams that there is blood in the beer, referring to Tom's violent work and his corruption of the sanctity of the home. Cagney's response makes use of body, gesture, and voice to clarify how different Tom is from Mike. Actors of this time tended to perform from the neck up, but Cagney uses his entire body: here he slouches back in his chair and hoists a beer. Cagney tended to perform aggression with a wicked, sneering smile. The gangster's voice is always instrumental to his aggression: in this film, we do not see Tom shooting all that much; more characteristic is the way he uses his voice for insult and attack. Tom lashes out at Mike, "You ain't changed a bit. . . . You killed and liked it! You didn't get those medals for holdin' hands with them Germans!" A reaction shot shows Mike visibly stricken by this line.

The grapefruit scene repeats a number of elements from the "beer and blood" scene. Furious with his family, Tom has left home and taken up residence in a hotel with his girlfriend, Kitty (Mae Clarke). The table in a hotel room is set, this time for breakfast. Seated with elbows on the table and running his hands through his hair, Tom demands a beer, but Kitty forbids it—her prohibition echoing Mike's. Once again, the clustering of oral terms—food, drink, domesticity—sets the stage for Tom's outburst. Kitty begins to make a wish. At first Tom seems to respond with a smile, "I wish you was a wishing well, s'tha I could tie a bucket t'ya an' sink ya." The line collapses a pleasantry—"I wish you well"—into murderous threat. Again displaying the sliding of moods in his speech, Cagney first smiles, then hardens into sarcasm, then moves into physical attack, shoving a piece of grapefruit into Kitty's face.

Although Cagney is usually remembered as a tough guy, this early performance exploits the androgyny of his features and the indeterminacy of his age. Cagney's vocal power is so important to the film that as Tom loses ground in later scenes, this is communicated through changes in speech. This begins in the relationship with the flapper Gwen, played by Jean Harlow. Because Harlow was the established star at the time of production, their scenes favor her over Cagney. The meeting of Tom and Gwen is filmed outdoors with moving camera shots that follow Gwen strolling on the street, while Tom and Matt drive by in an open car. The visual emphasis on open air and movement suggests that the gangster and the flapper are equals—both fast and free.

But Gwen has the upper hand. In a later scene set at her luxurious apartment, she is stretched out on a settee, her body taking up space in the foreground, while Tom sits hunched in a chair in the background. As if to reinforce the shift in the balance of power, Tom's voice changes in this scene. Gwen speaks very slowly, and she seems to have an effect on Tom, confusing him and slowing him down as well. The dialogue suggests that Tom has not been able to seize control of their relationship. He stutters, "You know, uh, all my friends, uh, think things are different than they are. They figure they know me pretty well, and uh, they don't think I'd go for a merry-go-round."

Near the end of the scene, Gwen sits on Tom's lap and pulls his face to her bosom, exclaiming, "Oh, my bashful boy!" In a variation on the maternal tensions characteristic of the oral stage, *The Public Enemy* depicts Ma Powers (Beryl Mercer) as a reduced type, while the threatening maternal function surfaces in the other women—Kitty, Gwen, and Jane. The crisis point in this pattern arrives in the meeting with Jane, mistress of Tom's mentor, Paddy Ryan. After gang war has broken out, Paddy takes Tom and Matt to Jane's for hiding. An initial action has Paddy confiscating Tom and Matt's guns, just as Jane arrives with a tray of drinks—another manifestation of the beer and blood motif. This time, Jane is an older woman who overpowers Tom, getting him drunk and seducing him against his will. The

Gangster Tom Powers (James Cagney) meets the flapper Gwen Allen (Jean Harlow) as friend Matt (Edward Woods) looks on in *The Public Enemy* (William A. Wellman, Warner Bros.). Collection Cynthia Erb.

scene of Jane's forced seduction is made more disturbing by her infantilization of Tom, as well as the incestuous overtones of their betrayal of Paddy. As she undresses the inebriated Tom, she tousles his hair and says, "Be a good boy and sit down. . . . Just a goodnight kiss for a fine boy." Tom struggles to come up with a rejoinder but cannot finish one: "Wha . . . in your hat . . . Get 'way from me. You're Paddy Ryan's girl."

The Public Enemy features a few more strong verbal turns from Tom, notably in the comic gun store scene. After the killing of Matt, however, Tom's vocal powers become gradually diminished, evident in his muted apology to his mother in the hospital scene. In the film's famous closing, the silencing of Tom seems strangely related to the stopping of a record that has been playing the period song, "I'm Forever Blowing Bubbles." This song appeared in an early scene with Putty Nose that signaled the start of Tom's career with the gangs. In the final scene, the song is playing on a record while the Powers family dines. After Mike opens the door and discovers Tom's corpse, the record ends abruptly, and only the scratching of the needle is heard. It is as if Tom's murder has ruptured the diegesis. In a striking fore-grounding of sound, the cessation of Tom's voice reverberates in the scratching of the sound track.

■■■■■■■■■ *Cimarron:* The Man Who Talked Too Much

Though Edna Ferber's novel *Cimarron* was the number-one bestseller in 1930 and the film adaptation won the Oscar the next year, the film has been largely ignored in studies of the western until recently, as scholars of the genre have increasingly emphasized revisionist histories of the West. Ferber's background resembled Hecht's: born and raised in the Midwest, she worked for a time as a journalist before moving to New York, where she wrote popular novels and Broadway plays. Lawrence Rodgers states that with *Cimarron* and other works, Ferber remained committed to her political roots in the liberal strand of the progressive tradition, as well as first-wave feminism (xvii). The film *Cimarron* has been criticized for being too concerned with the specifics of history and women's melodrama, but Ferber was apparently uninterested in pursuing the western as pastoral myth. *Cimarron* consistently departs from the standard western in its han-dling of history, gender, and language. It adapts the genre's conventions for the cause of reform. As such, its hero, Yancey Cravat (Richard Dix), talks too much.

Sarah Kozloff observes that the western's attitude toward language is contradictory. The model westerner is taciturn, yet nothing is of greater sig-nificance in this genre than "a man's word" (139–46). Westerns frequently associate talkativeness with women and other subordinate characters, while valuing a hard, stoical masculinity built on silence. *Cimarron* is a lib-eral western that requires its hero to talk—and talk and talk. Yancey is emo-tionally expressive and always ready to speak about any of the film's many reform causes—Indian rights, the corruption of oilmen, women's rights, antisemitism, miscegenation, and more. Like any westerner worth his salt, Yancey's skills as a gunman defy belief. But in the film's terms, his roles as attorney and newspaper editor are more important. His main weapon is language, and this is also his legacy.

As Peter Stanfield observes, revisionist studies of the western place more emphasis on "issues of national cohesion, American identity, and experiences of modernity" (12). Unlike the typical western, *Cimarron* is explicitly interested in the modern: it opens with the Oklahoma Land Rush of 1889 and follows the settling of a fictional town called Osage up to what was then the present—1930. It shares a theme—the disappearance of the

West—with later westerns such as *Shane* (1953) and *The Man Who Shot Liberty Valance* (1962), but *Cimarron* refuses to mourn this loss as do the other films. When the frontier finally closes, persons other than the westerner can take over.

Cimarron's opening sequence depicting the Oklahoma Land Rush features images of hundreds of horses and buggies, supported by a sound track of thundering hooves, that remains impressive and must have astonished the film's first audiences. Before the rush begins, Yancey, who is a trusting, good-natured man, announces to friends the stretch of land he plans to stake. Unbeknownst to him, a prostitute named Dixie Lee (Estelle Taylor) is listening. During the rush, she chases after Yancey and deceives him by deliberately driving her horse into a gulch and calling out for help. Yancey turns back to find her and dismounts, but Dixie steals his horse and races off, staking the claim for herself. Despite her deception in this scene, Dixie is the film's "prostitute with a heart of gold," and the image of her standing as possessor of the land at the film's outset establishes the feminist flavor of what is to come. Indeed, this is a rare western in which both the female types—wife and prostitute—prevail.

This setback forces Yancey to choose the life of the town over that of the frontier. This begins a long narrative, setting the fortunes of Yancey, his wife, Sabra (Irene Dunne), and their children against the gradual settling of Osage. At first little more than mud streets and flimsy wooden buildings, the town becomes more and more civilized. In one scene, piping is being installed for running water, creating open trenches in the streets. Yancey gets into a gunfight with a bandit named the Kid (William Collier Jr.), their showdown making use of the trenches in an apparent allusion to World War I.

Yancey's heroism transcends the gunfighter archetype, however. He sets up a newspaper called the *Oklahoma Wigwam* in which his powers with language prevail. As editor, he champions Indian rights. As lawyer, he takes up causes of the oppressed. In one early scene, Yancey is asked to serve as preacher at a Sunday service. His ability to make an all-inclusive community is stressed by the coexistence of several Christian denominations (listed by Yancey), as well as local Indians and a Jewish peddler named Sol Levy (George E. Stone), whom Yancey has rescued from being lynched in the street by a villain named Lon Yountis (Stanley Fields). The ideal of the western experience as melting pot is one of the film's central themes—reinforced in this scene's satire of a busybody named Mrs. Tracey Wyatt (Edna May Oliver), who chatters about how her ancestors can be traced back to the signers of the Declaration of Independence. The entire scene is designed

Yancey and Sabra Cravat (Richard Dix and Irene Dunne) and son Cim arrive in the town of Osage, which is still being built, in *Cimarron* (Wesley Ruggles, RKO Radio). Collection Cynthia Erb.

around Yancey's power as a speaker: while he is speaking to the assembly, his plan is to flush out Yountis, who killed the previous newspaper editor in town. After saying a few words about a passage in Proverbs, Yancey begins to expose Yountis's identity as killer: "I will tell you the name of that man is . . ." At this moment, Yountis shoots from the congregation. Yancey returns fire and kills him, finishing his speech, "*was* Lon Yountis." This action caps a Sunday service that has defied convention. The combination of gunfighting and speech does the job, but most of the time it is Yancey's speech that matters.

True to the genre, Yancey is a restless wanderer, who periodically leaves town—once to fight in the Spanish-American War, later just to drift. His disappearances, which become more pronounced as the film goes on, create openings for Sabra to take over his job, and eventually his legacy. The film's two great causes appear to be the promotion of women to jobs of authority and the melting pot vision of the West. This political vision creates several internal contradictions, some of which are noted problems of the progressive tradition. The only African American character, a boy named Isaiah (Eugene Jackson), is a stereotypical servant who dies early in the film. In addition, the treatment of Indian rights issues is inconsistent. More than once, new Indian territories are opened up by the government, and Yancey cannot wait to grab territorial land for himself. Yet he remains pious about Indian rights issues, repeatedly denouncing views of others— notably Sabra—that strike him as unenlightened.

At one point, Yancey disappears for five years. While he is away, Sabra is forced to take over his newspaper, though she leaves his name on the masthead. She is supported by Sol, who gradually rises from the status of street peddler to prosperous clothing merchant. The partnership of Sabra and Sol explicitly embodies Ferber's dual promotion of the contributions of women and ethnic immigrant groups in settling the West. (Ferber's father came from an immigrant Hungarian Jewish family.) Also assisting Sabra is Jesse Rickey (Roscoe Ates), a stuttering man who has worked with Yancey on the paper. As the film unfolds, Jesse gradually loses his stutter—a detail suggesting Yancey's influence through language. This film takes the western's conventional supporting characters—the immigrant settler, the comic sidekick—and promotes them to a central place. As Yancey's disappearances become longer and more frequent, supporting characters fill in, and the film inevitably proceeds into the modern moment.

In 1907, Yancey plans to run for governor as candidate of the Progressive Party. He and Sabra argue because Yancey wants to run a front-page story attacking government agents for stealing oil money from the Indians. He also wants to promote the cause of Indian citizenship, prompting Sabra to retort, "Give them the vote! The people here would mob you." Throughout the film, Sabra has displayed racist intolerance toward Indians. She changes partly because Yancey educates her, and partly because her son Cimarron marries a Native American woman. She also changes because Yancey finally just disappears, leaving her not only the paper, but also a life in politics. The closing scenes, set in 1930, seem to step out of the framework of the western and into the woman's film. Sabra has been elected to Congress on a Progressive platform and is being feted at a banquet in a hotel, where she is to give a speech. The mise-en-scène of the gathering accents the modern in the décor and the radio broadcast that will carry Sabra's speech. The scene strikingly features background music, which has appeared nowhere else in the film. As Claudia Gorbman has observed, sometimes the mere presence of a woman motivates music scoring in Hollywood cinema (80). The use of the music here gives the sound track a reflexive quality, as if it has caught up with modernity (in the sophisticated sound mix and the reference to radio). It also reinforces the dominant presence of the woman over the closing scenes.

After so many of Yancey's speeches, the film closes with one by Sabra: "The women of Oklahoma have helped build a prairie wilderness into the state of today. The holding of public office by a woman is a natural step." After the speech, all go out to visit an oil site on the Bear Lake reservation. A drifter is killed in an explosion, acting to sacrifice himself to save others. Of course, it is Yancey. Ferber had come up with this idea before the Wall Street crash, but the conceit of great man-turned-drifter probably acquired resonance in the Depression. At the same time, it is noteworthy that Yancey goes from being so famous and outspoken to such an abject state. In a conceit that anticipates *The Man Who Shot Liberty Valance,* Yancey is described by Sol as "part of the history of the great Southwest," but the westerner has to disappear in order that modern history can happen.

Conclusion

By mid-year, *Variety* was announcing a "reduction of chatter in pictures," one of many signs that the talkie style was finally receding in favor of the modulated sound track ("Less Talk"). The switch to the modulated sound track brought new possibilities—notably in the increased use of music scoring. The difference between pre-classical and classical sound styles can be detected in the contrast between the hybrid style of *Dracula* and the balanced classicism of *Frankenstein;* or in the contrast between the manic, nonstop vocal arrangements of *The Front Page* and the later *His Girl Friday* (which is slower, more classical). As the decade wore on, Cagney's vocal style became slower, more subdued—apparent in the differences between the early performance in *The Public Enemy* and later performances in such films as *Each Dawn I Die* or *The Roaring Twenties* (both 1939). Westerns disappeared from production schedules for several years. When they returned in the late 1930s, they featured heroes displaying more taciturn styles than that of *Cimarron*'s Yancey Cravat. Lest we assume that these latter movies and performances represent a standard in sound films from the beginning, however, we should not overlook the earlier films of this year, which were designed to exploit the power of the actor's voice.

NOTES

1. I am indebted to Kendall Phillips for noticing the significance of this passage (24–25). Lugosi was a political refugee who fled Hungary after taking a leading role in a movement to unionize theater employees. Though he later shrugged this off as the action of a romantic youth, he had been the type of socialist from Eastern Europe demonized by the film.

2. I am indebted to Matthew Ehrlich for noticing this application of Douglas's concept to *The Front Page* (20–21).

3. For detailed analyses of Cagney's acting style, see Naremore and Sklar *City Boys*.

1932

Movies and Transgression

DAVID LUGOWSKI

This year ushered in the worst of the Great Depression. Thirteen million Americans were unemployed, business losses were reported up to $6 billion, and industry was operating at half its capacity from before the Crash. Extremes, challenges, uncertainties, and episodes of upheaval set the tenor for the times, both at home and abroad. Japan took full control of Manchuria; over 10,000 Salvadorans were massacred in an indigenous uprising; Italy's Benito Mussolini met with Pope Pius XI to woo Catholics to fascism; the Nazis declared Adolf Hitler their presidential candidate; and French president Paul Doumer was assassinated. A hunger strike by Gandhi helped pass the Poona Pact, granting equal rights to India's "untouchables." On the domestic front, President Herbert Hoover's Reconstruction Finance Corporation failed to stem the economic devastation. Aldous Huxley's *Brave New World* predicted a grim future. Popular songs reflected desperation ("Brother, Can You Spare a Dime?"), denial ("Say It Isn't So"), melancholy ("Willow Weep for Me"), and even hope ("Happy Days Are Here Again").

Ordinary people enjoyed Walter Winchell's brash radio gossip, and those who could afford it were now able to purchase Revlon makeup, Campbell's tomato juice, and Frito's corn chips at groceries. The middle classes bought instantly developing Polaroid film and saw movies in an incredibly lavish new showplace, Radio City Music Hall. The underprivileged, too, had some moments of triumph. Women, facing increased pressure to enter into prostitution for money, found heroines in Amelia Earhart, making her transatlantic flight, and Hattie Wyatt Caraway of Arkansas, the first woman elected to the U.S. Senate. The Norris–LaGuardia Act passed, barring companies from requiring that employees promise not to join unions as a condition of their hiring. And the newly elected president, Franklin Roosevelt, promised a "New Deal."

Issues of flamboyant excess, poverty, violence, politics, and gender inevitably manifested themselves in the cinema. Hollywood, heavily invested in theaters and sound equipment, had believed that the "talkies" were Depression-proof. Nothing prepared the studios for the losses of this year:

Warner Bros. lost $14 million; Paramount lost $21 million and had to declare bankruptcy; and even Hollywood's newest "major," RKO, barely four years old, faced a punishing $10 million loss (Jewell 44). As capitalism and the "American way" seemed to fail, the studio system at once mastered much about sound cinema, preserved the classical paradigm established before the twenties, while also testing that classicism. Alternative cinemas, too, while unable to keep pace with Hollywood's costly technologies, responded to the Depression in surprising ways and with more honesty and realism about race, ethnicity, and class. Experimentation in genre and technique, overcoming the static qualities of earlier talkies; spectacle ranging from the uniquely exotic to the vaudevillian and the sweetly sentimental; controversy in matters sexual, criminal, and political; a pushing of the envelope alongside outcries about both film content and Hollywood's often conservative, middle-class escapism—all these mark the year in American cinema.

Troubles arose just when some things were going well—at least in terms of filmmakers and film style. Despite earlier triumphs, it was only now that the possibilities of sound were fully realized in Hollywood. The opening montage of picture and sound as Paris awakens in Rouben Mamoulian's masterly *Love Me Tonight* exemplifies this, just as the cross-class singing of "Isn't It Romantic?" promises a utopia hardly possible (Dyer, "Entertainment" 17–34). Musical scoring would come into its own more fully, confidently taking on its classical nondiegetic character. Even a year earlier characters would regularly be found listening to diegetic orchestras, or turning on radios before engaging in love scenes, so that audiences would not be confused about the music's origins. There were fine accomplishments in music quality, too, and composers begin to gain recognition. Max Steiner, uncredited for much of his earlier work, created a notable score for *Symphony of Six Million,* a Jewish-themed film of the kind that Hollywood would soon stop making, and his thumping score for *The Most Dangerous Game* became much imitated in the adventure genre.

Hollywood was also questioning what to do with the plays and novels it had purchased in its quest for dialogue. Speed was the order of the day; even a routinely plotted fifty-eight-minute courtroom drama, *The Trial of Vivienne Ware,* offered dizzying stylistic moments of the kind not expected with classicism, with William K. Howard replacing cuts with swish pans every chance he gets. An overdose of static musicals had all but killed the genre born with sound. The year found few musicals being made, but the genre survived with Mamoulian's contribution, the similarly Continental *This Is the Night,* the Eddie Cantor vehicle *The Kid from Spain,* and *The Big Broadcast,* one of many radio-influenced films.

The cliché about socioeconomic turmoil and political upheaval being good for art was an argument many filmmakers might have endorsed. Black, Yiddish, and Italian filmmakers were, in some cases, finally able to venture into sound, creating landmarks in U.S. independent film. Oscar Micheaux, working on a shoestring budget, created a reply to Hollywood's racist marketing of the American Dream with *Veiled Aristocrats*, a story of a light-skinned black man passing for white who attempts to get his sister to pass and intermarry. Questions of assimilation are also key to *Uncle Moses*, a film in Yiddish and English starring stage legend Maurice Schwartz. Filmed in New York's Lower East Side and in Fort Lee, New Jersey, it portrays a garment manufacturer who dominates his staff, hardly living up to the leadership status of his namesake, and finally brought low by his love for a poor woman and his striking workers. Bridging two worlds, the laborers must replace their transposed *shtetl* with the new community of a union (Hoberman, *Bridge* 163–64).

The studios, meanwhile, became even more "classical" in an organizational sense, with the producer unit system fully set in place (Bordwell et al. 320–29). The heart attack of MGM's Irving Thalberg spelled the end of a central producer system featuring one man overseeing a studio's output. Now a series of producers were each responsible for a smaller number of films per year. The corollary of this control was, ironically, that top directors enjoyed considerable autonomy under producers who favored them. The assemblage of talent and resources allowed creativity (the "genius of the system," in André Bazin's words) at the same time that studio hierarchy threatened to homogenize a profit-seeking product. Herein we have another tension aptly illustrated—how a classical cinema featuring "house" styles could, for a limited number of films, be an author's cinema.

Paramount allowed its top directors—Sternberg, Lubitsch, Mamoulian—their personal stamps on works, and another leading figure (if a lesser artist) returned successfully to the fold. Cecil B. DeMille, the studio's most financially successful filmmaker of the twenties, had struck out on his own. Several talkies released by MGM were not popular and, at the lowest ebb of his career, DeMille was given a one-shot deal at Paramount. The film turned out to be one of his most controversial ever, and hence one of his most popular, given that scandal often brought patrons to the movies. *The Sign of the Cross*, set during the age of Nero, proved to be an excessive yet quintessential expression of DeMille's showman-like, crass, but undeniably distinctive blend of extravagant "sinning" (lesbian seduction, torturing Christians) vanquished by sermonizing virtue.

Elsewhere, Universal gave elbow room to the unusual long takes favored by John Stahl (*Back Street*) and the even more attention-getting style of James Whale. Whale's *Impatient Maiden* features the roving camera and breakaway walls that belie both his theatrical roots and his love of cinema, and the extraneous asylum sequence indulges his gift for peculiar humor. Even little Columbia allowed one in-house "auteur" in Frank Capra, who quickly moved from slapstick to more prestigious assignments. *American Madness* was his most important film to date, a revelatory drama from a director who cut his teeth in silent farce. It was an indication of the times when escapist Hollywood made such direct social commentary and dramatized something that cut as close to viewers' lives as a bank run.

Some studios featured more homogeneous styles but even they afforded interesting directors notable opportunities. MGM's Edmund Goulding made his most prominent film to date with *Grand Hotel,* combining Art Deco glamour with the destitute aristocrats, corrupt executives, and ambitious working women that were such Depression archetypes. Another studio, Warner Bros., did not need to apologize for its studio style or lack of "auteurs," given the urban grit that typified its output. Indeed, directors flourished within the bounds of that style. Tay Garnett came into his own with the romantic yet tough-minded *One Way Passage,* its lovers parted at the finale, while Mervyn LeRoy handed down an equally downbeat ending—and a spectacular lack of closure—with *I Am a Fugitive from a Chain Gang.* "How do you live?" the fugitive's lover asks. "I steal!" George Cukor, a gay theater man like Whale, also entered the ranks of A-directors. He had to fight to keep his credit on Paramount's Lubitschean *One Hour with You* but, supported by rising producer David O. Selznick, found worthy projects at RKO. *A Bill of Divorcement* introduced a new star in Katharine Hepburn, while *What Price Hollywood?*, a dark, reflexive look at Hollywood, featured showy cinematic tropes (e.g., slow motion during an alcoholic director's suicide) that Cukor would rarely use later. Any rosy picture of studio support for emerging artists needs tempering, however. Although Paramount earlier had given her room to grow, Hollywood's lone woman director, Dorothy Arzner, opted to freelance, but not before making one of her finest films, *Merrily We Go to Hell.*

Menace was in the air too, generically and stylistically. Expressionistic lighting appears everywhere, from Maurice Chevalier's "I'm an Apache" number in *Love Me Tonight* to the low-budget *Mystery Ranch*. The U.S. frontier long since closed, the population now predominantly urban, and expensive failures like *The Conquerors* on hand, the western survives largely via B-pictures on the bottom half of another Depression-era development, the double bill. (A flurry of short-lived "Poverty Row" firms like Ajax and Chesterfield emerged to help fill this demand.) Horror becomes prominent, and indeed, in a generic mix typical of this odd year, *Mystery Ranch* plays like a horror film. Horror might have served as an imaginative refraction of the era's fears, or as the promise of escape to other lands with mysterious powers during a time when people felt trapped. The jungle picture vogue in fiction and documentary—*Tarzan the Ape Man, Congorilla*—served similar functions, and these featured horrific sequences as well. More problematically, horror was sometimes based on racial or geographic "Others." Indigenous Haitian practices inspire the first zombie film, *White Zombie,* while the mysteries of an Orientalized Egypt produce *The Mummy*. *The Mask of Fu Manchu,* meanwhile, finds its eponymous villain (Boris Karloff) labeled a "yellow monster." Jungle films participate in this racism too: the title of the colonial prison melodrama *Prestige* refers to the "privilege" of being white.

The tension between establishing new guidelines and playing with style amid cultural upheaval also pervades animated cinema. The first of Disney's Silly Symphonies, *Flowers and Trees,* experiments with conventions that would later become more set. More bizarre, however, are works by Max and David Fleischer, released through Paramount, but made at their own studio. Their Betty Boop cartoons were the most sexual, anarchic, and experimental. One of the richest of the political films in that presidential election year proposes *Betty Boop for President,* using elephants and asses to satirize the main parties, alongside caricatures that speak volumes on how far Herbert Hoover had fallen out of favor. No one is spared, yet the hardest sequence to fathom involves an unrepentant criminal being executed in the electric chair. He does not die, however (as Edward G. Robinson does in the incredibly grim *Two Seconds*), but rather receives a makeover in the chair, transformed into an effeminately groomed "pansy"! Here as in the films portraying the "lost generation" of World War I, this figure signals the crisis of masculinity in a culture where men could no longer provide for their families (Lugowski, "Queering" 3–5).

Other trends address generic—and gendered—inconsistencies, and narrative and performance excesses. The lingering influence of vaudeville dominates comedy, resulting in some of the Marx Brothers' best satire (*Horsefeathers*) and the anarchistic *Million Dollar Legs* (Jenkins 96–107, 214–36, 245–76). Gender play ranges from an explosion of "pansy" humor to the prominence of female comics Lyda Roberti, Polly Moran, and Marie Dressler. The "feminization of American society" during the Depression can even be seen in the way that women dominate box office polls (McElvaine

340). Female stars (Dressler, Janet Gaynor, Joan Crawford) occupy *Motion Picture Herald*'s top three spots, and five (including Greta Garbo and Norma Shearer) of the top six. The violent, male-dominated gangster film, with its own excesses, will not last the year; Hollywood looks to replace it with the female voice, frequently discussing sex. Wise-cracking gals like Ginger Rogers, Wynne Gibson, and Joan Blondell begin rising through the ranks, and Mae West, a key purveyor of excess on the subject of sex, debuts in *Night After Night* and steals the film in a supporting role.

Women and sex raised the issue of prostitution, the subtext wherever matters of women's "security" arose during the Depression. The prominence of films addressed to the most faithful spectators of the era, adult women, was not limited to comedy, however. The romantic melodrama, or "women's picture" as the industry scornfully called it, was in the midst of a vivid "confession" cycle. Shearer, Garbo, Crawford, Constance Bennett, Ruth Chatterton, Marlene Dietrich, Kay Francis, Ann Harding, Miriam Hopkins, and Helen Twelvetrees were sinning in high style, whether they were seduced, emancipated, sacrificing, or keeping their tongues firmly in cheek. These films were stylistically more subdued than the year's comedies, musicals, cartoons, and horror films, but their storylines and resolutions, in which transgressive women were seen as insufficiently punished by cultural bluenoses, were but one site of cultural, indeed ideological, struggle as the Depression worsened (see Jacobs 3–24).

The Monsters: *Scarface, Freaks, The Old Dark House*

Struggles over content became a key issue, leading to fascinating push-pull dynamics during the economic disaster. As profits slid, Hollywood did what Hollywood often does—it stepped up the sex and violence in films. Sound helped; risqué dialogue and gun blasts became more vivid with sound. The Studio Relations Committee (SRC), part of the overarching Motion Picture Producers and Distributors of America (MPPDA), worked to protect films from local censors by regulating content using the conservative Production Code written in 1930. Yet finger-wagging groups were noticing provocative costumes, unrepentant adulterers, "pansy" humor, and what they perceived as the endorsement of criminal violence. The gangster film, having made a splash in 1931, remained prominent, but would soon be shut down (Maltby, "Short and Dangerous" 159–74). Howard Hawks's *Scarface,* with possibly the highest body count amid a thinly disguised tale of Italian American mobster Al Capone (called Tony

Camonte in this film, played by Paul Muni), represents an apotheosis of the genre for the period. Spoofs would soon follow, and actors who became stars in gangster roles (James Cagney, Edward G. Robinson) would play good-guy enforcers in the genre's renaissance.

The hullabaloo over Hawks's landmark saga and the strange mixture of elements within the film show just how conflicted the year was. Its production history was drawn out and troubled; Boris Karloff, somewhat awkwardly cast as rival mobster Gaffney, essays a small part that echoed his journeyman character actor status before *Frankenstein* (1931) rather than his stardom afterward. As producer, the ever-eccentric Howard Hughes was determined to create a sensation, and his meddling involvement was one of the factors in play. Lee Garmes's masterful cinematography—he worked on three of the eight films considered here—shows the advances in fluid camerawork this year. The cinematography, though, alternately complemented and at times seemed upstaged by screenwriter Ben Hecht's cynicism and Hawks's atypically overt use of symbolism. It was certainly common for Hawks to tell of a man's world invaded by a woman, but whereas in other films she is accepted and assimilated into the group, here she is key to its dissolution. And never again would Hawks use symbolism as he does with the X's denoting death found everywhere. They are in the rafters of a ceiling, the shafts of light picking out a target, the Roman numeral for ten on an apartment door, the score on a bowling card when the bowler makes a strike just as the mob does as well, and even in Tony Camonte's facial scar.

So, too, do we find a rangy, flamboyant handling of the characters. Tony's sister Cesca (Ann Dvorak) and his mistress, Poppy (Karen Morley), are aggressively seductive, yet controlled and intelligently real. Tony's sidekick, and later Cesca's lover, Guino (George Raft), is also sleek but he is cool, still, and silent. (Raft, not the strongest actor but a signature face of the era, made an impression with Guino forever calmly flipping quarters. It is suggestive of the times that an actor who always looked sinister, and who reportedly had mob connections, could become a movie hero.) Camonte himself, by contrast, is at times monstrous, not only in the pleasure he gleans from power and violence but also in his often ape-like appearance. Paul Muni, also confirmed as a star with his work here, plays broadly but with compelling bravado, quite a switch from his quiet, simmering intensity in *I Am a Fugitive from a Chain Gang*. From the memorable opening tracking shots of a mob "hit" at a party, decorated with streamers, to the compelling gallery of attractive criminal characters (including Vince Barnett, both hilarious and poignant as Tony's factotum), this was one of the most stylish and stylized gangster films since silent days.

The style was part of the problem. Italian American groups were not happy and media watchdogs were up in arms. An awkward sequence was plunked right into the middle of the film, with concerned citizens having an angry "What are the authorities going to do about gangsters?" discussion, complete with direct addresses to the camera. The film was retitled *Scarface: Shame of the Nation*. Trims were made in the incestuous relationship between Tony and Cesca, but they remained, just as they did in MGM's *Unashamed*. The ending, too, after Tony kills Guino for his involvement with Cesca and then sees Cesca die in the climactic shootout, features what for some is a "gratuitously moral" yet ultimately "irrelevant" scene of Tony cowering before the police who shoot him (J. Baxter 94). Others, however, find the conclusion fitting, indeed essential, with Tony, a complex and sympathetic but never glorified figure, losing control even as he gains in awareness (Wood 65). However the film was read or tinkered with, its power, or what some saw as its subversive appeal, was hardly compromised. Any inconsistency in tone only made *Scarface* even more "1932." A film about the American Dream (an electric sign touting "The World Is Yours" lights up repeatedly throughout the film) going dangerously awry seems an apt message for the time. U.S. capitalism neared its lowest ebb, and Prohibition was clearly a failed experiment that would soon be abolished. The gangster film's short-term eclipse seems oddly fitting then, given that many mobsters were bootleggers, and *Scarface* was a fitting coda to the year's heady brew of monstrous violence and often monstrous "moral" hypocrisy.

The status of what defines an abnormal monster, the role of violence in society, and the place of community codes of conduct, all timely themes, were also in play in the year's most reviled film, *Freaks*. One could understand *Scarface* being produced by the rebel Hughes, helmed by the forever free-lancing Hawks, and circulated by United Artists, a company without a studio that distributed works made by semi-independent mainstream producers. But Tod Browning's bizarre morality tale of circus "freaks" and the revenge they take to protect their own was made at MGM. The glamour factory *par excellence* and the only major to turn a profit this year, it was dominated by its liberated female stars on one side and Louis B. Mayer's patriarchal and aggressively homespun tastes on the other. One balancing factor was central producer Irving Thalberg, with his usually keen story sense, his straining for artistic prestige mixed with profit, and his resistance to the Production Code. Browning was attracted to an old studio property whose circus setting evoked his youth. Circus stories were going out of vogue while horror was very much the order of the day, yet somehow the two were supposed to fit together. The "source" of the horror, and the reactions to it, made for a unique film and a very distinctive reception.

The Depression made the homeless and disabled more visible in U.S. culture, as ideas about the physically challenged were moving from their being "freaks" to those with a "medical problem" (Larsen 170). *Freaks* shows its unusual community trying, as so many were, to earn a living on their own. Many sequences focus on the actual physically challenged or mentally handicapped players performing routine, quotidian activities. When Randian the Living Torso (Prince Randian), a man without arms or legs, lights and then smokes a cigarette using only his teeth and head, one senses a progressive and humane documentary impulse flirting, in true Hollywood style, with an exploitation of his act as entertainment spectacle. (What then to make of his improbable menace at the climax, as he squirms slowly through the mud while the long-legged heroine tries to escape the vengeful "freaks"?) The film gives us two sets of more conventional people, played by established Hollywood players, as points of reference. The clown Phroso (Wallace Ford) and seal trainer Venus (Leila Hyams) are sympathetic and kindly to their disabled colleagues, Phroso flirting with some of the child-like "pinhead" women and being teased and flirted with right back. They are contrasted with trapeze artiste Cleo (Olga Baclanova) and strongman Hercules (Henry Victor), villains right out of silent melodrama who are ambitious for Cleo to seduce and marry the "little person" owner Hans (Harry Earles) and then kill him with slow poison. The handicapped denizens are taken in, even celebrating Cleo as "one of us" in the unforgettable wedding party sequence in which a loving cup is passed from person to person while Cleo and Hercules become more and more brazen with their scornful laughter. Finally, expected to drink from the cup and revolted at their acceptance, she drunkenly tells them off. A uniquely warm film in many respects, especially for Browning, *Freaks* thematizes and then problematizes the very issue of identification in cinema. "Little people" among each other lose their freakishness, and normalcy threatens to become monstrous—but could the film fully negotiate this point, let alone expect Depression audiences to do so?

Freaks was not the only horror film rife with contradictions. Their exoticizing and demonizing of the Other were tempered by the merits of everything from the poignancy of *The Mummy*'s undying romance, to *White Zombie*'s fairy-tale poetry, and the self-aware barnstorming camp of Fu Manchu's entertaining torture sessions. These sessions, notably, are inflicted upon male—rather than the standard female—bodies, signifying not only how "queer" the year was but also pointing to just how deeply the crisis of masculinity during the Depression was cutting. How fitting that the finest-ever telling of *Dr. Jekyll and Mr. Hyde* should combine the directorial control of Mamoulian (especially in the realm of fluid camerawork and a complex use of sound), a European atmosphere soon to vanish in an increasingly xenophobic U.S. culture, and an antihero with multiple personalities, well-suited to the age. With *Freaks,* however, the generic pigeonholing was even more loaded: in many ways it is not a horror film at all, yet it was marketed and made (by MGM, if not by Browning) to be one.

Sometimes the boundaries crossed in this era, when so much was in doubt, transgressed popular taste, especially when they questioned the very nature of humanity itself. When Thalberg supposedly demanded a film that would "out-horror" Universal's successes, Browning responded with a largely gentle and personal piece, flawed but full of unexpected poetry. He envisioned the freaks accidentally maiming Cleo, thus ironically making her "one of them." The ending as it stands, with Cleo inexplicably become a human chicken introduced to a horrified audience, unfortunately substitutes sensationalism for subtlety. It was even planned to show brawny Hercules with a squeaking voice—imagining MGM trying to represent a literal castration makes one reel—but instead he is merely knifed. *Freaks* had already crossed enough boundaries, generically and thematically.

A complex morality play, rife with its split intentions in a year of rapidly switching cultural and political loyalties, *Freaks* raised questions its audiences could not answer. How justified is the revenge of the "freaks" at the finale? Why does one feel the urge to cheer when one of them flicks a switchblade after Cleo's scheme is exposed? Is that finale a concession to the film's links to the horror genre? Are we asked to question our own sympathies and codes of conduct in desperate times? Or switch them back to the "normal" Cleo and Hercules when the "horror" starts? The whiff of exploitation was too strong, but "bad taste" alone was not at stake. Browning's vision asked, imperfectly, for a compassion that audiences could not give the way they did for Frankenstein's monster. Some horrors were too real.

Even Universal, which had kicked off the horror cycle with *Dracula* and *Frankenstein,* did not strike box office paydirt with every film. Such was the case with another borderline horror effort marketed as typical genre fare, *The Old Dark House.* Universal had *Frankenstein*'s gifted director James Whale under contract, but he did not want to be typed as a genre specialist. And genre was always a challenge for Hollywood every bit as much as it was a safe starting position anyway. Too much of one formula bores the audience, while not enough disappoints their expectations. So too with stars: audiences want a consistent persona they can purchase, like any reliable com-

Stranded traveler Gladys DuCane (Lilian Bond) finds out that there are worse things than rainstorms as she is menaced by brutish manservant Morgan (Boris Karloff) in *The Old Dark House* (James Whale, Universal). Collection Ina Rae Hark.

modity, but they need to cathect with the humanity and variety to be found within a distinctive performance style. Boris Karloff had scared audiences in *Frankenstein* even while they could see the monster as childlike, tragically pitiable, undeserving of the treatment it received. Universal tried to play things both ways in giving him big billing in Whale's quintessential "old house" chiller. An opening title card assures audiences that Morgan the butler, dangerous when drunk, is played by the same actor who essayed Mary Shelley's monster and that his role is a tribute to his versatility. And yet, while his performance is splendid, he is a mute character again, robbing audiences of the chance to hear their star's voice (which, as it turned out, was a marvelous instrument). He battles with the heroes and menaces the women, again as in *Frankenstein*; but Morgan is not this time dangerously uncomprehending. Rape is on his mind. What is more, his most tender moment is not reaching for sunlight or playing with a little girl's flowers, but weeping over a deceased, adult male member of the eponymous mansion. Thus new star Karloff plays a mute bisexual whose humane

moment appears at the very end, and who is more of a supporting character than he was in *Frankenstein*. Clearly, Whale's focus, and the film's, was
on more than promoting a new star or playing by the rules of genre.

His early success having enabled him to alternate smaller assigned
tasks with projects that gave him leeway with source material, casting,
and crew, Whale worked with writer friends like Benn Levy (as he did
here) and R. C. Sherriff, and his stock company of British-imported
eccentrics whenever he got the chance. Based on a novel by J. B. Priestley,
The Old Dark House appears to tell a standardized tale of five travelers in
the Welsh countryside forced to take refuge in a menacing mansion
peopled with five counterparts including the effeminate, waspish Horace
(Ernest Thesiger); his hostile religious fanatic of a sister (Eva Moore);
their bedridden, cackling centenarian father (played by actress Elspeth
Dudgeon); the ever-hovering Morgan; and the deceptively disarming Saul
(Brember Wills), actually a murderous pyromaniac. This film, combining
maximum theatrical flamboyance with formidable cinematic grace and
superb character acting, seems to guy its material and then outsmart us by
playing it "straight" when needed (Everson, *Classics* 82). As an openly gay
director who had served in World War I and had extensive theatrical background, Whale knew how to shift gears. He also understood the entire
range of characters he was pinpointing with such detail. His "lost generation" hero was a key fixture in films this year, as were the cynical "jibes"
at heterosexual marriage, family propriety, and even "Christian morality"
(Benshoff 41). They were simply supposed to be confined to moments
within cocktail comedy and self-serious drama, not form the basis of a
brilliant horror movie.

Eventually, the English-flavored and the Continental horror film would
become increasingly Americanized. *Murders in the Rue Morgue*, however,
potently shows the lingering impact of Weimar's *Caligari* impulses. *Dr. X*
looks toward more contemporary impulses, beginning with wisecracking
journalists in New York before unfolding in a European-style Gothic mansion on Long Island. Despite Whale's extraordinary flair for Expressionist
touches, *The Old Dark House* did not veer entirely toward the past of screen
horror or its future, nor did it attempt to straddle them. Rather it followed
its own deliberately campy, dryly sophisticated, and remarkably personal
path. As a film with a classy pedigree, it was critically respected and mod-
erately popular; many films of the day with that tone did well enough in
New York and Los Angeles to justify their being made. But *The Old Dark
House*, as a nonpareil parody of "family values," a culturally and indeed
regionally specific cross-section of lingering Victorian mores, and a horror

film with no supernatural content, relatively little Karloff, and more style and wit than menace, could not appeal to a very wide audience.

■ Return to Gender: *Smilin' Through, Blonde Venus, Call Her Savage, Trouble in Paradise*

Smilin' Through, a completely different, unabashedly romantic, and very effective tearjerker also featuring a World War I–battered hero, had no such problems. Norma Shearer was one of Hollywood's biggest names, having survived the coming of sound beautifully. Fredric March was a fairly new and hot star who had come to Hollywood with talkies, and Shearer's other leading man was the highly promising Leslie Howard. An old canard about filmmaking claims that one can make money by doing things cheaply or by splurging. Sumptuously produced (Thalberg), designed (Cedric Gibbons), costumed (Adrian), and photographed (Lee Garmes again), and frequently playing the haunting, well-known title tune, this film illustrates the second budgetary policy. While some of the critics did not anticipate Shearer's versatility after a series of "naughty" modern-day sex dramas, audiences were not fazed by her new screen persona and made the film a smash hit.

And yet it too features a couple taking refuge from a rainstorm in a frightening, run-down mansion. It too deals with the subject of fear, and features one-legged and otherwise handicapped men, just a bit like *Freaks.* Even the split personality of the era manifests itself, as Shearer and March take on dual roles. He gets to play to one of his great strengths, the ability to convey palpable mental anguish. His Kenneth Wayne, an American come over to England in 1915 to sign up, falls in love with Kathleen Sheridan (Shearer) but is unable to marry her because of the prohibitions of an elderly guardian, her uncle Sir John Carteret (Howard). Flashbacks to the Victorian era reveal that Kenneth's father Jeremy Wayne (also played by March) was the hysterical, possessive, and ultimately murderous childhood sweetheart of Moonyeen Clare (also played by Shearer), who was set to marry the young Sir John. Jeremy disrupted the wedding and tried to kill Sir John, only to shoot Moonyeen accidentally. Sir John cannot accept the son of Moonyeen's killer into the family and threatens to disown Kathleen. Ken must go off to war and refuses to marry Kathleen for fear of leaving her destitute, a situation many in the Depression could empathize with. He comes back seriously wounded, planning to close up the mansion and return to the United States, and he puts off the faithful Kathleen because he does not want her pity. Sir John, however, prodded by the ghost of

Jealous Jeremy Wayne (Fredric March, right) tries to kill his rival Sir John Carteret (Leslie Howard, left) but instead destroys the woman they both love, Moonyeen Clare (Norma Shearer). The deed will haunt the next generation as well in *Smilin' Through* (Sidney Franklin, MGM). Collection David Lugowski.

Moonyeen to let the lovers come together, helps to reunite them. He is then free to die and join her.

Smoothly directed by MGM house artist Sidney Franklin, *Smilin' Through* is one of the best renditions of Frank Borzage–style soft-focus romanticism, where enduring love conquers all barriers and death is a force that reunites lovers. As the comforting flip side to all the screen horror, Sir John argues, "I get a great deal of contentment out of what you call conjuring up ghosts." It is not surprising that such a style and message would find their place along with the year's violence, cynical wit, and urbane sex.

Smilin' Through shows the savvy managing of Norma Shearer's talent and that essential mix of sameness and difference needed to keep tantalizing patrons at a time of plummeting receipts. Shearer moved from prestige projects to the occasional comedy, from more old-fashioned topics to her specialty of the period, the modern woman who faces the double standard. Finding herself cheated on by men, she becomes liberated and fools around in turn, only to be brought back, chastened, to traditional marriage. Other stars performed similar parts, but none more successfully than Shearer. She embodies the restless upscale woman who plays to a heterosexual male voyeurism by suddenly becoming available, while also giving her female fans a mixture of escapist fantasy and moments of feminist protest and open desire (Everson, *Love* 69). While she does no sinning as either Kathleen or Moonyeen, she once again must face the unreasonable jealousies, possessiveness, and economic or physical dominance of men. A crazed lover shoots the blonde Moonyeen at the altar, while her modern-day brunette counterpart denies herself fulfillment at every level. And, for a time, her doughboy fiancé goes along with the older man's strictures. Kathleen is quite frank that even her sexual desire is at stake. When Ken is waffling about marrying her, he weakly declares, "I love you so." "Is that all?" Kathleen asks. "Don't you *want* me too?" Later on she adds, "I want you too— I'm not ashamed to say it" and even "By the time I'm through with you, you won't be able to fight anymore." Sir John's windows may rumble as he and Kathleen sit by helplessly while fighting rages across the Channel in France, an apt portent of rising fascism. But the political and the national are bound up as well with the economic, the historical, and the sexual. Women, who had the vote for only a little over a decade, who were working more than ever yet earning less, who faced the prospects of prostitution and separation from lovers and families, could identify with *Smilin' Through*'s timely gender realities while seeking solace in its more timeless fantasies.

No director ever conjured up more ethereal fantasies than Josef von Sternberg. Of course his uniquely decorated films, so stunningly designed and photographed as to be often described as painting with light, did not deal with faith, devotion, or sweet romance. His obsession, rather, was obsession. His films with his muse Marlene Dietrich, who clearly was both someone (and her persona some *thing*) entirely under his control and yet completely out of his reach, are essays on the cruelty and flippancy of possession. The films are dreamlike experiences of the masochistic pleasures of the visual tease, much as the male characters almost seem to enjoy their self-immolation before a femme fatale at once chilly and maternal (Studlar 108–34). Dietrich's acting may strike the viewer as subtle and sensuous or as ironic, distancing, deliberately empty posing, or, intriguingly, as both.

In a time of economic crisis, Sternberg's work was downright decadent; his first films with Dietrich were highly popular, like the year's earlier *Shanghai Express,* but there were concerns his exquisite hothouse dramas could not maintain their appeal. Such was the Depression that even Sternberg chose to address it via the "confession cycle" with his first Dietrich film set in the United States, *Blonde Venus*. Unlike its immediate predecessor, the film was their first box office disappointment. Perhaps audiences did not buy the Continental Dietrich, or her two British-born leading men (Herbert Marshall and a young Cary Grant), as Americans living in the United States. An exotic China or Morocco was fine for Dietrich's erotic adventures, but the Deep South, where Helen (Dietrich) flees with her son, was maybe less persuasive as a setting. The resulting film, nonetheless, is on par with the duo's other strange works. It richly reconsiders the conventions of melodrama and family unity, the malleability of Dietrich's androgynously liberated persona, the immigrant Sternberg's adopted terrain, and the phony mythology of the "American Success" story (P. Baxter 94–96, 102, 124–25).

Ned Faraday (Marshall), poisoned by the materials used in his own scientific research, needs money to travel to Europe for treatment. This requires his wife Helen to go to work—a situation that many women knew well and to which many men objected during the Depression. Returning to the nightclub singing she had done before marriage and motherhood, she is pursued by Nick Townsend (Grant). When suspicions break up her marriage and lead Helen to flee with her young son, the film clearly evokes the kidnapping of the Lindbergh baby, the human interest story of the year and one that the studios were dying to exploit but could not dare to do directly (P. Baxter 132–36). The hints of adultery for financial gain, and the depths of degradation to which Helen descends while in flight, flirted with censorship. And whether being aided in her flight by a lesbian-coded businesswoman and mother, or caressing a chorine's cheek before performing onstage in top hat and tails, she shows that queer gender play, as it relates to socioeconomic realities, was not limited to men.

In a year filled with racist yet complex imagery in its many jungle-set films, another number in this near-musical, "Hot Voodoo," more than earns its prominence. A gorilla with a slightly runny nose meanders menacingly among the patrons of Nick's nightclub. Darkly tinted chorines begin their jazzy shuffling to the heavy thump of the song's introduction. An astonishing moment occurs when the gorilla takes off its paw—it is only a furry glove—to reveal a white woman's graceful hand. It is Helen/Dietrich under that get-up, and she eventually transforms herself into the fetishistically costumed "Blonde Venus," capping off her costume with a frizzy wig seemingly inspired by one of Hollywood's most beloved blonds that year, Harpo Marx. Dietrich's butch androgyny had been seen; she and Sternberg had never before attempted to transcend species. Despite its racist elements— black culture, represented by the gorilla suit, is at once foregrounded openly while also reduced to a costume doffed by an ultra-white star—the number is too ridiculously stylized and extravagant to take at face value, much like the gorilla, or Helen, or Dietrich-Sternberg. The lyric, barely audible as Dietrich growls it, is about a woman's uncontrollable drives, things that lead Helen from poverty to fame in one gorgeous Sternberg sequence of dissolves or back to a reconstructed family mythology with her most convincing love object, her son. Ultimately, the number, and the film, serve as a microcosm of the excesses of pre-PCA cinema that the Code itself could not regulate fully.

Whereas at least part of the transgressive glory found in *Blonde Venus* comes from Sternberg's baroque visuals, another film lacked its style but went double on the excess in terms of its narrative and incidental highlights. Fox's *Call Her Savage* would prove to be the penultimate film of the embodiment of the late twenties flapper, Clara Bow, let go from Paramount the year before. Bow's film did not stem the slide brought on by a string of mediocre films, her own insecurities, scandalous personal problems with lovers and grasping hangers-on, and an image still identified with the carefree, reckless twenties. But as a bizarre stew of themes and motifs that distill the year's essence, it remains unique.

Yet another melodrama combining fallen woman and mother love motifs, *Call Her Savage* tells of Nasa "Dynamite" Springer (Bow), daughter to a sympathetic mother not telling all she knows about her paternity and to a rancher father fed up with her unmanageable ways. We are introduced to Nasa as, obviously braless, she wildly whoops it up on her horse and fearlessly whips a snake that threatens her. When Native American ranch hand Moonglow (played by Mexican American Gilbert Roland) laughs at her, she starts flogging him too. Sadomasochism, whether it suggested the performative sexual freedoms and taboo-smashing culture of the twenties or the beaten-down status of the American male, was in the air. Boris Karloff, as the eponymous villain in *The Mask of Fu Manchu,* rubs his hand across the bare chest of the bound and nearly naked Terry (Charles Starrett) and, in the same film, Fu's daughter (Myrna Loy) gets erotic pleasure when Terry is whipped. In the realm of comedy, the unabashed gold-digger heroine of *Red-Headed Woman* toys with an obviously masochistic lover. And she herself enjoys a slap he gives her during an argument: "I like it! Do it again!" Nasa's flogging of Moonglow has a similar frisson, although her fickleness changes her fury to affection, and his passive acceptance of her act contains a nonjudgmental good humor. Such an attitude pervades *Call Her Savage,* pushing the envelope on innuendo in indirect ways that the SRC could do little about. Even a lengthy scene of Nasa roughhousing with her dog has a playfully kinky air about it.

As with *Blonde Venus,* the highlights, ellipses, and lapses in story logic speak volumes of the tenor of the times, money being acquired and lost with incredible speed. Attempts to polish Nasa largely fail, but she ends up mingling with high society anyway, only to get involved with a caddish husband (Monroe Owsley). She also hires a male escort to see to her entertainment and he takes her slumming, to the first gay bar in American film ("Only wild poets and anarchists go there"). Her fighting skills prove handy when, after a pair of transvestite singing waiters entertain the crowd with a tune about sailors in pajamas, she and her escort must escape because they are recognized as wealthy capitalists by a Communist. Nasa even has to fend off an attempted rape by her drug-crazed husband. "Don't get up," she tells him at one point, to which he gives the multiply suggestive reply, "I get up every afternoon." She eventually finds herself destitute with an infant to provide for but, unlike Dietrich's Helen, pays the price for prostitution rather immediately. Trying to pick up a man on the street, she discovers her apartment building on fire. Her baby dead (another Lindbergh connection), a humble Nasa leaves the city for the wide open spaces again, only to find out the "explanation" for her turbulent personality. Her biological father is not the white man she has known, but rather a Native American her mother was once involved with. Understanding her "true" nature and her place in life better now, she is free to love the patient Moonglow.

The racist explanation of Nasa's hedonistic ways enables the film to make a U-turn away from the city to hearth, home, and a happy ending, but as with other films this year, it only fitfully contains the problematic issues it has raised. And yet one finds a positive glimmer in Moonglow, since minority characters such as Native Americans would not be likable romantic leads in films for much longer. (Indeed, the Tim McCoy western *The End of the Trail,* with its sincere denunciation of governmental policies against the Native American, would be one of the last films of its kind for a generation.) Complexities surround issues of gender as well. The death of Nasa's baby seems a punishment for her near-prostitution, and yet Bow's cheerfully brash persona and performance style unabashedly celebrate her sexuality. Bow could not continue in this vein, however. The performance of prostitution, social-climbing, or "gold-digging" came to the fore in the image of one of the year's most prominent new stars, and Bow's successor, Jean Harlow. After several years as a strident peroxide-blonde ingénue lacking in confidence, Harlow comes marvelously into her own as a prostitute in the racy *Red Dust* and the even more scandalous *Red Headed Woman.* The latter film calls attention to many of the same details as *Call Her Savage,* from see-through dresses to homosexuality. Harlow's character, however, does not suffer, but rather ensures her security through sexual chicanery, and the film even includes a wish-fulfillment finale where she is gloriously unpunished for her deeds and has a gigolo chauffeur in tow. Still, Clara Bow, almost ready to bow out, got the chance to run a greater emotional and generic gamut, from bitchy wisecracking repartee to highly emotional melodrama, from camp to an almost innocent cheerleader charm.

A similarly surprising range of tones also marks a much more coherent piece of filmmaking and one of the most accomplished, stylish films of the year. Often considered Ernst Lubitsch's greatest film, the superbly acted comedy *Trouble in Paradise* also links money gained and lost, gender play and risqué sex, but not via a story of female prostitution. (If anything, it's the man who must worry, warned at one point about the dangers of becoming a "good-for-nothing gigolo!") Gaston (Herbert Marshall) and Lily (Miriam Hopkins), thieves employed as staff to Mariette Colet (Kay Francis), scheme to fleece the wealthy perfumer, but Gaston proves to be far from immune to her charms. Noted for its stunning Art Deco design, the film illustrates the mastery of music and movement not present in most earlier talkies. For all of the film's glamorous trappings, however, it shows an awareness of the differences between romantic illusion and socioeconomic realities. The singing gondolier who actually collects garbage sets the tone early on, later reinforced as the film cuts from a witty montage of ads for Colet's products to shots of factory workers and a boardroom discussion of proposed salary cuts. The ultra-suave Gaston and Lily have to work to earn their living, and the clever Mariette, far from being merely a spoiled heiress, proves that she can use her femininity to both protect worker wages and manage the many men who pursue her (Paul 43, 46–49). Gaston, "a self-made crook," highlights the film's satire of capitalism and the "American Way" when he quotes a phrase that would haunt Herbert Hoover—"Prosperity is just around the corner." By "applying the laws of capitalism, Gaston undermines the system from within" (Hake 181).

And yet the central trio, faced with messy financial deceptions, never lose their sense of style. "When you don't have any money—and in the Depression nobody had any—manners, morals, ethics are coin of the realm," wrote dance critic Arlene Croce in another context, but she might just as well have been writing about the erotic dance of the principals here ("Ginger Rogers" 70). *Trouble in Paradise* is a film where champagne is ordered so that moonlight will be reflected in it. Lovers recline on a lounge and dissolve sensuously (and cinematically) into thin air, while later, potential lovers' shadows are cast across beds, and clock faces and staircases become

Lavish décor pieces such as this clock become richly repeated metaphorical motifs in the stylish comedy of love and larceny, *Trouble in Paradise* (Ernst Lubitsch, Paramount). Here Gaston (Herbert Marshall) romances his wealthy employer Mariette (Kay Francis) before deciding to return to his partner in crime Lily. Collection Ina Rae Hark.

richly repeated metaphorical motifs. Butlers, wealthy but feckless rival suitors, and corrupt board members might get confused in the scramble of identities and bedroom doors, but the able thieves and their sympathetic, savvy prey reach moments of sly and even touching understanding where money, sex, and honor are concerned. One of the great scenes of erotic foreplay in cinema occurs as Gaston and Lily hilariously keep one-upping each other at stealing objects off the other's body. Gaston might end up with his fellow crook rather than the upscale Mariette, but the film never telegraphs its political targets, narrative twists, or memorable one-liners. "That's the thing about mothers. First you get to like them, and then they die," notes Mariette, a character who can play passive when hiring a secretary for "a good spanking—in a business way, of course," but who can also actively drive a man crazy with desire by snapping her fingers. Gaston and Lily's reconciliation at the end reprises their thieving foreplay, as he stuffs his big wad of cash into the eager, open purse sitting on her lap.

Although signs existed that the Continental flavor of *Trouble in Paradise* would soon fall out of favor as the Depression bred xenophobia, the film's influence was both lingering and immediate. Gritty Warner Bros., not normally inclined to imitate Paramount's sleekness, produced a delightful confection, *Jewel Robbery,* well handled by William Dieterle. The title alone evokes Lubitsch's masterwork, as does the casting of Kay Francis, here playing the spoiled wife of an older husband who falls for a good-humored thief (William Powell) even as he fleeces the store where she shops. At its best the film's risqué humor matches Lubitsch's, most outrageously when, in the thief's lair, the straying wife seductively requests of the crook, "Show me your jewels." The film's cheerfully amoral coda shows her planning to leave her dull spouse and rendezvous with her lover, whose *modus operandi* includes a uniquely pre-PCA touch—making his victims too happy to pursue him by giving them marijuana to smoke!

Inside Outsider Perspectives: *A Bronx Morning*

Trouble's skewering of capitalistic excess, including exposing the chairman of Mariette's company as a crook, doubtless sat well with the "Thunder on the Left" prominent in union organizing. The film's satirical jibe at communism (Leonid Kinskey's "Phooey!") probably did not. But then liberal, union-oriented, and radical leftist viewers were used to Hollywood's politics and its marketing of glamour to those who could still afford movie tickets. In contrast, the on-the-street labor documentaries of the Film and Photo Leagues (*Hunger, Bonus March*) give us the Depression at its most raw. While later government documentaries display a classical polish, these guerrilla-style works eschew voiceover commentary and narrative progression toward any easy solutions to poverty and injustice. A still photographer who had been involved with the Leagues, Jay Leyda, working alone, made a major contribution to both documentary and the avant-garde with *A Bronx Morning*. Inspired by city symphony films, the European avant-garde, and political montage, sometimes only via stills he saw in magazines, Leyda created both an exercise in abstract modernism and a rich commentary on the emptiness and emasculation created by unemployment.

"Premiered" at the Julien Levy Gallery, Leyda's silent eleven-minute short explores many aspects of film style and renders a memorable impression of the Depression. It does not follow the chronological "day in the life" structure of many city symphonies but rather is organized by its own formal play and three ironically used intertitles. "The Bronx does business . . ." is followed by shots of businesses that have lost their leases. "And the Bronx lives . . . ," while followed by shots of tenements, nonetheless does not show any people, as if to connote the difficulty of living in such conditions. The last title, " . . . on the street," ushers in shots of garbage and a possibly homeless woman's legs sprawled on the pavement. The film uses elevated trains to achieve tracking shots, and is marked by the use of empty space and carefully decentered compositions. The film's playfulness, meanwhile, encompasses intertextual references—the baby carriage shots recalling Sergei Eisenstein's *Potemkin* (1925)—alongside reflexive graphic matches (e.g., a capitalized "LOOK" on a sandwich board sign). We also see examples of the Kuleshov effect (e.g., shots of a cat followed by shots of birds flying off, apparently frightened), and self-consciously impoverished devices (e.g., sacks and awnings used as wipes).

While many city symphonies highlight men at work, *Bronx* shows little productive labor, focusing instead almost surrealistically on body parts, especially feet—clearly a sign of the still photographer at work, traipsing about. It also highlights a world of women, children, pets, cleaning, and the street, a "feminine perspective" that importantly highlights the same "crisis in masculinity" that Hollywood reflected, less deliberately, through very different means (Horak 401; Lugowski, "Bronx" 147–49).

That connection with mainstream, "classical" cinema is worth highlighting during a year when Hollywood was achieving new artistic peaks in sound cinema while also struggling to survive. Experimentation did exist in Hollywood, if not quite in the same way as in Leyda's film or other examples of alternative cinema. Minority representation that would soon diminish is quite visible in mainstream fare. A somewhat broadly played, stereotype-prone, but warm-hearted Jewish comedy from Warner Bros. like *The Heart of New York* finds its parallel in the businesses in Leyda's film that sport Hebrew lettering in their windows. The women and children in the street of the Bronx resonate with Dietrich escaping into the Deep South, or Bow walking the streets to earn money for her baby. The problematic status of the male breadwinner, the World War I "forgotten man" or the "monstrously" aberrant figures of the day, be they gangsters, stock horror film types, or the handicapped, is rendered by Leyda mostly as a structuring absence—we don't really see men at work. But the messages, themes, and cultures on display are very much the same. The urban life, the socioeconomic upheaval, the mixing of hard-edged reality with playful style, and loose ends in the storytelling mark both Hollywood and the avant-garde because they mark the year so prominently. There is nothing in Leyda's film as transgressive as marijuana, "pansy" humor, or attempted rape, but his unique, virtuoso exercise does feature one overt reference to Hollywood and thus to the connections we are making. The elevated train at one point passes a movie marquee in the street below, and shows Janet Gaynor's smiling face advertising *Daddy Long Legs* (1931). When he won the presidency by a landslide, the public did not know that Franklin Roosevelt's long but polio-afflicted legs did not function, but he was clearly the "Daddy" figure the country wanted. And so he, Hollywood, independent film artists, and the country all soldiered on.

1933

Movies and the New Deal in Entertainment

MARTIN RUBIN

"Life is bare / Gloom and misery everywhere / Stormy weather / Just can't get my poor self together," so crooned Ethel Waters in Harold Arlen and Ted Koehler's hit tune "Stormy Weather," linking the singer's personal heartbreak with the atmospheric conditions around her. It would not have been difficult for listeners to make a further leap from the song's inclement weather to the political and economic turbulence that had been gripping the country.

The storm clouds abroad loomed even more darkly but, to isolationist America, still distantly. Adolf Hitler became chancellor of Germany on 30 January. Japan expanded its imperialist aggression in China and withdrew from the League of Nations. News of massive famine began to leak out of the Soviet Union.

While President Franklin D. Roosevelt cut the rest of the world loose by sabotaging July's World Economic Conference in London, New Deal America sought images of the Old World in the romanticized settings, remote in time or place, of such popular novels as Hervey Allen's *Anthony Adverse* and James Hilton's *Lost Horizon*. Domestic-themed bestsellers countered foreclosure-fueled farmer revolts and the nascent Dust Bowl with such nostalgic rural visions as Gladys Hasty Carroll's *As the Earth Turns*, Louis Bromfield's *The Farm*, Bess Streeter Aldrich's *Miss Bishop*, and, in a more hardscrabble vein, Erskine Caldwell's *God's Little Acre*.

Outside of fiction, conditions were more difficult to embroider. The winter seemed agonizingly long as the country waited out the four-month gap between Herbert Hoover's defeat and Roosevelt's inauguration—the last such interregnum before ratification of the Twentieth ("Lame Duck") Amendment on 23 January. On 5 January Hoover's predecessor, Calvin Coolidge, died, as if to confirm the sweeping away of past familiarities in anticipation of an increasingly uncertain future. In this vacuum of delay and drift, anxiety expanded, and many considered a coup d'etat or popular revolt inevitable. "Meet me at the barricades" and "Comes the revolution" became popular phrases in salutations and punch-lines (Cowley 153). Such grim fears were nearly realized in Miami on 15 February when five bullets fired by assassin Giuseppe Zangara missed the president-elect, killing Chicago mayor Anton Cermak instead.

The Chicago World's Fair opened on 27 May, and by that time the country had rebounded enough so that the exposition's official title, "A Century of Progress," did not seem bitterly ironic. Its top attractions included the edifying Hall of Science, the undulating Sally Rand, the emulsified wonder Kraft Miracle Whip, Buckminster Fuller's innovative but ill-fated Dymaxion automobile, and, in another instance of the year's rural fixation, Grant Wood's painting *American Gothic*. On the radio, "Amos 'n' Andy" continued to rule, vaudeville veterans such as Eddie Cantor and Ed Wynn rode high, and a rising genre of heroic narrative was reinforced by "The Lone Ranger" and "Air Adventures of Jimmie Allen," but the biggest radio hero of all was FDR, whose "Fireside Chats" drew record audiences. Although the New Deal recovery faltered in the latter part of the year, enough progress had been achieved to encourage tempest-tossed America to hope that it might, as the lyrics of "Stormy Weather" ventured, "walk in the sun once more."

It was a time of stormy transition in American film history as well. Like Forty-second Street ("where the underworld can meet the elite," in the words of the title song from the musical film of the same name), the year is a crossroads. It represents the intersection between the downtown dens of gangsters and fallen women where moviegoers slummed so frequently in the early thirties, and the uptown precincts of the prestige pictures and screwball comedies that spiffed up the latter part of the decade. It is the swing year between the early 1930s upheavals unleashed by the coming of sound and the stock market crash, and the mid-1930s move toward regulation, regularization, and the growth of the youthful film industry into what has been called "a mature oligopoly" (Izod 97) or "a modern business enterprise" (Balio 8). Robert Sklar terms these two eras of 1930s moviemaking "The Golden Age of Turbulence" and "The Golden Age of Order" (*Movie-Made* 175–76).

Two dates loom large in the early part of the year, both representing turning points, one for the country at large, the other for the film industry. The first is 4 March, when all eyes turned toward Washington, D.C., and the inauguration of Franklin D. Roosevelt, marking the end of the twelve-year Republican presidency that had overseen both the Roaring Twenties and the Crash. The inauguration set in motion a burst of intense activity, commencing immediately with the bank holiday[1] and continuing through the celebrated "Hundred Days" period, producing a whirlwind of new policies, legislation, and government programs. The most highly publicized of these programs was the agency of business assistance and regulation known as the National Recovery Administration (NRA), whose blue eagle emblem began appearing on films in the latter part of the year.

These events, signaling the presence of a more vigorous government and enhanced by the charisma of FDR himself (a media star of the first magnitude), led to a rise in confidence and consensus. As important as the actual programs of Roosevelt's first months in office (which were a very mixed bag in terms of actual accomplishments) was the boost in public morale that resulted. The phrase "new deal," first used by FDR in his nomination acceptance speech and later applied to the innovative programs of his administration, became a slogan of this renewed optimism. It pops up in a number of films of this period as a metaphor or catch phrase, without any specific reference to Roosevelt's policies, reflecting instead a general feeling that change was in the air and that, even if happy days weren't exactly here again,[2] at least some decisive action was at long last being taken.

American movies were caught amid these shifting tides of national temperament, reflecting them and sometimes being reshaped and reinterpreted in light of them. Some films are characterized by what Thomas Doherty calls "A New Deal in the Last Reel," wherein the body of the story expresses a bleak pessimism appropriate to the Hoover era, only to be reversed in the final minutes by an evocation of FDR and/or the intervention of a benevolent authority figure (85). The most blatant example of this confusion is *Wild Boys of the Road*, a harsh, uncompromising depiction of the hardships endured by a group of homeless juveniles . . . until a fatherly judge (the NRA emblem hanging on the wall behind him) takes them under his wing with the assurance, "Things are going to be better now . . . all over the country."

The second significant event, as private as the inauguration was public, occurred the next day, on the evening of 5 March. In a mood of crisis framed by the ever-deepening box office slump and intensified by Roosevelt's announcement that day of the bank holiday, movie censorship czar Will Hays called an emergency meeting at which leaders of the film industry were pressed to reaffirm their support of the Production Code, Hollywood's formula for government-co-opting self-censorship, which had been on the books since 1930 (Maltby, "Production Code" 57).

This resolution marked a crucial escalation in the long-running campaign for regulation of screen content, setting the stage for a series of

heated censorship battles that raged over the next fifteen months. They cul-
minated in July 1934 with the creation of the Production Code Administration or PCA (aka the Breen Office, after its zealous leader Joseph Breen),
a fortified advisory body credited with bringing to an end the less rigorously
regulated interlude now referred to as the pre-Code era. These events sig-
nified far more than specific issues of film censorship; they were part of the
general movement toward a regularization of the industry, an entrench-
ment of the major studios' system of monopolistic control, and a shift in the
balance of power away from the Hollywood studio bosses to their more
cautious East Coast financial managers.

The films discussed in this chapter illuminate all or most of the issues
Throughout the year, Hollywood was under widespread attack by religious organizations, women's groups, morality crusaders, legislators, and
social scientists. It faced the possibility of not only federal censorship but
also increased taxation and antitrust regulation. The film industry was
placed on the defensive as never before. On the one hand, Hollywood
maintained that movies were merely entertainment (and therefore should
be excused from moral and educational responsibilities) and, on the other
hand, that they were a social necessity (and therefore should not be financially or legally penalized by the government) (Doherty 45–46; Maltby,
"Production Code" 47, 57). Questions regarding the function and value of
movies as entertainment were especially pressing, and they provide an
important framework for interpreting the year's films.

The films discussed in this chapter illuminate all or most of the issues
introduced above: the shift from early 1930s "turbulence" to mid-1930s
"order," the upswing in morale inspired by the FDR administration, the
battles over screen censorship, and the debate over the function of entertainment. As always, fluctuations in movie genres and gender roles provide
important indicators of major trends in a pivotal period. The trio of Warner
Bros. musicals with numbers by Busby Berkeley, the most important
American filmmaker of the year, are particularly significant. Looking at
films chronologically reveals many developments in this year of rapid and
dramatic change.

Cavalcade and the Twentieth-Century Blues

Hollywood released at least seven World War I–centered
films: *Ace of Aces, Captured!, The Eagle and the Hawk, Hell Below, Storm at Daybreak, Today We Live,* and *The White Sister*. Although that number might not
seem earthshaking, it is more (in most years, many more) than in any other
year of the 1930s. The number of fictional war films was augmented by

compilation documentaries such as *The Big Drive, Forgotten Men,* and *Hell's Holiday*. In addition, there were several films in which World War I combat scenes are incorporated into a wider narrative, such as *Heroes for Sale, Men Must Fight,* and *Pilgrimage,* or in which World War I figures as a key offscreen plot device, such as *Ann Vickers, The House on 56th Street, The Secret of Madame Blanche,* and *Turn Back the Clock.*

The most prominent example of this war-conscious trend was *Cavalcade,* whose story (based on the 1931 play by Noel Coward) ends with the ringing in of the New Year of 1933, just a few days before the film's New York premiere on 5 January. *Cavalcade* went on to become one of the biggest grossing and most honored films of the year. As is often the case with award-winning movies, a large part of *Cavalcade*'s success can be attributed to novelty—in this case, the novelty of fashioning a historical overview of the twentieth century. The still-young century was coalescing as a coherent entity with a shape and breadth of its own, defined by such milestones as the sinking of the *Titanic,* the Great War, the Jazz Age, the Crash, the election of FDR, the rise of Hitler. The recent upheavals of history had produced a heightened sense of the past, of moving from one era to another; it was a time for looking back and taking stock.

Cavalcade begins in London on New Year's Eve 1899 with the upstairs/downstairs paralleling of two families: the veddy proper Marryots (Diana Wynyard, Clive Brook) and their boisterous servants the Bridgeses (Una O'Connor, Herbert Mundin). As the Boer War and Queen Victoria's funeral roll by, the Bridgeses leave service and become uppity and boorish. The Marryots lose both of their sons, one on the *Titanic* and one in the war, while the Bridgeses' daughter, Fanny (Ursula Jeans), becomes a singing star. World War I is presented in a discordant montage of marching cannon fodder and thudding corpses to the tune of "It's a Long Way to Tipperary." The twenties are dispatched in a similar cacophony of Bolsheviks, atheists, warmongers, and headlines shrieking divorce, sex, and murder. Battered but still plucky, the aged Marryots totter to their balcony to greet another New Year.

Cavalcade is not a musical, but it contains a wealth of period songs and a pocket history of musical entertainment forms, including operetta, music hall, busking, fan dancing, musical comedy, and cabaret. Popular entertainment in *Cavalcade,* although it serves nostalgia and national unity, often seems disconnected, even heartless. Fanny Bridges dances obliviously beside a sidewalk band while her father, flattened by a fire engine, lies dead a few yards away. Three Loreleis in a nightclub sing a peppy recruiting song to lure young men into the army; later their faces appear superimposed in ghoulish close-ups over the montage of war casualties. Near the end of the film, Fanny dispassionately delivers Coward's languid lament "Twentieth Century Blues" ("Why is it that civilized humanity can make the world so wrong?") in a decadent cabaret. Ultimately, entertainment seems just another weary participant in history's endless, indifferent procession, rather than a privileged means of transforming or transcending it.

Directed by British-born Frank Lloyd as a mixture of shapeless crowd scenes and stiff dramatic passages, *Cavalcade* is not highly regarded today. That same year, in the less heralded *Pilgrimage*, Lloyd's Fox studio-mate John Ford evoked a more vivid sense of passing history with one quietly devastating scene of bereaved Gold Star mothers[3] filing onto a France-bound ship than there is in all the pomp and circumstance of *Cavalcade*. Nevertheless, the film marks an important step in the evolution of what might be called century consciousness.

Cavalcade shares many of its concerns with a contemporaneous series of American-set business sagas, such as *The Power and the Glory*, about a railroad magnate (Spencer Tracy); *Sweepings*, about a department store magnate (Lionel Barrymore); and *The World Changes*, about a meat-packing magnate (Paul Muni). Like *Cavalcade*, these films view the twentieth century as a downward slide: the American Dream turns sour, the younger generation goes to pot, the capitalist patriarch dies with the bitter taste of futility in his mouth. It remained for Franklin D. Roosevelt and the New Deal to turn those twentieth-century blues into the blue skies of anticipated recovery, and to transform the war from a bitter memory into a stirring symbol of national purpose and renewal.

She Done Him Wrong and the Risen Woman

Unlike their male counterpart, the gangster films (which had been rubbed out by the morals mob in 1932), the censor-incensing fallen woman melodramas, though on the decline, kept doggedly plying their trade. Carny dancer Ruth Chatterton loses an illegitimate baby, takes a lover, and ends up in a sexless marriage to a drunken cripple in *Lilly Turner*; saintly bad girl Loretta Young seduces a gangster to protect the man she loves in *Midnight Mary*; touring American showgirl Irene Dunne marries a British rotter, has her child taken away, and becomes proprietress of a French hot-sheets hotel in *The Secret of Madame Blanche*.

These and other unfortunate floozies were given stiff competition by some new girls on the block: more inclined to rise than fall, less victimized and stigmatized, more comic and powerful than their sorrowful sisters. Just as anxiety over masculinity and gender roles famously produced the figure of the film-noir femme fatale in the late 1940s, the equivalent concerns of this period spawned a less numerous and less sinister predecessor that could be called the *femme forte*.

Notable examples include Greta Garbo in *Queen Christina* (mostly tragic), Barbara Stanwyck in *Baby Face* (mixed comic and tragic), and Ruth Chatterton in *Female* (mostly comic). These swaggering gender benders often claim the prerogatives of men: running countries (Garbo), running businesses (Chatterton), ruining businesses (Stanwyck), and guiltlessly enjoying multiple sex partners (all three—and Garbo even smooches her lady-in-waiting!). Even if they end up domesticated or lonely in the final reel, the scintillating spectacle of women riding high ultimately outweighs the less entertaining lesson of their comeuppance.

This healthy trend had been anticipated by Jean Harlow in her 1932 scarlet sensations *Red Dust* and *Red-Headed Woman*. Although Harlow was being toned down and made more family-friendly in films like *Hold Your Man* and *Bombshell,* the torch was snatched up and held high by the most potent female symbol of life, liberty, and the pursuit of happiness since the Statue of Liberty: Mae West.

After serving a long vaudeville apprenticeship, West had gained notoriety in a series of scandalous plays she herself had written or co-written. She was considered too hot for Hollywood even in the pre-Code era, but, with his company in receivership,[4] new Paramount production chief Emanuel Cohen declared his intention "to be as daring as possible" and signed West to a contract (Maltby, "Production Code" 53).

She Done Him Wrong, directed under West's thumb by Lowell Sherman, was her first starring movie role. It was based on her 1928 stage hit *Diamond Lil,* which had been placed on the Hays Office's list of banned books. By taking evasive action and making some selective concessions (including a title change and a last-minute trimming of the provocative song, "A Guy What Takes His Time"), Paramount was able to get West's bombshell on the screen relatively intact. Premiering on 27 January, it became an enormous hit and, combined with her even more successful fall release *I'm No Angel,* made the forty-year-old West the year's hottest new movie star, especially popular with women (Hamilton 200; Watts 164, 178).

West plays Lady Lou, the queen of a Gay Nineties Bowery saloon, who collects men and diamonds with equal aplomb. She holds her own against some rough characters, entertains the customers, and sets her sights on a missionary (Cary Grant) who turns out to be a federal undercover agent. The plot is a pretext for West's charismatic presence—her sumptuous costumes, her suggestive songs, her bawdy zingers. In her first entrance, in response to the compliment, "You're a fine gal, a fine woman," West cheerfully agrees, "One of the finest women ever walked the streets." Later, Grant implores her, "Haven't you ever met a man that could make you happy?" and she purrs, "Sure. Lots of times."

No fallen woman, West is at all times ascendant. She surveys her domain from the landing outside her second-story room and uses variants on her "Come up and see me" signature line at least five times. Whereas the other risen-women films were sometimes uncomfortable mixtures of melodrama and comedy, West lifted her even more brazen archetype wholly into the realm of comedy, without any last-reel remorse or regrets. Her "taming" at the ends of both *She Done Him Wrong* and *I'm No Angel* is qualified at best, delivered with a broad wink to the audience.

A plump film for lean times, *She Done Him Wrong* fills its cluttered frames with plush, overstuffed furniture and beefy, overdressed men. West's already ample figure is decked out with furs, feathers, flounces, ruffles, spangles, sequins, and, of course, diamonds. Ostentatiously licking its lips in anticipation of the repeal of Prohibition, the film festoons the foregrounds of shots with great brimming goblets of frothy beer.

The sound track is equally stuffed. *She Done Him Wrong* begins with a barrage of vintage favorites (including "The Bowery," "Daisy Bell," and "The Old Gray Mare") accompanying street-scene vignettes. In the second half of the film, in addition to West's singing performances, there is an almost continuous flow of music emanating from the saloon stage and heard in the adjacent rooms. The use of offscreen sound links West's boudoir to the stage and reinforces the ideas that sex is a form of entertainment (no more, no less, no strings attached) and that entertainment (at least, in the hands of a pro like Mae) is a form of sex, as well as an enabler of easygoing social cohesion.

Although *She Done Him Wrong* is set in the 1890s and the Mae West persona was primarily a product of the twenties, her image was repackaged for Depression relevance. For return engagements of *She Done Him Wrong* during the bank holiday, ads pictured West with the legend "You Can Bank on Me" (Watts 155). Her popularity brought the full-figured look back into fashion, and, although a teetotaler herself, she managed to work beer into the equation, telling reporters, "Now that beer is really back and we are all drinking it, why not wage a campaign for a return of the woman's natural figure?" West identified such brew-bolstered physiques with "a return to normal, the ladies' way of saying that the depression is over" (Watts 165). She claimed a similar economic punch for her bluenose-baiting sexuality: "My fight has been against depression, repression and suppression" (Leider

257). Mae West wrapped up sex, beer, prosperity, entertainment, and her own copious curves into a generous package that offered a red-hot antidote to the Depression blues.

42nd Street and the New Deal Express

Although it had existed for barely five years, the movie musical had already gone through a cycle of boom and bust. The darlings of the talkie-takeover year of 1929, musicals were considered box office poison by mid-1930. Now, amid the accelerated evolutionary pace of the early sound era and the sense of impending change inspired by Roosevelt's ascension, this inherently optimistic genre would come roaring back to life. Moreover, its revival occurred in a subgenre that had been deemed especially dead and buried: the backstage musical, centered on the relationships among show people putting on a show.

The turnaround musical was the Warner Bros. release *42nd Street*, which premiered in Denver on 23 February. Its success made the genre fashionable again and generated two follow-ups that same year, *Gold Diggers of 1933* and *Footlight Parade*, featuring similar personnel and musical spectacles staged by Busby Berkeley.

The starting point for any consideration of the Warner Bros. backstage musicals of this period is the obvious but essential observation that they are composed of two sides, the narrative and the numbers. The relationship between these two sides, although not nonexistent, is considerably looser than it is in the more "integrated" style of musical that was then being developed by such directors as Ernst Lubitsch, Rouben Mamoulian, and Mark Sandrich. Berkeley, whose name became synonymous with a certain style of spectacular production number, was responsible for the three numbers that come back to back to back at the end of *42nd Street*. The narrative portion of the film was handled by Lloyd Bacon.

Although Berkeley has received the lion's share of the credit for the film's impact, the unsung hero of the production is Bacon, a journeyman director currently residing in nobody's pantheon, who took over the reins late in the preparation process when Mervyn LeRoy fell ill (Barrios 374). The numbers of *42nd Street* are inventive and lively, but, in retrospect, with the entire Warner Bros./Berkeley cycle unfolded before us, they seem tame compared to the more audacious and ambitious showstoppers that would erupt from *Gold Diggers of 1933*, *Footlight Parade*, and points beyond.

"Shuffle Off to Buffalo," the most successful and small-scale of the three final numbers, gets its bittersweet kick from the ability of the cash-shy honeymooners (Ruby Keeler and Clarence Nordstrom) to maintain their romantic mood in the face of an anti-romantic environment that includes lack of privacy, a tiny sleeper-car berth for their bridal suite, cynical divorce-predicting neighbors, and, at the end, a porter snoring loudly in close-up. "Young and Healthy," an upscale contrast to "Buffalo," focuses on technical effects such as revolving platforms and kaleidoscopic bird's-eye shots, which became Berkeley trademarks. "42nd Street," the film's most expansive number, is a frenetic jumble of street-scene vignettes, dances, gags, trick cuts, and stage effects lacking the rigorous design that underpins Berkeley's later and greater spectacles.

The narrative side of the film, on the other hand, is the strongest of any of the 1930s Warner Bros. musicals, even the snappy, Cagney-charged *Footlight Parade* (also directed by Bacon). Although the screenplay is commendable for its slangy dialogue and interwoven subplots, and Warner Baxter delivers an unforgettably hyperbolic performance as the show's high-pressure director, Julian Marsh, the most impressive aspect of the narrative is its vigorous, dynamic direction.

The key to Bacon's approach is his handling of the audition and rehearsal scenes. In Warner Bros. backstage musicals by other directors, these types of scenes are more peripheral, a backdrop to the main storylines. Here and in *Footlight Parade,* they are given more prominence, and in *42nd Street* they are the heart of the film, more so than Berkeley's numbers. The purpose of these scenes is less plot development than the elaboration of a bustling milieu characterized by speed, energy, movement, camaraderie, friction, and a constant barrage of wisecracks pitched in from the sidelines and flavored with pre-Code saltiness.

Bacon's fragmentary, caught-on-the-fly style breaks up the scenes with bits of business, asides, cutaways, punchy camera movements, and varied angles. In one characteristic segment, a crane up on the weary company rehearsing a number is followed by a swift lateral track to a showboy ("Where ya sittin'?") with showgirl Una Merkel ("On a flagpole, dearie!") squirming on his lap, a rafters-level bird's-eye view, a fall-back with Merkel and fellow chorine Ginger Rogers exchanging catty gossip, a close shot of exasperated director Baxter, a medium shot of bored onlookers in the orchestra, a medium shot of Rogers cracking wise with the assistant director, an oblique angle of the stage from behind the silhouetted Baxter, and a medium-shot return to the misadventures of the saucy Ms. Merkel, her eyes widening as she is goosed by two showboys in succession: ten shots, all different camera set-ups, in just over a minute. The rehearsal scenes set the tone for the entire film, their energy carrying over to the plottier, relatively

Spunky showgirls (center, left to right) Ann Lowell (Ginger Rogers), Peggy Sawyer (Ruby Keeler), and Lorraine Fleming (Una Merkel) hoof their way through one of the many rehearsal scenes that form the heart of *42nd Street* (Lloyd Bacon, Warner Bros.). Gene Siskel Film Center.

slower (but still brisk) scenes set outside the theater; and the multiple, decentralized storylines keep the narrative hopping from subplot to subplot without standing still too long.

Before Roosevelt had even taken office, Warner Bros. executives divined an affinity between their hot property and the incoming president, and they played it for all it was worth. "Inaugurating a NEW DEAL in ENTERTAINMENT!" trumpeted ads for the film (Fumento 39). Production chief Jack Warner, an ardent FDR supporter, hammered home the connection by launching the "42nd Street Special," a chartered train filled with Warner Bros. stars whose cross-country publicity tour was timed to arrive in Washington on Inauguration Day (Barrios 377). The studio's ad campaign instructed exhibitors to sell the film "not merely as an improvement over the old, but as something vastly different and sensationally new" (Fumento 29).

To what extent was *42nd Street* new and/or New Deal? Much of such claims was undoubtedly hype, opportunism, and piggybacking on the

Roosevelt band wagon. *42nd Street* was entirely written and mostly shot before FDR's election. The basic ingredients of the backstage formula had been laid down years before; the trade paper *Variety* aptly dubbed the film *The Broadway Melody of 1933*, a reference to the 1929 ur-backstage musical (Barrios 378).

42nd Street's newness now seems more a matter of style than of basic structure or content. More evolution rather than revolution, the film did basically the same things that first-wave backstagers had done, but it did them more vividly. As instructed by producer Darryl F. Zanuck, Bacon and the screenwriters ramped up the gritty topicality of the narrative; Berkeley did the same for the rowdy spectacle of the musical numbers; and between them they generated a chain reaction of speed and intensity that was atypical for the musical genre and that connected the film to the excitement surrounding Roosevelt's inauguration.

The film's backstage structure—especially its emphasizing and energizing of the rehearsal scenes—is crucial to its topical relevance. By dwelling on the process of production so much, *42nd Street* provides a rationale for its own value as Depression-era entertainment. Entertainment is presented as *work*—demanding, exhausting, and ultimately productive. Moreover, it means *jobs*. In two impassioned speeches, Marsh harangues the show's unreliable investor (Guy Kibbee) and its untested star (Keeler) that their failure to deliver will affect not only themselves but the livelihoods of two hundred people. Broadway—and, by extension, Hollywood—might deal in the stuff of dreams, but those dreams gild the hard currency of labor, income, and employment.

King Kong and the Backstage Horror Film

Following the gothicized classics of 1931–32 (*Frankenstein, Dracula, Murders in the Rue Morgue, Dr. Jekyll and Mr. Hyde*), the horror film became less Eurocentric, either by going further afield to more primitive and exotic environments (*Island of Lost Souls*) or by importing archaic and foreign elements into familiar contemporary settings (*Mystery of the Wax Museum*). Combining both trends is the legendary *King Kong*, one of the most resonant fables of the twentieth century.

The film's lucid three-act structure begins with the outfitting and sailing of a motion-picture expedition from New York, proceeds to the discovery and capture of the giant ape Kong on uncharted Skull Island, and returns to Manhattan where Kong is exhibited on Broadway before going on a rampage that ends at the Empire State Building.

Complicating the clear-cut vector of the film's adventure story is a quad-rangle centered on starlet Ann Darrow (Fay Wray). Ann is virtually the only woman in the film, outside of some anonymous extras. On the other hand, the leading male role is split three ways: entrepreneur/adventurer Carl Denham (Robert Armstrong), square-jawed sailor Jack Driscoll (Bruce Cabot), and simian antihero Kong. All three have difficulties relating to the opposite sex: Denham seems to be asexual or prepubescent, with a "No Girls Allowed" sign on his clubhouse door; only grudgingly, out of sheer box office necessity, does he consent to put a woman in his latest jungle picture. Jack freely expresses his aversion to females ("They're a nuisance. . . . Women just can't help being a bother"), which he eventually overcomes in Ann's case, using the alibi, "You aren't women." Kong doesn't share his human rivals' reticence toward women, but the size and interspecies prob-lems put up insurmountable obstacles to any successful consummation.

Aided immensely by composer Max Steiner's ominous/plaintive score and chief technician Willis O'Brien's expressive animation, Merian C. Cooper and Ernest B. Schoedsack's film evokes tremendous ambivalence toward the monster. Besides sending numerous Skull and Manhattan Islanders to horrific dooms via chomping, stomping, and dropping, Kong develops a deep passion for the heroine, abducts her twice, gallantly pro-tects her from prehistoric beasts, and bids her a poignant farewell before taking his final plunge from the top of the world's tallest building.

Despite its fantastic elements, *King Kong* begins with its feet firmly planted in Depression America, as Denham scouts a leading lady among the haggard denizens of Skid Row before he spots starving Ann in the act of stealing an apple. Both the opening shot of the film and the final embrace of Ann and Jack show in the background the clustered towers of Wall Street—ground zero of the Crash, whose aftershocks were being acutely registered by the film's production company RKO, then in receivership. The site of the towering climax has similar resonances. Although it has since been enshrined as a monument to American power and progress, at the time (two years after its opening) the Empire State Building was widely considered a folly—a relic of the pre-Crash real-estate boom whose approx-imately 75 percent unleased space earned it the nickname "Empty State Building" (Tauranac 276).

King Kong's generic indeterminacy contributes greatly to its universality and durability. Now it can be seen as the granddaddy of all monster-rampage movies, but during its first release it was perceived and promoted more as a jungle movie in the tradition of *Chang* (1927), *Trader Horn* (1931), and *Tarzan the Ape Man* (1932) (Erb 54–56). Andrew Bergman, in his valuable

Astonished spectators, including (on stage below, left to right) Jack Driscoll (Bruce Cabot), Ann Darrow (Fay Wray), and Carl Denham (Robert Armstrong), watch temperamental star Kong prepare to break through the proscenium in *King Kong* (Merian C. Cooper and Ernest B. Schoedsack, RKO Radio). Collection Martin Rubin.

thirties overview *We're in the Money,* sees it as a variation on the formula of country boy bamboozled by city slickers—*Mr. Kong Goes to Town* (Bergman 73). *King Kong* can also be related to the backstage musical. Determined to put on a big show, Denham is an obsessive, visionary showman in the vein of Julian Marsh (*42nd Street*) and Chester Kent (*Footlight Parade*). As in Busby Berkeley's most audacious numbers, this spectacle is far too excessive to be confined on a normal stage. However, here the stage space does not expand magically to contain the surplus, and Kong literally breaks through the proscenium to wreak havoc on the world outside. (For an analogy, imagine the torrents of *Footlight Parade*'s "By a Waterfall" overflowing the confines of the stage and dousing the on-screen audience like a tidal wave.)

Although some commentators have judged Denham in light of later attitudes as an imperialist/capitalist/racist/inhumane evildoer (Mayne 381, Ollier 69, Peary 12), it is difficult to find evidence for such a harsh verdict in the film itself. It is true that Denham was a villain in early drafts of the screenplay (Erb 48–49), but in the finished film he is never vilified, even though his hunger for a big box office results in widespread death and destruction. The cop at the end doesn't arrest Denham but treats him with friendly respect.

King Kong is perfectly, purely ambivalent about Denham and the value of entertainment he represents, just as it is about the monster-victim Kong and those Wall Street towers that loom in the background, the Crash behind Kong's crash. Is entertainment in the midst of disaster irresponsible or therapeutic? Does it deserve dispensation for its alleged sins? How much do we need our shows?

Though it premiered shortly after *42nd Street*, on 2 March, *King Kong*, longer in conception and production, seems to belong to an earlier era, and, unlike *42nd Street* or *Three Little Pigs*, it did not contain elements that could be so easily repackaged to greet the incoming New Deal. More precisely, the film seems poised amid the crosscurrents of two eras, suspended in an enchanted calm where it can be propelled in almost any direction by the forces of interpretation and imagination that it so marvelously incites.

■ *Three Little Pigs* and the Wolf at the Door

Three Little Pigs, an entry in Walt Disney's Silly Symphony series, premiered on 25 May, toward the end of the Hundred Days. Although response to its opening at Radio City Music Hall was unremarkable, the nine-minute cartoon later caught fire at neighborhood theaters and became a cultural phenomenon—held over for months, often billed above feature films, and generating a hit Depression-era anthem, "Who's Afraid of the Big Bad Wolf?" (Thomas 114).

In the opening scenes, each of the pigs (identified in the script as Fifer Pig, Fiddler Pig, and Practical Pig) introduces himself by singing to the camera. Fifer and Fiddler build flimsy dwellings and prefer play to work. Practical Pig, pugnacious and tenacious, devotes himself to a solid construction of brick and stone.

As the two little twits chirp "Who's Afraid of the Big Bad Wolf?" the Furry One himself creeps up, drooling copiously. After flattening Fifer's straw domicile, the wolf tries subterfuge rather than lung-power to gain entrance to Fiddler's wooden home, posing as an orphan lamb left on the doorstep. At the brick house, he again resorts to trickery, disguising himself this time as a Jewish peddler with baggy overcoat, thick glasses, bushy beard, and huge nose. (This touch of ethnic spice was expunged from re-releases of the film.)

When the wolf's huffing and puffing fails to blow the house down (but succeeds in blowing his own clothes off), he sneaks down the chimney, where Practical is waiting with a pot of boiling turpentine. The wolf scurries off on all fours, dragging his scalded butt and howling like a dog—this igno-minious exit completes the forfeiture of anthropomorphic status that began with his loss of clothing. Fiddler and Fifer sing and dance in celebration, but Practical reins in their high spirits by rapping on the piano, causing his chicken-hearted companions to scurry under the bed.

Another sardonic counterpoint to the film's triumphant spirit is provided by the Pig family portraits glimpsed in the backgrounds of several shots: Mother is portrayed as a sow with a row of suckling piglets alongside her, while poor Father is seen as a string of sausage links in one portrait and as a ham hock in another! These provocative bits of marginalia gain significance from the fact that the family portraits appear only in Practical's house. Not only do the pictures align Practical as a parental role model for his less mature brethren, but they also expand his hardheaded work ethic into a wider program of practicality and productivity. Cute though they may be, pigs must serve a function: mama pigs produce little pigs, and papa pigs produce, from their own chubby carcasses, sausages and hams and all the other porkalicious products that will feed a hungry nation. Meanwhile, little pigs grow up to take their parents' places in either the farrowing pen or the processing plant. One imagines that Practical Pig, like his father before him, would face the butcher's block with the same satisfied sense of accomplishment that he derives from building his house—a job well done!

But what about the other pigs? Are all of us cut out to be so pragmatic? And what about the wolf? It is but a matter of packaging that enables us to hiss the wolf when he slavers over the three little pigs but to slaver ourselves when confronted with a juicy pork chop. Also, the wolf is lean and hungry, unlike the plump and presumably well-fed pigs—his hobo-like attire adds an element of class conflict to his efforts.

As in the classic fairy tales to which Disney is heir, such factors complicate the story and give it life as a suggestive fable rather than limiting it to a straightforward moral lesson. These submerged ambivalences are supplemented by the film's surface attractions. Although Practical is the locus of *Three Little Pigs*' message, most of its fun resides in the simpleton pigs' unquenchable high spirits and burbling inanity, and in the gleeful machinations of Mr. B. B. Wolf, with his pricelessly sly expressions and conspiratorial glances toward the audience.

Even more so than *42nd Street* or Mae West's image, *Three Little Pigs* is an example of a cultural object's elasticity enabling it to stretch across different interpretations in a mutating era. The film was embraced by the public as a Depression-razzing allegory, but the terms of that allegory are slippery. Disney chronicler Richard Schickel surmises that Practical evokes Herbert Hoover by virtue of his jowly countenance and prudent policies (Schickel 154). However, by the time *Three Little Pigs* achieved wide popular success, its political subtext had been hijacked to suit the rising optimism of the FDR presidency, with a particularly irresistible connection between the theme song's fear-banishing lyrics and Roosevelt's celebrated inaugural-address phrase, "The only thing we have to fear is fear itself."

Baffled by all the significance that had been attached to his short cartoon, Disney protested, "It was just another story to us and we were in there gagging it just like any other picture" (Schickel 156). But such disclaimers do not negate the relevance of *Three Little Pigs* in affirming the value of the musical genre, entertainment, and Hollywood itself in this year of tribulation and transition. Just as raising morale was an important (in retrospect, perhaps the most important) accomplishment of the early New Deal, the very levity of cartoons, musicals, and other upbeat entertainments validated their function in Depression-dejected America.

Song, dance, and musicality are carefully situated in Disney's minimusical. Only the pigs have access to song; the gravel-voiced wolf is restricted to dialogue. Although Practical grumbles, "I have no chance/ To sing and dance/ For work and play don't mix," he later demonstrates that he can pound a mean piano (made of brick, of course!) while off-duty. Music is elevated from mere frivolity to anti-Depression blues-chasing when Wolf-at-the-Door's strenuous but futile puffs and knocks are each answered by a lilting piano run from Practical. Despite the stern work ethic espoused at the beginning of the film, *Three Little Pigs* ultimately opts for a sensible balance of work and entertainment. All work and no playing the piano would make Practical a dull pig, just as all business and no funny business would make America an incurably demoralized nation.

Gold Diggers of 1933 and the Sexual Depression

Producer Darryl F. Zanuck embarked on *Gold Diggers of 1933* in November 1932, shortly after *42nd Street* had completed principal photography. Made in the uneasy, rudderless period between FDR's election and his inauguration, the film was rushed out for a 27 May premiere to capitalize on the success of *42nd Street*, with Warner Bros.' publicity urging theaters to play up the similarities between the two movies (Hove 17). *Gold*

Diggers of 1933 was even more successful than its predecessor, although it did not have the same groundbreaking impact.

Despite the undeniable tie-ins, there are also striking differences between the two films. Though laced with humor, *42nd Street* is primarily a melodrama—a grittier, speedier variation on the *Grand Hotel* (1932) model. *Gold Diggers of 1933* is a comedy through and through—or, more accurately, a pair of awkwardly joined comedies. Spinning off from *42nd Street,* the first act is a bustling, Depression-drenched backstage story centered on a trio of destitute showgirls (Joan Blondell, Ruby Keeler, Aline MacMahon) whose salvation lies in the new show that producer Barney Hopkins (Ned Sparks) is struggling to get off the ground. The second act, derived from Avery Hopgood's 1919 play *The Gold Diggers,* is a drawn-out 1920s-style sex comedy centered on the cynical stratagems of two of the girls (Blondell, MacMahon) to fleece a pair of stuffed shirts (Warren William, Guy Kibbee).

Whereas Bacon's supercharged rehearsal scenes provided the heart of *42nd Street,* this time, with the narrative under the less dynamic direction of Mervyn LeRoy, it is Berkeley's musical spectacles that shape the film, ultimately transforming the mixed 1920s/1930s signals of its narrative into a coherent vision of the relationship between the two eras. Unlike *42nd Street* and *Footlight Parade, Gold Diggers of 1933* does not stack all the big Berkeley numbers at the end. It opens with "We're in the Money" (aka "The Gold Diggers Song"), a tongue-in-cheek paean to prosperity featuring literally inflated currency and chorines wearing little but some strategically placed coins. The number is interrupted by a posse of repo men, one of whom strips the coins fore and aft from cowering, nearly nude showgirl Ginger Rogers ("You could at least leave me car fare!")—an equation of loss of economic power and loss of sexual power that will be extended to the male side of the ledger in the "Remember My Forgotten Man" finale.

Inserted at the end of the first act is "Pettin' in the Park," a full-scale comic-erotic spectacle in which Dick Powell's determination to fondle sweetheart Ruby Keeler expands into a vision of Central Park as a pettin' paradise—featuring neckers and spooners of all ages and colors, cops who wink at the widespread hanky-panky, girls who use roller skates to stay ahead of their pursuers, a lecherous infant (homunculus Billy Barty) who joins in the fun, a seasonal shift from winter frolics to spring showers (all the better to soak those flimsy dresses), and a punch line in which the girls don protective armor only to be foiled by good old American know-how in the form of a can-opener. "Shadow Waltz," featuring chorines with neon-illuminated violins, is the most spectacular and least consequential of the numbers, serving mainly to provide an elegant contrast to the earthy "Pettin' in the Park."

"Remember My Forgotten Man" picks up the themes introduced in "We're in the Money." A streetwalker (Blondell) laments the common man's closely linked losses of earning power and sexual virility, in poignant contrast to his forgotten World War I military glory. This downfall is depicted in a series of short, stunning blackout tableaux: men marching off to war, erect, proud, *employed*; soldiers trudging back from battle, wounded, bleeding, sagging; and (Berkeley's most powerful stroke) a line of unemployed men at a chilly soup kitchen, shivering, sheepish, subdued.

Several dramas of the period, such as *Heroes for Sale* and *Turn Back the Clock*, draw a parallel between the catastrophes of World War I and the Crash. Unlike those films, Berkeley's dreamlike condensation of history cuts out the buffer period: there are no victory parades, no wild parties, no soaring stock indexes. The men go directly from the front line to the breadline, reinforcing a series of sliding connections: war/castration/Depression.

The final grand tableau shows women watching from the sidelines as the men kneel before the unattainable Woman, in the form of Blondell, and images of their bygone glory, in the form of rifle-toting doughboys circling on Sisyphean treadmills in the background. Like the finales of the other classic Warner Bros. musicals, "Remember My Forgotten Man" combines social and sexual dimensions, but here the separate male and female choruses do *not* merge as they do at climaxes of "42nd Street" and "Shanghai Lil." The economic disaster of the Depression has inhibited sexual relations between man and woman. (The facts confirm the number's theme: between 1929 and the present year, the marriage rate and birth rate declined 22 percent and 15 percent, respectively [Kennedy 165].)

Although their relation to the narrative is loose, Berkeley's numbers are often richly interconnected to each other. This is especially true of "Pettin' in the Park" and "Remember My Forgotten Man," the first two great numbers of his career. "Pettin'" shows us what has been lost in "Forgotten Man": a paradise of heterosexual bliss (in part, it is an idealized version of the era that is elided from "Forgotten Man"). Central Park becomes a democratic Eden, open to all races, ages, classes, sizes, and species—petting, even more than parading, brings everyone together. A mock, comic war (the battle of the sexes) gives way to real wars on both the military and economic fronts, but Berkeley also retains a utopian vision of an idealized, recoverable past, somewhat like Mae West's vision of the Gay Nineties in *She Done Him Wrong*.

More than the other musicals in the year's Warner Bros./Berkeley triptych, *Gold Diggers of 1933* proposes a concept of entertainment as social consciousness, a means of commenting meaningfully on the times. "It's all about the Depression," as producer Hopkins says of the all-star revue he is putting together. However, this relevance is accomplished not in the somber and narrativized terms of *Wild Boys of the Road* and *Gabriel Over the White House* but with the tools of sexuality, showgirls, and spectacle (i.e., some of the very elements then under attack by reformers and regulators) best suited to both the musical genre and its current golden boy, Busby Berkeley.

████████████ *Footlight Parade* and the Hundred Days

History was moving fast in this year, and even Warner Bros., with its forced-march production schedules and flair for topicality, was hard pressed to keep up with the pace of events and the national mood. Bridging the period from the last grim days of Hoover to the shaky but sanguine dawn of the New Deal, the three classic Warner Bros./Busby Berkeley musicals trace a rainbow arc that rises in the direction of optimism, progress, and harmony. Following the hard-boiled melodrama of *42nd Street* and the cynical sex comedy of *Gold Diggers of 1933*, *Footlight Parade* is a more affirmative, generous-spirited diversion centered on the necessity (and ability) of entertainment to reinvent itself. *Footlight Parade* went into production in June (Hoberman, *42nd* 67), right on the heels of Roosevelt's Hundred Days, and the film's emphasis on speed, innovation, and dynamic leadership marks it as a product of that action-packed period.

Many of the elements central to the two earlier films are either pushed to the margins or given a breezier spin. Chief among these is Chester Kent (James Cagney), the washed-up Broadway producer who revives his career by staging live musical "prologues" for movie theaters. A less neurotic, more resilient variation on Julian Marsh from *42nd Street*, Kent cracks plenty of jokes about winding up in a coffin or an insane asylum, but he never actually sinks into Marsh's morbid, depressive funk.

The materialistic gold-digger maneuvers of *Gold Diggers of 1933* are shunted off onto a secondary character: a phony sophisticate (Claire Dodd) whose amiable attempts to entrap Kent are easily deflected by his adoring secretary (Joan Blondell). *Footlight Parade* even makes light of the ongoing censorship wars by treating a fatuous bluenose (Hugh Herbert) as the harmless butt of numerous jokes.

The "New Deal in Entertainment" concept that was opportunistically tacked onto the publicity campaign of *42nd Street* is developed more organically in *Footlight Parade*. The story begins with an electronic news headline announcing the advent of talking pictures—and the consequent decline of stage musicals. The suddenly unemployed Kent observes, "So musicals are out, eh?"—conflating the situation on Broadway in 1929 with that of Hollywood in 1931–32 (i.e., before *42nd Street*), just as his prologues fudge the boundary between the theatrical and cinematic worlds (a billboard touts the prologues as "The Ultimate in Picture Theatre Presentation").

The film identifies the Old Deal in Entertainment as the venerable Broadway spectacle tradition of Ziegfeld and the Shubert Brothers, represented by such concepts as Girls of France, Girls of South America, and, hoariest of all, Girls as American Beauty Roses (when the last is pitched to him, Kent howls, "Stop, you're killing me! I almost fell out of my cradle when the Shuberts did it back in nineteen hundred and twelve!"). Entertainment has to (and, the film presumes to demonstrate, is able to) grow up and change with the times. The innovative Kent applies the cost-cutting "chain-store idea" to the production of his prologues. Then, trapped by his own Frankenstein monster, he is a slave of novelty, compelled to come up with a constant supply of fresh ideas—Gay Nineties, Bridesmaid, Baby Doll, Voo Doo, Russian Revolution, and so on—that evokes the blizzard of new bills Roosevelt rammed through the Hundred Days congressional session.

Lloyd Bacon, the speed king of *42nd Street,* was back as director. Although not as audaciously splintered as in *42nd Street,* Bacon's fast-and-loose style fashions *Footlight Parade* into a rat-a-tat series of brief scenes and lively frames filled with casual detail. In general, the density and pacing of *Footlight Parade* are less frenetic, more exhilarating than in *42nd Street,* and the hard work of the rehearsal scenes seems less of a grind, more of an adventure. Again, it is the pace of FDR's Hundred Days: pressing, purposeful, productive.

Berkeley's three big production numbers, stacked into a juggernaut at the end of the film, advance beyond their predecessors in terms of scale, complexity, and boldness in flouting the realistic boundaries of the stage space in which they are purportedly taking place. In keeping with the tone of the rest of the film, they are also less raunchy, more upbeat, more New Deal.

"Honeymoon Hotel" shifts the focus from petting to procreative productivity ("Bridal suites are never very idle/ At the Honeymoon Hotel") in its wholesomely naughty depiction of an establishment devoted to connubial bliss. The aquatic rhapsody "By a Waterfall," featuring the glistening bodies and geometric group-formations displayed by a bevy of water nymphs, pushes its central tension between form and flesh to a level of ecstatic merger where depth collapses, the distinction between light and water dissolves, and human bodies mutate into elemental cell-like units.

Beginning as a parody/repudiation of the guilt-ridden fallen woman melodrama, the finale "Shanghai Lil" transforms rakish oriental decadence into rousing New Deal morale-boosting, with a climactic parade in which vigorously marching U.S. troops merge with orientalized chorus girls to produce composite images of the American flag, FDR, and the NRA eagle, guns firing from its flanks. Roosevelt and his inner circle frequently invoked America's World War I experience as a glowing example of government-led collective action in facing a national emergency—"the great cooperation of 1917 and 1918," as FDR called it (Kennedy 178). That is the spirit in which "Shanghai Lil" uses the war analogy (and in which Kent uses it when, after sequestering his company to avoid security leaks, he declares, "This is war! A blockade!"), while "Remember My Forgotten Man" in *Gold Diggers of 1933* had conceptualized the war more in pre–New Deal terms, as a reference point for disillusionment and trauma.

Premiered on 30 September, *Footlight Parade* received mixed reviews and was less successful at the box office than either of its predecessors (Parish and Pitts 198, Roddick 276). This relatively tepid response is puzzling, because *Footlight Parade* is the most consistent of the three films, with Bacon, Berkeley, and Cagney all in top form; and it is the one most in tune with the euphoric spirit of the early New Deal. Perhaps the 1933 Express was moving too quickly, and the hybrid form of these musicals, although appropriate for the Hoover-to-Roosevelt transition period, was already being left behind.

▰▰▰▰▰ *Little Women* and the Charms of Harmony

Premiered on 16 November, RKO's *Little Women* vied with Mae West's second release of the year, *I'm No Angel,* for the title of the year's biggest fourth-quarter hit. These two blockbusters represented trends moving in opposite directions: West was about to be toppled from her throne by declining box office receipts and stepped-up Breen Office interference, while *Little Women,* held up as a model by Will Hays and other industry reformers, solidified the reign of literary-credentialed prestige pictures as Hollywood's most reliable big earners for the rest of the decade (Balio 63, 187).

Although West's big mama and Louisa May Alcott's diminutive damsels (soon to be reinforced by the biggest little star of the 1930s, Shirley Temple) present a convenient contrast for defining the passage from pre-Code wickedness to post-Breen wholesomeness, their tweakings of traditional gender hierarchies are not so diametrically opposed. Like several other films

Precocious writer-director Jo March (Katharine Hepburn) demonstrates proper melodramatic histrionics to her overly dainty sister Amy (Joan Bennett) in *Little Women*
(George Cukor, RKO Radio). Gene Siskel Film Center.

of the period, *Little Women* blurs together the specters of war and economic
hard times (albeit the war here is the Civil War), and, as in *Gold Diggers of
1933*'s "Remember My Forgotten Man," these twin traumas produce a
shortfall of masculinity. Not only are men in scarce supply, but those available do not project a strong patriarchal or masculine authority.

Many of these implications are already present in Alcott's 1869 novel,
but the RKO movie version, helmed by quintessential "woman's director"
George Cukor, accentuates the story's feminized world more strongly than
do subsequent film adaptations of the book. Daubed with heavy makeup
and lipstick, Douglass Montgomery's boy-next-door Laurie becomes a formidable sissy counterpart to Katharine Hepburn's rambunctious tomboy Jo
March. Compared to later versions, Laurie's reputedly ferocious grandfather turns out to be even more of a pussycat (while Jo's Aunt March is
more commandingly cantankerous); Jo's stammering, shambling suitor
Professor Bhaer (Paul Lukas) is declawed into a less romantic, more avun-
cular figure; and the paterfamilias Reverend March is reduced to even
more of a cipher.

Growing up in Concord, Massachusetts, with her close-knit sisters—starchy Meg (Frances Dee), sickly Beth (Jean Parker), and saucy Amy (Joan Bennett)—Jo is the center not only of the story's coming-of-age component but also of its positions on art and entertainment. As a professional writer, Jo achieves early success with lurid potboilers. In contrast to the rationales for entertainment found in most of the other films discussed in this chapter, her stories' providing of pleasure and distraction is not considered sufficient value, nor is their economic function (even though Jo notes, "'The Duke's Daughter' paid the butcher's bill"), nor is their populist appeal (they are eagerly consumed by the servant class). Mirroring Hollywood's contemporaneous quest for a more middle-class audience (Balio 62), the mild but persuasive mouthpiece Professor Bhaer is used to advance a concept of entertainment that is respectable, grounded in the truth of experience, full of "simple beauty," and unsullied by "artificial plots, villains, murderers, and, and, and such women!"

Although *Little Women* embodies certain tendencies that will flourish during the rest of the thirties, it is ahead of its time as well as of its time. Cukor embraced the screenplay's casual structure ("It wasn't slicked up. The construction was very loose, very episodic, like the novel" [Lambert 76]) and extended it to the film's style. In a manner that seems more inclusive than inconsistent, *Little Women* encompasses two different styles. One serves a Katharine Hepburn star vehicle, centered on her recklessly broad performance and punctuated with soft-focus close-ups that showcase her emotional arias. The other serves a more ensemble-oriented depiction of social cohesion, at times revealing Cukor as a forerunner of the long-take aesthetic developed more famously by Orson Welles and William Wyler in the early 1940s. The film's deep, roomy, fluid, extended shots establish the spatial continuum of Hobe Erwin's solidly but not fussily detailed sets, reinforce connections between the characters, pull back to take in the whole group, and crystallize into idealized images of familial and communal togetherness.

Episodic in structure and light on sustained conflict, the narrative maintains a balanced rhythm in which moments of resolution are quickly answered by bursts of disruption, and vice versa. The principle of disruption is often physicalized via spills and pratfalls, mostly supplied by Jo's galumphing impetuosity—as when she knocks a kiss-seeking Laurie to the ground, or topples the scenery of her home-staged melodrama (the uproar provoked by the latter is quickly contained by the maid summoning the boisterous audience to a neatly laid supper). One sequence underlines this hubbub/harmony process by literalizing the pictorial component: Amy is sketching an idyllic scene of little men and women lounging on the lawn when the maid rushes up with news of Reverend March's hospitalization, unleashing a small flurry of tumult and tears that resolves itself in an idealized image of the four girls lined up prettily on the porch in obedience to their departing mother's request ("I want to carry away a picture in my mind of my brave little women to take to Father").

This finely tuned sense of balance extends to the complementary personalities of the four sisters, the visual style's blending of fluidity and pictorialism, the central thematic opposition of transition and stability, the moderate gender politics of feminine assertion tempered by discrete exercises of patriarchal authority, and the essentially optimistic view of history as an eternally renewable achievement of equilibrium, rather than an inevitable process of decline as in *Cavalcade* and its American-set counterparts such as *Sweepings* and *The World Changes*. *Little Women* was a key film in the establishment of Hollywood's "Golden Age of Order." There would be much to regret in the passing of the rowdy, raunchy, stormy, and occasionally subversive temper of the early 1930s, but Cukor's extraordinarily lovely vision of harmony offered a gracious invitation to a new era.

NOTES

1. The first decisive act of Roosevelt's presidency, the bank holiday stemmed a rising financial panic by closing all banks until 13 March.

2. Milton Ager and Jack Yellen's "Happy Days Are Here Again" (1929) was adopted as the theme song of FDR's 1932 campaign.

3. It was traditional in World War I for families that had lost a son in combat to hang a gold star in their window in memory of the fallen soldier. One such woman, Grace Siebold, decided to found an organization open to all mothers who had lost children in combat. After years of planning, twenty-five mothers met in Washington, D.C., on 4 June 1928 to establish the national organization, American Gold Star Mothers, Inc.

4. Receivership refers to the placing of an insolvent company in the hands of a court- or creditor-appointed receiver (such as an accounting firm or a professional trustee) until the company's financial status is resolved.

1934

Movies and the Marginalized

CHARLENE REGESTER

A Year in Flux

If the departure of Babe Ruth from their team might have demoralized Yankee fans, far more fearsome changes were afoot. In Europe, totalitarianism was solidifying its hold. Adolf Hitler had secured his grip on the Nazi Party with the "Night of the Long Knives" on 30 June, a series of police raids that resulted in the execution of chief rival Ernst Roehm and many of his supporters. The death of President Hindenburg on 2 August allowed Hitler to claim the title of Reich chancellor and Führer and to abolish the presidency after a plebiscite in which more than 90 percent of voters approved of the move. In the Soviet Union Josef Stalin also eliminated dissent, bringing to an end a period of relative liberalism in the Politburo when he began his Great Purge in December.

At home, Americans witnessed another devastating year of drought and dust in the plains. Great dust storms spread from the Dust Bowl area, eventually covering more than 75 percent of the country and significantly affecting twenty-seven states. Bonnie Parker and Clyde Barrow continued to rob banks and kill policemen and John Dillinger broke out of jail using a wooden gun, although all three were dead by year's end. In more positive developments, FDR's ongoing New Deal initiatives targeted the country's financial infrastructure. He took the nation off the gold standard, forbade the export of silver, and established the Securities and Exchange Commission (SEC), the Federal Deposit Insurance Commission (FDIC), and the Federal Communications Commission (FCC). The Tennessee Valley Authority (TVA) contracted its first rural power customer, the town of Tupelo, Mississippi. And farmers impacted by the dust storms were protected by the Frazier-Lemke Farm Bankruptcy Act, which restricted the ability of banks to dispossess farmers in times of distress.

Comic strip icons continued to be a dependable product of lean times. "Li'l Abner," "Terry and the Pirates," and "Flash Gordon" made their debuts. It was a great year for soon-to-be classic fiction as well: *Tender Is the Night, I Claudius, And Quiet Flows the Don, Call It Sleep, Good-Bye, Mr. Chips,* and *Murder on the Orient Express.* Pop song standards written this year included "What a Difference a Day Makes," "Blue Moon," and "I Only Have Eyes for You." Notable beginnings of other sorts were also prevalent. In Canada, the five Dionne girls became the first quintuplets to survive their initial days of life. The Masters golf tournament was played for the first time, and the first Walgreens drugstore opened, as did the Los Angeles Farmers Market.

Also in Los Angeles, things were looking up financially for the film studios. After several years of declining movie attendance since the Crash, ticket sales increased. But the industry was still beset by worries. One major issue was the quantity of pictures compared to their general quality. In response, the studios launched an initiative aimed at reducing the number of pictures produced and releasing higher quality films. One report noted, "There are too many pictures and . . . the majors have seen the light and are ready to concentrate on fewer and better pictures" ("Majors to Cut" 18). Comments by studio executives demonstrate, however, that concerns about focusing on quality films rather than quantity were primarily driven by economic forces as opposed to artistic concerns (see Ramsaye 9–11).

As the executives at large debated this issue, the companies they oversaw experienced management changes that would dramatically affect the industry. Reports circulated that talks were ongoing between the Cohn Brothers and DuPont-Schlesingers for control of the newly formed Columbia Pictures ("Sam Katz" 18). While Columbia was undergoing a change in management, William Fox was resurrecting his career with Fox Film Corporation after a favorable Supreme Court ruling granted him an estimated $100 million in damages in a suit against RCA Photoplay and Electrical Products. The case involved copyright infringement on sound equipment utilized by nearly every theater in the country, and after the court's decision, it was revealed that Fox was "in complete control of the recording and reproducing sound situation in America, and every studio must pay him for the privilege of making sound pictures and every theater must pay to show the pictures" ("William Fox's Comeback" 19; "Fox Wants" 19).

Amidst these concerns, changes, and struggles, the industry was also confronted with increased government scrutiny when an investigation was launched to monitor the exorbitant salaries received by studio executives. President Roosevelt commanded them to disclose their salaries, citing the disparity in pay that existed between management and workers, particularly at a time of looming national debt. A Senate investigation was scheduled to interrogate them after their salaries were disclosed to the public

("Film Executives Costly" 20). These salaries were considered gratuitous compensation in an industry where wages were seen to be a primary factor driving the high cost of film production, where theater owners complained that film rentals were too high, where stockholders were not receiving dividends, and where office workers were subjected to pay cuts.

Studios also had to contend with self-censorship concerns arising from the Motion Picture Producers and Distributors of America's implementation of the Hays Office–mandated Production Code. In an attempt to encourage the industry to enforce its standards, Will Hays, the president of the MPPDA, issued the following proclamation: "'It behooves all producers to observe the moral code and it might be well for a few of them, now manifesting an inclination to take short cuts, to mend their ways. That's because the industry is going to crack down on any offending members. The industry will develop a means to put bad boys in their places'" ("Hays Whipping" 5). Others soon joined the call to censor those films deemed objectionable. The president of one theater association publicly expressed his views in a *Billboard* editorial: "We find well meaning, intelligent, broadminded people in all parts of the country banding together in a determined effort to stop the dishing out of dirt by producers who have but one thought: to make money. To do this they are continually injecting sexy situations of the most lousy nature into good and wholesome pictures" ("An Exhibitor Gives" 18).

The Catholic Church echoed such views and encouraged its members to boycott films deemed offensive and to promote so-called "clean films" ("Seek 5,000,000" 20). Despite these protestations, Cecil B. DeMille spoke out against censoring the industry: "Censorship is un-American and I don't believe the American people want it. . . . Censorship—that is, control by any person or group or organization—is dangerous to liberty. If it comes to pictures it will come to the press, and this would put a ring thru the nose of the people and the politicians could lead them whither the politicians desire" ("Censorship" 19). In the end, the accord reached in July was, according to Richard Maltby, "best seen not as the industry's reaction to a more or less spontaneous outburst of moral protest backed by economic sanction, but as the culmination of a lengthy process of negotiation within the industry and between its representatives and those speaking with the voices of cultural authority" ("Production Code" 40).

In spite of all these controversies, the studios continued to produce a significant number of films that showcased the talents of their creative personnel. Claudette Colbert, Clark Gable, Wallace Beery, Bette Davis, Marlene Dietrich, William Powell, Myrna Loy, and Will Rogers had signature roles. Shirley Temple made her feature debut in *Stand Up and Cheer*. Some of the more prolific directors spotlighted that year in the press were Mervyn LeRoy, with *Sweet Adeline* and three other films released; Lloyd Bacon, with *Wonder Bar* among his four; and John Cromwell, with *Of Human Bondage* among his. Other significant films produced in this year included Cecil B. DeMille's *Cleopatra,* Wesley Ruggles's *Bolero,* W. S. Van Dyke's *The Thin Man,* Jack Conway's *Viva Villa!,* Victor Schertzinger's *One Night of Love,* and Josef Von Sternberg's *The Scarlet Empress.*

Affected by industry concerns associated with the economic demands confronting the motion picture industry and plagued with censorship difficulties inherited from previous years, the year can best be described as a year of ebbs and flows. This instability is reflected in a number of films that dealt with the fluidity of gendered, racial, and class positions: *Imitation of Life, Judge Priest, Manhattan Melodrama, It Happened One Night,* and *Our Daily Bread.* At a time when many people experienced great dislocations from positions once thought secure, films not only examined traditionally marginalized or disempowered groups like women, Blacks, and the poor but also portrayed the barriers between them and the socially prominent white male becoming porous and permeable. Some films showed the formerly marginalized gaining power, while others displayed members of a more privileged race, gender, or class occupying the place of the socially marginalized.

Otherness Chosen: *Manhattan Melodrama* and *It Happened One Night*

W. S. Van Dyke's *Manhattan Melodrama* reconstructs the tragic tale of two boys whose friendship as adults becomes strained by circumstances that lead one, Jim Wade (William Powell), to become governor while the other, Blackie Gallagher (Clark Gable), assumes a life of crime, ultimately leading to his execution. The film opens aboard a steamship where crowds of people dance jubilantly on the deck. However, a fire soon erupts on the ship, forcing people to jump overboard. Two of the youngsters on board—Blackie and Jim—survive the ordeal and because they are now without parents they are later adopted by an elderly gentleman, Poppa Rosen (George Sidney), who decides to raise them in the absence of his own son who was killed in the disaster. When Rosen first extends his offer to take care of the youngsters, Blackie remarks, "I'm not a Jew," to which Rosen responds, "Catholic, Protestant, Jew . . . what difference does it matter now?" Blackie's comments on his ethnicity certainly demonstrate how difference will be a subtext in the film. Moreover, Jonathan Munby contends that "ethnic marking," introduced early in the narrative, was clearly related to class status, and that gangster dramas produced in the 1930s were "dependent on a mass interest in the realm of ethnic urban lower class experience. The genre's mass popularity testified to the fact that even if the American 'others' continued to be historically and politically marginalized they were becoming culturally central to the life of the nation" ("Manhattan" 102).

Following Rosen's attempt to provide some semblance of a family in its absence for the two boys, they join others similarly displaced by the disaster in a makeshift camp. When an unnamed Russian professes his views that a revolution among America's working class is inevitable, Rosen denounces him, proclaiming that although he too is Russian, he starved in his home country, while in America he was able to eat. The other Russian refers to Rosen as a "capitalistic stooge"—a remark that inflames those who are supportive of American democracy and that results in riots. In the aftermath of the melee, Rosen is killed and the two youngsters survive yet another tragedy.

The film then moves forward to portray Blackie and Jim in adulthood, where each of the boys has come to assume a position for which he had seemed predisposed. Blackie, who at an early age had engaged in a lifestyle of trickery and bribery, now owns and operates an illegal gambling casino, while Jim, who had always been devoted to his studies, becomes a lawyer and then the district attorney. One film reviewer observed, "If Jim Wade is straight as a die, Blackie Gallagher is crooked as his own dice" ("Cinema: *Manhattan Melodrama*" 24).

Many thirties gangsters are marked as ethnic outsiders, but Clark Gable is not as recognizably from immigrant stock as gangster characters who are overtly Italian, Jewish, or Irish. Instead, the film marks his character with metaphorical racial difference. Starting with his name, he is identified with blackness. Conversely, he has an aversion to whiteness. At one point he advises Jim not to paint his "big time house" white because "I hate white." Blackness becomes synonymous with evil and crime, but it also suggests that anyone who is not completely Anglo-American white might be more likely to succumb to that temptation. Munby contends:

> While "Anglicization" was understood by some ethnic urban community [*sic*] as a necessary phase in assimilation, the gangster vehicles which catapulted ethnic stars to national fame questioned precisely the boundary which separated Anglo-America from ethnic 'others' and the consequent uneven terms of assimilation. In recasting this conflict as one between the law and the outlaw the 1930s gangster film drew attention to the ethnocentric order of things.   ("Manhattan" 117)

The contrasts between Blackie and Jim are underscored by the scene in which Jim's election victory is juxtaposed with Blackie's collection of money from some of his criminal associates. Because Blackie is busy with his criminal exploits, he is unable to meet Jim to celebrate his election victory, so he sends his girlfriend, Eleanor (Myrna Loy), instead. This begins a relationship between Eleanor and Jim, and results in her losing interest in Blackie. According to Munby, "Eleanor . . . oscillates between narratives, falling in and out of love with both . . . acting as an internal (within the text) witness to the two men's good characters" ("Manhattan" 105). Later, Blackie attempts to convince Eleanor that her relationship with Jim is doomed to failure: "Jim is as much out of your class as he is out of mine." Yet these class differences are not as fixed or insuperable as Blackie thinks they are.

At the film's end, Jim marries Eleanor and is elected governor of New York. However, Jim's election is only possible after Blackie murders his assistant, who had been attempting to sabotage his victory. Ironically, during his campaign for governor, Jim is forced to prosecute Blackie for the murder, resulting in his being sentenced to death. Eleanor, aware that Blackie killed to save Jim's career, pleads with her husband to commute his sentence. She even threatens to end their marriage, proclaiming that he has become so preoccupied by his career that he ignores the plight of his lifelong friend and that Blackie has higher moral character than he does. Convinced by Eleanor, Jim rushes to the prison to halt Blackie's execution, but finds that Blackie has confessed in order to invite his own death, conceding, "If I can't live the way I want to, at least let me die the way I want to." Following Blackie's execution, Jim resigns as governor and publicly admits that Blackie committed murder to save his election. Jim and Eleanor are reunited, and she embraces him for engaging in this ethical act.

Blackie's metaphorical racial otherness is underscored by his ultimate fate—the death penalty being a sentence disproportionately administered to black males.[1] Even when Blackie walks toward the death chamber, he stops to exchange words with a black inmate, another attempt by the film to associate Blackie with nonwhites.

We should not, however, ignore the film's intentional parallel between Jim and Blackie, which speaks to the fact that Blackie and Jim represent two sides of the same self. Blackie represents the dark or immoral side and Jim represents the light or moral side, but neither is a fixed position. The two characters reverse their roles when for a time Jim seems wrong in his refusal to commute Blackie's sentence, while Blackie assumes the more selfless position by making a commitment to save his lifelong friend. Of course, at the film's end, Jim's good character is restored, but not without the death of Blackie, who represents Jim's potential for moral "blackness."

Ironically, *Manhattan Melodrama* went on to become part of historical legend when real-life gangster John Dillinger was shot by federal agents after sneaking into a screening of the film at the Chicago Biograph Theater. This film, among others, would force Will Hays to institute a moratorium on gangster film production in the following year (Munby, "Manhattan" 103–04). While the coincidental combination of Dillinger and a gangster film had grim consequences for both the criminal and the genre, the "happy accident" of Frank Capra's *It Happened One Night* led to wild success for all who came together to film it.

Often regarded as the first screwball comedy, the film begins with a splash—literally—as pampered heiress Ellie Andrews (Claudette Colbert) jumps overboard because her father (Walter Connolly) objects to the man she plans to marry. Her engagement to King Westley (Jameson Thomas), like her temper tantrum on the ship, stems more from a rebellion against the family patriarch than true love. To elude his massive search for her, she boards a bus traveling from Miami to New York, where she meets Peter Warne (Clark Gable), a drunken reporter recently fired by his boss. Peter detects that she is on the run and decides to protect her. He also tries to get her to come to terms with her privileged, aristocratic upbringing, which he strongly resents. Frequently, he refers to Ellie's upbringing as having turned her into a spoiled brat. At the same time, Peter sees in her attempt to avoid capture by her father a story that could help him resurrect his journalism career. During a series of misadventures on the bus and off, the two manage to set aside their class differences and coexist, eventually leading them to fall in love.

Despite the fact that the film is a lighthearted romance, it also serves as a commentary on normative and dominant cultural codes and expectations. Ellie transgresses her upper-class status and takes on a number of social positions other than her own, such as living without money (she runs away from her father with only her watch to pawn) and learning humility from Peter (he repeatedly outmaneuvers her and has an answer for her every remark). When their bus ride is interrupted due to adverse weather, they have to stay together in a cabin at a motor court. Because she has no luggage of her own, Peter offers her his pajama top, a gesture that forces her to transcend her feminine self and assume the gendered place of the masculine. For the first time in her life, she is denied the accoutrements associated with her status and sexuality, even to the degree that she has to bathe in the

Newspaperman Peter Warne (Clark Gable) and spoiled heiress Ellie Andrews (Claudette Colbert) fall in love during a road trip on the run in *It Happened One Night* (Frank Capra, Columbia). In this publicity still their hitchhiking skills are tested. Collection Ina Rae Hark.

communal outdoor shower. However, Ellie finds such hardships liberating. She remarks that being with Peter is the first time that she has been alone with a man, as she has always had bodyguards.

The sequence at the motor court is one of the most celebrated in the film. Peter plays on Ellie's sense of propriety by nonchalantly undressing in front of her, deferring the removal of the most crucial items of clothing like a practiced strip-tease artist. (When he removes his shirt to reveal the absence of any garment beneath, the revelation supposedly depressed undershirt sales to would-be Clark Gables in the audience.) A gentleman at heart, who poses no sexual threat to his companion, Peter both enjoys and resents having to deflect her fears of what can happen when a young woman shares a bedroom with a strange man. His solution is to string up a rope with a blanket draped over it between their beds, offering privacy but clearly no protection from a determined suitor. He jokingly invests this weak barrier with biblical strength, however, dubbing it "the Walls of Jericho." Much of the scene plays out with the frame divided between the two characters as they are together in the same space yet separated by Ellie's lingering distrust.

When detectives search their cabin for Ellie, she pretends to be Peter's wife—a plumber's daughter—and they engage in a staged argument to deceive them. When their masquerade is finally revealed, they are forced to abandon the bus and decide to continue their journey on foot. They are further marginalized when they seek refuge on an abandoned farm where she has to sleep on a makeshift bed in the hay; later he uses a knife as a toothpick to remove a stalk from her teeth. Despite her previous refusals, Ellie even resorts to eating raw carrots out of hunger.

Peter similarly occupies the margins of his own class in that he has been dismissed from his job at the newspaper and is depicted as a drunk.[2] His confrontational nature becomes glaringly apparent early on when he boards a bus and yells at the driver about a seat occupied by a pile of newspapers. He responds by throwing the newspapers out the window, and he and the driver exchange words. This initial characterization marks him as oppositional and nonconformist, as is further apparent when he informs Ellie that he is not interested in her money, even though he is interested in her story. His dismissal of her family's wealth, class, and aristocratic lifestyle is captured in his remark, "You all are a lot of hooey to me." His willingness to pose as Ellie's husband also marks his departure from conservative sexual norms by masquerading as something he is not.

Peter's nonconformity is represented by his helpful behavior as well. He engages in a degree of role reversal with Ellie when he waits on her hand and foot in the cabin—he prepares her breakfast, presses her dress, and provides her with toiletries—actions customarily associated with women. His unconventional behavior marks him as a person who lets no dominant ideology determine his actions.

For most of their journey Peter serves as tutor to Ellie, showing her how "the other half lives" and breaking down her class-based assumptions and behavior. One other example occurs when he teaches her how to dunk her doughnut in coffee, a practice that would certainly be frowned upon in view of her class position. Because both her father and Peter know better what Ellie needs and wants than she does herself, *It Happened One Night* cannot be read as the triumphant story of a brave young woman seeking to take control over her own life and destiny by acts of rebellion. Despite her defiance she is still guided, controlled, and influenced by men. To this end, Sidney Gottlieb observes that "Capra presents his heroine as 'a spoiled brat' so that he will not have to deal with her as a real woman" (135). He notes further that the one instance when she teaches Peter a lesson, rather than the reverse, may not be as empowering as it first appears. In the film's most famous scene, the pair are hitchhiking. Peter claims to have a mastery of all the various techniques for flagging down a ride. None of them causes a car to stop, until she tries her own technique: "Ellie shows that she possesses a certain amount of power but only as a sexual object: she hikes up her dress to stop a car for a ride, proving that her 'limb' is stronger than his 'thumb' but this is a dubious victory" (Gottlieb 132). However, the liberations supplied by screwball comedy are all about sex, so Gottlieb's objection may be beside the point. Ellie is not freed of class and gender restraints so that she can live independently of men; she is freed to find the right man for her.

When the couple has exhausted their finances, Peter returns alone to New York to inform his editor of the story he has written about the now-famous aristocratic runaway who is in love with him, and uses this as leverage to borrow $1,000 so that they can finish their journey together. This action results in a misunderstanding characteristic of the genre. Ellie, upon discovering that he has left her in the motel without saying goodbye, believes that he did not in fact love her and only kept up their relationship in order to obtain the reward offered for her return by her father (who also has agreed to drop his objection to her original choice of husband). Although she admits she is still in love with Peter, she decides to go through with her marriage to Westley. Yet when it comes time for her to walk down the aisle in an elaborate ceremony, her father tells her that he has ordered a car to wait nearby for her in case she changes her mind. In a parallel to her jump overboard at the beginning of the film, she suddenly makes a dash for the car with her wedding veil flowing behind. The film ends with a married Peter and Ellie reunited in the same type of tourist cabin in which they had earlier stayed, bringing down the "Walls of Jericho" as they consummate their love. The lovemaking is of course offscreen, but the sound of a toy trumpet tells the audience all it needs to know.

Otherness by Appropriation: *Imitation of Life* and *Judge Priest*

Following Colbert's success in *It Happened One Night*, she returned to the screen in *Imitation of Life* as Bea, a widow struggling to continue operating her husband's maple syrup business while attempting to raise her daughter as a single mother. Her life takes a turn when she meets another single mother, Delilah (Louise Beavers), a black woman who is seeking employment as a maid in order to provide for her daughter. The two first meet when, in response to an advertisement, Delilah confuses Aster Street with Aster Avenue and shows up at Bea's house just as Bea is feeling overwhelmed by her household duties. Delilah's confusion about the address serves as a metaphor for the misrecognition that occurs throughout the film, exemplified most significantly in Delilah's light-complexioned daughter, Peola (Fredi Washington), who desires to pass as white. The misrecognition that Peola strives for can be read as embodied also by Bea, who is symbolically a black woman in a white skin; she thus mirrors the contradiction embodied by Peola, who wishes to be white despite her black ancestry.

Even though she has arrived at the incorrect address, Delilah recognizes that "Miss Bea" needs some assistance. After making herself indispensable by helping her with the nearly burnt food on her stove, Delilah proposes that she would be willing to serve as her maid without pay in exchange for a place to stay for her and her daughter. Delilah attempts to convince Bea that she will not be a burden: "I don't eat like I look . . . I'se very light at the table"—a remark that reflects the film's racial politics by contrasting the oversized black (conceived as unattractive) Delilah with the thin white (conceived as attractive) Bea. Jeremy Butler observes that "Delilah fits comfortably into the 'mammy' type: large framed, self-effacing, religious to the point of superstition, uneducated but 'wise' in matters of the heart, and above all else totally committed to nurturing not just her own daughter but Bea's daughter and Bea herself" (292).

As the two women join forces, Bea launches a successful pancake business—a business derived from Delilah's secret recipe. Confronted with unprecedented success, Bea becomes a wealthy entrepreneur, while Delilah, who declines her share of the pancake company because of her commitment to Bea, descends into a state of declining health brought on by her daughter's identity crisis and their ensuing conflicts. At the film's end, Delilah dies—a death hastened by her daughter's rejection. In contrast, Bea denies herself the love of her life, Stephen, by rejecting his marriage proposal in order to save her relationship with her daughter, Jessie, who has herself fallen in love with Stephen.

Although Bea is primarily constructed to represent the antithesis of the racial Otherness embodied by Delilah, she might also be seen as masquerading as a racial Other. This is not to deny Bea's narrative function as the white foil to the black Delilah. Were it not for the black characters existing within the context of a world in which whites are dependent on Blacks, the film's plot would have no basis. The asymmetrical relationship that develops between the two is highlighted as Delilah remains committed and devoted to Bea, in one scene relieving her of a briefcase and rubbing her tired feet when she returns home after a long day at work, a racial slight that disregards Delilah's labor at the expense of her white employer. Even *Time* magazine noted, "The real heroine of *Imitation of Life* is not Bea Pullman but Aunt Delilah, and of the many problems which the picture investigates by far the most exciting is that of the aging colored woman whose good fortune emphasizes her daughter's racial unhappiness. By dodging this problem with dogged determination, *Imitation of Life* relinquishes all claim to artistic honesty" ("Imitation" 47).

Yet there are a number of ways to read Bea's character so as to stress her parallels to rather than contrasts with Delilah. Both women are nurturing single mothers who defy normative codes and enter worlds where they are a minority. Bea enters the male-dominated world of business entrepreneurship and Delilah enters the white world of black domestication. Their commonality is visible when the two combine their business acumen to establish the successful pancake venture. Delilah volunteers her secret pancake recipe and expresses concern regarding the families' limited finances, while Bea negotiates with the repairmen when opening her restaurant and later incorporating her business. Added to this, the two women share the same physical space. Living in the same quarters reflects their indispensability to one another, despite the fact that Bea lives upstairs—an indicator of her white privilege—while Delilah resides downstairs—a signifier of her subservient status. A further parallel between the two is Bea's embrace of Delilah's superstitions in that Delilah's rabbit foot brings Bea good luck when Stephen enters her life. Finally, Bea complies with Delilah's request for an appropriately elaborate funeral. Susan Courtney declares that "Delilah's presence, and eventual death, also works to eventually restore Bea to the feminine roles of mother and potential wife" (152).

While the film may have established these parallels between Bea and Delilah to demonstrate how Bea is closely linked to her black counterpart, Bea's Otherness is also indicated by the fact that she attempts to establish a business in the male-dominated world during a period when women were predominantly confined to domestic spaces. By the end of the film Bea is seemingly punished for her decision to become a working mother because, despite her economic success, she is denied her love interest, Stephen. Ultimately she is constructed as an "ineffective" mother who has to rely on her black maid to nurture and care for her own daughter. Yet while Bea is displaced by Delilah as a mother to her own daughter, she at the same time serves as the authoritative voice and stands in for the commanding mother-figure that Delilah is not to her daughter, Peola.

Peola Johnson (Fredi Washington, left) is caught passing for white by her black biological mother, Delilah (Louise Beavers), to whom she is less likely to listen than her mother's white employer, Bea Pullman (Claudette Colbert) in *Imitation of Life* (John Stahl, Universal). Photofest New York.

For example, when Peola returns home from school after passing as white and Delilah informs Bea, it is Bea who reprimands Peola by telling her that she must not feel that way; it is Bea who instructs Peola to remove her wet clothes after she refuses to do so for Delilah; and it is Bea who suggests to Delilah that she should send Peola to a different school. That Bea assumes such a prominent role in her relationship to Peola speaks not only to Peola's affinity for whiteness, but also speaks to Bea's affinity for blackness. Peola leaves school and decides to pass as white and work in a store without her mother's knowledge. When Delilah discovers her working in the store, Peola speaks disrespectfully to her own black mother; it is Bea who intervenes and retorts "how can you talk to your mother that way?"

Later, as Peola confronts her mother and asserts her decision to pass as white, Bea tries to excuse herself from the conversation, but Peola insists that she remain in the room: "You don't know what it is like to be black and look white." However, perhaps she does understand. Bea, the "ineffective" mother, now gives advice to Delilah, the "effective" mother, telling her not to worry because once Peola experiences a few hard knocks in life, she will return to her mother. That the "ineffective" mother is now advising the "effective" mother demonstrates how Bea comes to displace Delilah as a mother figure to a black daughter. More importantly, that Peola obeys the white mother rather than her own black mother reflects her belief that whiteness is privileged, but also hints at Bea's association with blackness.

The many instances of misrecognition in the film serve to point up not only Peola's problematic identity complex but also Bea's. At one point Delilah remarks of Peola's intellectual capacity, "We all start out smart—we don't get dumb until later." Such commentary, although infused with racial politics, suggests how Blacks frequently masquerade, and it is this masquerade that characterizes the Otherness embodied by Peola and appropriated by Bea. When Peola passes as white at school, her assumed identity is in part constructed by her black mother. Bea's ability to disguise her own identity is shown by the fact that she does not reveal her business ownership when she first meets Stephen; he is surprised when he discovers that she is the "Pancake Queen." Other examples of misrecognition occur when Stephen meets Jessie after having seen only her photo and is surprised to learn that she is no longer a juvenile but a college-age woman; and when Peola is found working in the store and attempts to conceal her identity with the claim, "I am sure that you've got me confused with someone else."

The various forms of misrecognition portrayed in the film hint at a possible misreading of Bea who, despite her whiteness, often functions as black. If, as Susan Courtney suggests, "'black' female subjects at times appear to be 'white'" (142), then is it not possible for a white female subject to appear black? This implied racial hybridity for Bea then serves as a metonymy of her more overt gender hybridity as a woman inappropriately succeeding in men's endeavors.

Another film of this year that foregrounds the interdependency of Blacks and whites is John Ford's *Judge Priest*. Thomas Cripps describes it as having "a crusty Southern ambience clothed in wisps of racial satire. . . . Negro women tote 'white folks' washing'; a potbellied Kentuckian lazes on a verandah under the fanning of a black boy; Blacks and whites doze in the courthouse square as a harmonica trills. Inside, a judge hears a 'gangling, lazy mumbling negro' charged with chicken-thieving but acquits him because both would miss their fishing trip" (272). However, the satire hardly has any urgency. This film seems designed to celebrate the South's perseverance in the aftermath of the Civil War—including the perseverance of the racial hierarchies of slavery, which the film softens but nevertheless tacitly approves.

The film opens with a courtroom scene in which Judge William "Billy" Priest (Will Rogers) sits reading a newspaper while hearing the case of Jeff Poindexter (Stepin Fetchit [Lincoln Perry]), a black male accused of stealing chickens. The prosecuting attorney's determination to teach him a lesson seems to be attributable more to Jeff's blackness than to the crime of which he is accused. The prosecutor recommends to the judge that Jeff be sentenced to six months on the chain gang because, to his knowledge, Jeff has never done any honest work. After the prosecutor makes his case, the camera cuts to Jeff, who is portrayed as a slow-witted buffoon so uninterested in his fate that he is asleep during his own trial. Judge Priest commands, "Hey, Boy! Wake Up!" and immediately Jeff's subordinate status as a black male is affirmed by the fact that he is not named. Jeff rises slowly while scratching his head to reflect a state of confusion and discontent. He then tells the judge his name and declares his innocence. He testifies that instead of stealing chickens, he was actually fishing in the "Sleepy River," using beef liver to catch catfish. Jeff's case is quickly resolved when the judge decides he would rather join him fishing.

This is the first indication of the judge's affinity with black characters.[3] By aligning himself with the black racial Other, Judge Priest transgresses the boundaries not only of race and class but also even morality since he is a court-appointed official fraternizing with the accused. Certainly, the judge's behavior is an indication of the ambivalent relationships between southern whites and Blacks in an era when both crossed these—real or imagined—racial boundaries.

In the next scene, the camera cuts to Aunt Dilsey (Hattie McDaniel), the quintessential black "mammy" figure, as she removes clothes from the clothesline while singing. She sings overzealously, as though this is the highlight of her life, before being greeted by the judge's nephew, Jerome Priest (Tom Brown), who has just returned from law school. Jerome informs Dilsey that he has "stomach trouble," to which she replies, "What them Yankees feeding yo'?" Here Dilsey is utilized as the means by which to invoke the divide between North and South while serving as the nurturer to the white family for whom she works. Following his encounter with Dilsey, Jerome becomes reacquainted with his uncle, who is intent on helping him rekindle his romantic interest in Ellie May Gillespie (Anita Louise).

From this point on, the film's plot is primarily concerned with Jerome's attempt to renew his relationship with Ellie May. Although Ellie May seems to epitomize the white southern belle, Jerome meets resistance from his mother, who insists that she is unsuitable for him because she is from a lower-class background and lacks family pride. Judge Priest thinks otherwise and ends up playing a pivotal role in getting the two reunited. On one occasion, when Ellie May appears on the verge of becoming involved with Flem Talley (Frank Melton), the judge disrupts their relationship by speaking in two different voices and fabricating a conversation suggesting that Flem is being hunted by a posse. Flem, overhearing what he believes to be a real conversation, fears for his life and flees: "The camera pans to the bushes, revealing Judge Priest hiding alone; he has been doing blackvoice" (Rogin 171). That the judge imitates "black speech and dialect" while constructing this fake conversation demonstrates how he is able temporarily to transgress his racial identity and participate in blackness while remaining white. The fact that the judge is so skilled at speaking in "blackvoice" that Flem interprets his imitation as real further demonstrates the judge's ease in adopting a black identity.

When a man overhears Flem disrespect Ellie May in the barbershop and proceeds to retaliate violently by knocking him out, the film makes its circuitous return to the courtroom. In revenge for the assault in the barbershop, Flem and his friends decide to retaliate against this man, which results in Flem's being injured. The case goes to trial and Judge Priest is set to preside, but because of his association with those involved in the case, he recuses himself from hearing it. However, Jerome, in his first case as lawyer, defends Flem's attacker—a man who, because of his shady past and involvement in a previous murder, seems destined to lose.

The night before the end of the trial, the town's minister visits Judge Priest, who now serves as associate counsel for the defense, and proclaims his willingness to "break a pledge of secrecy." When the trial resumes the next day, the minister is called to testify on behalf of the accused and provides a moving testimony regarding his character. The minister testifies that the man had been a prisoner-turned-soldier during the Civil War and that he had performed many outstanding feats, including saving the lives of those wounded in battle. Michael Rogin, in his review of this scene, notes: "To enlist sympathy for the stranger, the Judge has arranged for the story of his Civil War bravery to be interrupted by the sounds of 'Dixie' from outside the courtroom" (172). The minister then reveals a secret he has kept for a long time: that the accused man is actually Ellie May's father, Roger Gillespie (David Landau). With this revelation, the courtroom erupts in jubilation as those assembled celebrate Roger's heroism during the war and the fact that Ellie May's father is alive, contrary to what everyone had previously believed. The film ends as the courtroom attendants march in a parade to celebrate this discovery and to pay tribute to the Confederate war hero; the march includes other Blacks and is led by none other than

Judge Billy Priest (Will Rogers) often abdicates his position of white male authority to side with Blacks and social outcasts in *Judge Priest* (John Ford, Twentieth Century Fox). Collection Ina Rae Hark.

Jeff Poindexter, who wears a raccoon coat and top hat (given to him by Judge Priest for delivering a letter of importance) while beating a drum ecstatically.

The black characters' odd enthusiasm for the Lost Cause is mirrored by Judge Priest's close affinity for Blacks, as illustrated through his relationship with Jeff, his constant companion throughout the film. Jeff fans the judge to keep him cool when he sits on the front porch; Jeff retrieves the judge's croquet balls; Jeff accompanies the judge on a fishing expedition; and Jeff desires the judge's raccoon coat. As a result of their close association, the judge both identifies with Jeff and even imitates him when he engages in "black discourse." Correspondingly, Jeff ends up dressed in the judge's clothing. Rogin further speculates about the interdependency between the judge and Jeff: "Speaking Jeff's voice to invoke paternal prerogative, the Judge and [Jeff] together stand in for Ella [sic] May's absent father" (171).

The judge's camaraderie with Blacks is further apparent when he joins Aunt Dilsey and her associates in singing. His non-normative racial position is set in direct contrast to that of the prosecuting attorney. While the prosecutor demonstrates a desire to distance himself from blackness by accusing Jeff of not only stealing but also being lazy, the judge aligns himself with Jeff by not only acquitting him, but joining him on a fishing trip. Although Jeff has little dialogue in the film, he is an almost ubiquitous presence, appearing onscreen nearly as often as some of the white characters. This, in addition to the star billing he receives, speaks to his importance in the film, however problematized his role may be. Richard Dyer's affirmation that even though "whites hold power in society [they] are materially dependent upon black people" ("White" 48) seems particularly relevant to the relationship between Jeff and the judge.

The judge's abdication of his class privilege is also apparent, marked by the way he stands with Ellie May in opposition to his sister-in-law, Carrie, who wants to keep her and Jerome apart. Ellie May is constituted as socially marginal because of her class position and orphan status. However, the judge defends her and insists on helping to pair her and Jerome, regardless of their social differences. In the end, *Judge Priest* suggests that the judge is willing to transgress his intrinsic racial and class identities, relinquishing his position of symbolic white male authority and power in order to occupy black social spaces and champion the socially marginalized.

Otherness Imposed: *Our Daily Bread*

King Vidor produced and directed *Our Daily Bread* after becoming frustrated with the reluctance of the major studios to film his depiction of Depression-era subsistence farming. *Time* magazine reported:

> More than two years ago Director Vidor read an article on subsistence farming by Professor Malcolm McDermott of Duke University. What he felt about subsistence farming seemed too radical for the producers to whom Vidor offered his ideas. Besides, they believed the subject would be outdated before

it reached the public. But Vidor's friends told him to go ahead and for a year Vidor hired a girl to do nothing but clip newspapers. Convinced that the common people were as interested in his theme as he was, he produced *Our Daily Bread*.   ("Cinema: *Our Daily Bread*" 36)

The film employs a semi-documentary style to solicit sentiment for those displaced by the Depression, resulting in broken lives, false hopes, financial struggles, and a persistent desire to return to the land as a means of carving out a living. The religious allusion of the film's title speaks to the fact that in times of uncertainty individuals on the brink of disaster frequently return to their religious doctrines in order to sustain themselves.

The opening sequence to *Our Daily Bread* is designed to engage the audience with the characters' plight and also to engender sympathy for their monetary troubles. Mary Sims (Karen Morley) answers the door to a rent collector and asks for more time to secure the payment due. She succeeds in convincing him that her husband, John (Tom Keene), should have the money in the next few days. When John arrives, having narrowly missed the rent collector on the stairwell, Mary tells him that she has invited his uncle to dinner, because she hopes that he might be able to help John get a job. In spite of the dire circumstances facing them, Mary is eager to impress John's uncle, and she insists on preparing chicken. Although they have few resources, John manages to negotiate with the local grocer and convinces him to accept John's guitar in exchange for one scrawny chicken. When Mary and John meet with Uncle Anthony (Lloyd Ingraham), he presents them with an opportunity to occupy his abandoned farm in hopes that they can refurbish the farmhouse and revitalize the land, thus making the property become valuable to the bank.

Having little other choice, they make the transition from city to rural life only to be confronted with a number of new obstacles. Arriving unprepared for farming, John decides to invite those similarly displaced by the Depression to join him in creating a cooperative community. Lured by his offer, several economically disenfranchised families pool their resources and together build dwellings, establish a community bank and food store, and attempt to reconstruct their lives. This collective sharing of resources within the community is more socialistic than capitalistic, perhaps an attempt to denounce capitalism in the face of an economic depression. Raymond Durgnat and Scott Simmon suggest that "the film touches on the implication that the whole American democratic system is corrupt and should be left behind by this community" (149). In fact, the group debates whether or not they will establish a democratic or nondemocratic form of government. And despite their inability to come to an agreement, they elect John to lead this community. Durgnat and Simmon add that "the coincidence of owner-ship and leadership in *Our Daily Bread* may just be a convenience for the purposes of political ambiguity; but that fusion itself owes something to Jef-fersonian democracy, which puts its faith in the yeoman farmer, distrusted Eastern mercantilism, and anticipated later reactions against big business and demagoguery" (152).

The fact that the film explores a group of individuals dispossessed by economic circumstances automatically renders them as marginal in a country once known for its thriving economy and abundance of resources. Moreover, the group is quite heterogeneous in its vocations and ethnicities: "Farmers, carpenters, masons, plumbers, a heavily accented tailor, bricklay-ers, even a concert violinist, all of varying nationalities" (Bergman 77). While the film examines the instability of class positions during the Depres-sion, John also struggles to maintain his moral stability after the camp is invaded by the slick, city-wise Sally (Barbara Pepper), who arrives during a rain storm (a signal of foreboding) and declares that her father has died dur-ing their travels. Following his burial, Sally's lack of grief alerts us to the fact that she will sow the seeds of conflict. She brings a new, metropolitan tone to the community in that she is a peroxide blonde, smokes cigarettes, and plays jazz music. When she becomes attracted to John, Louie (Addison Richards) warns her that John is married and that she needs to "lay off." Despite Louie's efforts, Sally continues attempting to seduce John and eventually succeeds in persuading him to leave his wife and the farm to be with her. *Time* describes what happens next: "Gloomily John is about to go off with a wench [Sally] who has joined the group, when he hears a sound which he knows means the mountain stream is filling" (36). The sound comes from the powerhouse, and John has an epiphany, realizing that he can pump water from the powerhouse to the fields to provide the irrigation system necessary for the crops to thrive again. Although tempted by Sally's seductiveness, he decides to go back to his community.

In the final scenes of the film, John returns with his idea of creating an irrigation system, and the community, although disappointed that he almost abandoned them to run off with Sally in a time of need, throw their support behind his idea. They work through the night digging trenches, building bridges and troughs, so that the water can flow downhill to the fields: "The lithe speed of men rushing downhill, keeping pace with the first wave, is broken up by the monumentality of John pushing an aqueduct up from beneath and a bare-torsoed muscleman crouching over the boulder he is lifting from the stream" (Durgnat and Simmon 159). When the water trickles through the ditches into the fields the men, women, and children rejoice at the fact that their backbreaking labor has paid off and that their collective efforts will again allow them to thrive as a community. Regarding this last scene, often considered one of the film's best, Vidor said, "I tried to develop it like a ballet. I aimed to get the effect of mounting drama through the movements of the diggers' bodies. With the use of a metronome whose tempo was kept constantly on the increase, I set my actors to work with their picks and shovels. I believe I have gotten what I wanted" ("Cinema: *Our Daily Bread*" 36).

John's decision to return to both his wife and the community reestablishes his moral authority as it also restores his virility, represented symbolically by the rebirth of the crops. According to Durgnat and Simmon, "As John and Mary watch their little shoot sprouting . . . the scene celebrates fertility in the truer sense—the shoot is no more a phallic symbol than the phallus is a vegetation symbol. . . . It's as if John's work had imbued him with a steadfast maleness, where passion has no need of the vamp, but grows from his own labor, toward the woman" (156–57). As a virile, moral, and productive member of society John has now defeated the forces that marginalized him.

Conclusion

Films produced in this year often foregrounded Otherness, whether or not this was always intentional. *Manhattan Melodrama* considers differences of morality, class, and, symbolically, race, as it portrays two friends torn apart by socioeconomic circumstance. *It Happened One Night* chronicles the union of two nonconformists who develop an attraction for each other despite being class opposites. *Imitation of Life* features two women who, while one is black and the other white, share parallel journeys, with the white character constructed as embodying the hybridity associated with the mulatto character in the film. *Judge Priest* centers upon a white judge who engages in blackvoice and occupies black spaces. And *Our Daily Bread* explores the plight of those disenfranchised because of the Depression who work collectively to overcome their marginalization. Through examples such as these, we can see Hollywood's undeniable fascination with the constant slippages between one social position or identity and another in a nation profoundly unsettled by economic dislocation.

NOTES

1. A study by the Black Radical Congress noted that 1930 was a turning point in increased state-sponsored execution of Blacks: "After 1930, extralegal race riots and legal executions replaced lynching as means of social control. All white or predominantly white

juries and government officials merely extended societal racial discrimination to executions. More than half (53%) of the 4,220 persons executed between 1930 and 1996 were Black" (Hart and Cha-Jua). Figures on all executions in the United States, from 1608 until 1972, when the Supreme Court ruled the death penalty as then practiced unconstitutional, showed that more Blacks (49 percent) were executed than those belonging to any other racial group; whites, despite their overwhelming majority status, made up only 41 percent of those executed (Espy and Smylka).

2. We may also consider the significance of casting Gable as Peter, given the fact that his predisposition or affinity for blackness/Otherness is well known in his other screen roles, such as in *Gone with the Wind* (1939). In fact, historian Joel Williamson argues that when Margaret Mitchell wrote the novel upon which the film was based, the protagonist, Rhett Butler, played by Gable in the film version, was constructed as a black character: "Margaret Mitchell wrote a strikingly white novel, so white in fact that some of the white characters seem black. The most important of these is Rhett Butler . . . dark, mysterious, and a slightly malevolent hero loose in the world" (97, 99). Even though *GWTW* had not yet been filmed, audiences could certainly have recognized Peter's affinity for blackness. Gable's dark complexion highlighted by his dark hair and moustache, along with his unconventional behavior, infused his characterization of Peter with a type of Otherness closely aligned with blackness.

3. Judge Priest's ease in occupying nonwhite spaces is given another level of complexity in that Rogers was born in the Indian territory of Oklahoma to parents who both claimed Cherokee ancestry. He invoked his Indian heritage as a significant component of his star persona.

1935

Movies and the
Resistance to Tyranny

INA RAE HARK

As the second half of the decade began in Hollywood, the turmoil that had marked the first half mostly subsided. This year saw either the continuation or the culmination of trends that would leave the studio system a mature oligopoly with a stable, vertically integrated system of production, distribution, and exhibition. The last of the major studios took on its familiar contours when Fox Film Corporation merged with Twentieth Century Pictures to form Twentieth Century Fox. The financial recovery in the industry continued as Fox and Paramount emerged from debt after successful reorganization, and theater admissions rose by ten million after a ten million increase the year before (Balio 30–31). Also this year, long experimentation with various color processes came to their culmination with the premiere of the first studio feature film using three-strip Technicolor, RKO's *Becky Sharp,* directed by Rouben Mamoulian.

The year also saw significant films starring many of the iconic stars of the era. Some had first came to prominence at the beginning of the thirties, while others only made their marks at its conclusion; for some, their careers (or lives) ended before the decade did, or continued for several decades beyond. Will Rogers starred in five films this year, two of which were released by Fox after he was killed in a plane crash in August. Meanwhile, surging to prominence at his studio was ticket-selling powerhouse Shirley Temple, who began a run of four straight years as "the number-one box-office attraction in the world" (Balio 147).

Elsewhere, Warners was discovering the romantic chemistry of Errol Flynn and Olivia de Havilland in *Captain Blood.* Jean Harlow and Wallace Beery joined Clark Gable in *China Seas,* in which Gable found himself on the opposite end of a mutiny from the one he would lead in *Mutiny on the Bounty.* Greta Garbo was *Anna Karenina,* Katharine Hepburn was both *Alice Adams* and *Sylvia Scarlett,* supported in the latter by a Cary Grant not quite emerged into stardom. James Stewart got his first onscreen credit in *Murder*

Man, as did his friend Henry Fonda in *The Farmer Takes a Wife.* Mickey Rooney was Puck to James Cagney's Bottom in *A Midsummer Night's Dream;* Cagney also played a *Devil Dog . . . of the Air* and a *G-Man.* Edward G. Robinson (along with Jean Arthur) was the reason *The Whole Town's Talking,* while Mae West was *Goin' to Town.* Spencer Tracy ran *Dante's Inferno* and Bette Davis was *Dangerous.* The Marx Brothers spent *A Night at the Opera* while Fred Astaire was putting on his *Top Hat* for Ginger Rogers. Boris Karloff gave the finest performance in his signature role as the Creature in James Whale's *The Bride of Frankenstein.*

While things were stabilizing at last in Hollywood after the chaos caused by the advent of sound, the stock market collapse, and the wrangles over the Production Code, in the world outside instability prevailed. The National Recovery Administration, including a set of codes that governed labor practices in the film industry, was declared unconstitutional in May. Although some protections for labor were reenacted through the National Labor Relations Act (also known as the Wagner Act), signed into law on 5 July, "Hollywood's response to the act was simply to ignore it" (Balio 154), and so the Screen Actors Guild failed to enter into collective bargaining with the studios. Some infamous careers were cut short by violence: Ma and Pa Barker, Dutch Schultz, and Huey Long were all slain. Less contentious change manifested itself in the world of sports and the arts. The first Orange and Sugar Bowls were played, as were the first major league baseball night games. *Porgy and Bess* had its premiere and Benny Goodman reigned as "the King of Swing." Kodachrome film and the Jolly Green Giant made their trademark debuts, and, for the first time, nylon and canned beer were on the radar (also invented this year.)

On the international front, shocks were so frequent as almost to register on the Richter scale (developed this year to measure earthquakes). The first indication of the expansionist aims of the fascist governments of Europe was Mussolini's invasion of Abyssinia in February. By October, the *Motion Picture Herald* noted that the conflict was bound to influence Hollywood decision makers: "The thunder of hob-nailed marching feet of Mussolini's Italian infantrymen, mingled with the softer retreat of Haile Selassie's unshod but calloused tribesmen echoes with the roar of bombing planes from Abyssinia across 3,000 miles of ocean and then 3,000 miles of land, and Hollywood is listening, even as the world listens to the newer rumblings of Mars on the Russo-Japanese border and on the waters at Malta and the Suez Canal" ("Hollywood Starts" 18).

Even with films produced before the advent of these hostilities, this year boasted many pictures that dealt with occupying armies and rebellions against internal tyranny. Such scenarios had long been part of Hollywood's stock in trade, and the vogue for prestige pictures increased the likelihood of their being produced, especially if they were set in a distant place and time, since, according to *Motion Picture Herald,* two of the biggest sources of the "presold properties" upon which prestige pictures were likely to be based were nineteenth-century European fiction and biographical and historical subjects (Balio 179–80). So the year gave audiences everything from Cary Grant and Claude Rains embroiled in the Turkish persecution of the Armenians in *The Last Outpost* to the French Revolution and its aftermath in *A Tale of Two Cities* to the British occupation of Ireland in *The Informer* to the domestic tyranny of Mr. Murdstone in *David Copperfield* to the conjugal rebellion of Titania against Oberon, set within the context of the conquest of Hippolyta by Theseus, in *A Midsummer Night's Dream.*

Condoning Colonialism, Fearing Communism

The number of prestige films that dealt with issues of tyranny and oppression, with special emphasis on resistance and rebellion, is not surprising. The events of the year made them particularly timely, but these are themes deeply imbedded in the history of the United States and the stories it tells, including the films that Hollywood produces. After all, it is a nation born out of rebellion against a ruling colonial power. Yet a close look at the films cited above reveals that they are far from straightforward accounts of morally justified violent resistance to systemic state oppression. Whatever its own history, America feared worker revolt at home and was not inclined to commit itself to opposing the rising tide of fascism abroad. When the Abyssinians appealed to the League of Nations in the face of Mussolini's invasion in October, the League enacted half-hearted sanctions six weeks after the request. The United States, however, was not even a member of the League, and one excuse given by the membership for not putting an embargo on oil exports to Italy was that "Italy would simply get her oil from America—a non-League country" ("Abyssinia"). Mussolini represented the invasion as simply an extension of the colonialism practiced by the major European powers throughout Africa. Having been denied key holdings on the continent during the rapacious nineteenth century, Italy was simply making up for that lack at a later date, and the colonial investment of the rest of the European powers left them on shaky grounds to oppose the land grab. Despite its own origins as a British colony, the United States did not vigorously side with the Abyssinians either.

To find significant American opposition to fascism, one had to look to the American Communist Party. In this year the Seventh Congress of the Comintern agreed to form a "popular front" with other antifascist organizations, including labor unions: "In the United States, the Communists abandoned opposition to the New Deal; they reentered the mainstream of the trade union movement and played an important part in organizing new unions for the Congress of Industrial Organizations (CIO), for the first time gaining important positions of power in the union movement. As antifascist activists they attracted the support of many non-Communists during this period" ("Popular Front").

The U.S. government was anxious to forestall the drift of unions leftward and also to head off a full-fledged war between labor and management at home. The enactment of the Wagner Act was intended to defuse often violent conflicts between workers seeking to unionize and employers using tactics of intimidation to prevent them from doing so. The act guaranteed that "employees shall have the right to self-organization, to form, join, or assist labor organizations, to bargain collectively through representatives of their own choosing, and to engage in other concerted activities for the purpose of collective bargaining or other mutual aid or protection." It established compromise and negotiation as the paths toward protecting worker rights while at the same time keeping interstate commerce free from disruption ("Transcript").

Hollywood's films about the opposition to tyrannies against workers and colonized peoples also advocated this middle road of compromise and negotiation, and made particular efforts to stigmatize radical and violent liberation movements. As a prime example, the revolution against the despotic Bourbon monarchy soon turns into the deadly "Terror" that claims the life of Sydney Carton, protagonist of *A Tale of Two Cities*. *The Informer* spends far less time depicting the justifications for Irish resistance to the occupying "Black and Tans" than it does Gypo Nolan's betrayal of his best friend and Sinn Fein colleague. This betrayal in turn has resulted from the rebels' ongoing efforts to deal with traitors in the ranks.

Tyrants as Bad Bosses: *Captain Blood*, *Mutiny on the Bounty*, and *Lives of a Bengal Lancer*

More nuanced ambivalence about rebellion as a political tool is portrayed in three films, each highly acclaimed and successful at the box office. All belong to the broadly defined genre of "adventure," of whose politics Brian Taves observes: "Adventure films belong completely neither to the left or the right; they project portions of both viewpoints. Liberation and conservatism are blended, compatibly, each making the other more palatable, lending a polysemy to the politics of adventure. . . . The genre mixes adversarial elements, the narrative sometimes contradicting the tenor of the political statement" (171). Each film is set in a narrative of British colonialism, yet the relation between the British imperialists and their colonial subjects is not the site of the interrogation of tyrannical practices. Those non-Europeans who are enslaved, occupied, or exploited receive little attention. Rather it is the poor treatment of one group of Britons by their rulers, owners, or commanders that is the focus.

All the films posit as antagonist a British official whose conduct toward those over whom he has authority appears tyrannical. In Warner Bros.' *Captain Blood*, directed by Michael Curtiz, Colonel Bishop (Lionel Atwill), later the governor of Jamaica, is a brutal slave owner, mirroring the repressive rule of his sovereign, James II. In MGM's *Mutiny on the Bounty*, directed by Frank Lloyd, William Bligh (Charles Laughton) is a captain in the British Royal Navy who rules over his men with a sadistic regime he justifies as rightful discipline in the service of the Crown. In Paramount's *The Lives of a Bengal Lancer*, directed by Henry Hathaway, Colonel Stone is a martinet whose rigid command style alienates many of his men, not least his estranged son. Thus, all three manage to map issues of colonialism and rebellion onto a discourse about counterproductive business practices.

One might well expect each of these films to play out a narrative of justified rebellion against and defeat of these tyrants, thus symbolically replaying the narrative of the American Republic's founding. As will soon become apparent, this is not in any way the case. Corrupt regimes or venal imperialism are represented less as political problems than as problems of businesses with poor management philosophies. A few labor reforms, and all is well. The films all disregard the fact that although corrupt individuals may be replaced or censured, the systems that facilitated tyranny remain in place, ready to oppress again should oppressive men inhabit them. As Andrew Bergman observes, Hollywood in the thirties insisted on "the reduction of complex social ills to instances of personal evil" (103).

Of the three, *Captain Blood* comes closest to advancing a revolutionary critique. The protagonist, Irish physician Peter Blood (Errol Flynn), is condemned to slavery in the Caribbean because he has treated a man wounded while acting as an adherent of the Duke of Monmouth's rebellion of 1685. He escapes, turns pirate, and then is restored to good citizenship by the Glorious Revolution of 1688. Peter Valenti asserts that the film conveyed a powerful, topical message to Depression audiences:

> By sustaining his individual dignity, Flynn-Blood was demonstrating that even the most abject victims of social circumstance have hope—their servitude is only a temporary shackle. One day the system will be corrected and then all will be well—they too will have another chance, will know the opportunity when it comes by. Blood was not only a pirate but the persevering victim who will one day assert his true position in the world. (61)

The bloodless revolution that removes the tyrannical king is about as far as Hollywood would go at this time to endorse forcible regime change, and the film is nevertheless careful to undercut Blood's political radicalism in a number of ways.

In the first scene of the film, Blood's housekeeper informs him that his pro-Monmouth neighbors are suspicious of his sitting out the rebellion. Half assume that he is a "papist," and thus a supporter of the Catholic-leaning James; the others think he is a coward, an opinion no doubt bolstered by his tendency to worry about the health of his geraniums. On the first count, Blood makes clear that he is no ideologue but rather judges the leader behind the ideology. He has concluded that Monmouth would be just as unsuitable a ruler as James.

A more detailed defense of his bravery, necessary for the protagonist of a swashbuckler adventure, follows: "I've been most everywhere where fighting was in evidence. I fought against the French for the Spanish, against the Spanish for the French, and learned my seamanship in the Dutch navy." Although such a resumé might prompt accusations that Blood is a mercenary with no national loyalties, it is a consistent part of the film's depiction of a man whose freedom from any sort of factional loyalty is a positive, not a negative. At any rate, whatever the motivations that caused him to take up the sword, Blood is now a man of peace. He abandoned fighting and became a healer.

Adjudged guilty of treason under the king's law for giving aid and comfort to a wounded rebel, Blood refuses to accept such a law, and while every other accused rebel at his session of the Bloody Assizes pleads guilty, he proclaims, "It's entirely innocent I am." Questioned by the notorious hanging judge Lord Jeffreys (Leonard Mudie), he announces his humanist philosophy. He treated not a rebel but an injured man, out of his "sacred duty as a physician," and his business was "with his wounds, not his politics." Reminded that his sacred duty is rather to his king, Blood retorts, "I thought it was to my fellow man."

However, the lack of due process inherent in the proceedings politicizes Blood. He wonders what kind of king could allow a cruel and unjust man such as Jeffreys to administer his law, and he gives up his claim of innocence: "My chief regret is I didn't try to pull down the filthy fellow that sits on the throne." He will later compare himself unfavorably to his fellow slaves because of this failing to be a true opponent of the king's tyranny. "They're all honest rebels," he tells Arabella Bishop (Olivia de Havilland). "I was snoozing in my bed while they were trying to free England from an unclean tyrant."

Once Blood and his comrades are transported to Jamaica and sold into slavery, the brief against tyranny acquires a second focus, the one *Captain Blood* shares with the other two films under consideration: a depiction of English superiors acting in an abusive way to their fellow English subordinates. On the one hand, the slavery constitutes the punishment for treason handed down by Judge Jeffreys, commuted from hanging for economic reasons. And, as a metaphor for an illegitimate relationship between ruler and subject, it is completely apposite. A tyrannical and oppressive ruler does not work to ensure his people's welfare and fundamental liberties but rather subverts them, rendering them virtual slaves to his will. On the colonial plantations, this metaphor is literalized. The exhausting physical labor and harsh punishments, such as being branded, flogged, and denied water, reflect, less fatally, the draconian measures applied to those accused of supporting the rebellion; in both instances, there is no due process and no appeal. The plantation owner, Colonel Bishop, eventually succeeds the ineffectual governor of the colony, thus making him, like Jeffreys, another surrogate for a very bad source of state authority.

Blood leads his comrades on an escape from the plantation during a Spanish raid on Port Royal, seizing the Spaniards' galleon to be their pirate ship, and the focus turns from indicting the monarchy to presenting an alternative model of group leadership. Blood drafts a series of articles for all his men to subscribe to. The articles include specific "workmen's compensation" payments for those who lose eyes or limbs in the pursuit of the pirate trade and stipulate that all their takings, minus expenses, be pooled and shared equally. As captain, he does not rule as an unchallengeable autocrat. When his senior officers advise against attacking an English ship they have sighted, he jokes about having a mutiny on his hands, but in the end complies with their wishes. When he feels more strongly about their opposition to his plan to return a captured Arabella to Port Royal, he volunteers to step down as captain, then proceeds to persuade them by force of reason that his plan has sufficient merit. Few labor leaders could wish for a more utopian vision of workplace relations.

All the difficulties that have plagued Blood from the beginning of the film are resolved when Lord Willoughby (Henry Stephenson), the emissary from the new King William, offers the pirates amnesty. They accept and end up saving the colony from the French after Governor Bishop has left it vulnerable by taking his fleet out to sea in obsessive pursuit of Peter Blood. For his heroism, Blood gets not only amnesty, but appointment as the new governor of Jamaica. Just as the replacement of James by William and Mary has restored right rule in England, the replacement of Bishop by Blood suggests that right rule will subsequently prevail in the colony.

Despite Blood's earlier embrace of violent revolution as an accepted means of fighting tyranny, this outcome positions the film's ideology firmly on the side of nonviolent regime change. Just as the citizenry "roused themselves at home" (because "the English people will go so far . . . and then they get up on their stubborn hind legs") and forced James to flee, but did not take his life as they did his grandfather's, Blood prevents his men from killing Bishop when the colonel has come aboard the commandeered Spanish ship to thank Port Royal's saviors. He gives Bishop a fighting chance, tossing him overboard to make a successful swim to the nearby shore. Blood rightly calculates that the humiliation is a far worse punishment than death for the arrogant plantation owner, but *Captain Blood* is able at the same time to keep its hero's hands free of the blood of a British official.

The film also posits that there are no bad systems of government, including monarchies and colonial appropriations; there are simply bad men who will corrupt any system. This point is emphasized also when the pirate Levasseur (Basil Rathbone) agrees to sail under Blood's articles but ignores them as it suits him, leading to his unlawful seizure of Arabella and a duel in which Blood kills him in order to rescue her. Blood and his crew oppose tyrannical English individuals, but the film is careful never to portray them as enemies of broader English interests. Although dialogue tells us that they have seized English vessels, we never witness such a seizure; indeed, we never see them attack any civilian ships. What we do witness, in the film's two most elaborate action sequences, are the escaped slaves saving Port Royal from the Spanish raiders and then the attacking French warships. (Although both bombardments of Port Royal, filmed using miniatures, often suggest toys in a bathtub, the action onboard the dueling ships makes brilliant use both of the moving camera and of vertical motion in what it films: men swing down from the rigging; broken masts and other debris, often on fire, fall to the deck; the French flag comes down and the Union Jack rises, all to the pounding rhythms of Erich Wolfgang Korngold's rousing score.)

In the end, *Captain Blood* advocates dissent rather than rebellion. Our final point of identification is not Blood and his pirates but Arabella Bishop

Pardoned by King William, erstwhile slave, thief, and pirate Peter Blood (Errol Flynn) takes on two roles of which he is more deserving: governor of Jamaica and lover to Arabella Bishop (Olivia de Havilland) in *Captain Blood* (Michael Curtiz, Warner Bros.). Collection Ina Rae Hark.

and Lord Willoughby. Willoughby is shown as one of the circle of James's advisers who criticizes his policies and works through the political process to bring about his ouster. King William then sends him as envoy to bring the outlaw rebels on Blood's ship back into the fold of legitimate Englishmen. Arabella is shown to object to the enslavement of the English rebels and their treatment at the slave auction ("As if he were buying horses!") and to approve of Blood's refusal to submit to its humiliations. She purchases him herself to save him from the mines (apparently a more hellish place than her uncle's brutal plantation), brings his medical skills to the attention of Governor Steed, and lies to protect him from discovery when he has been shopping for boats. Yet when they met again after his career as a privateer is well underway, she scorns him as "thief and pirate," even though he has just gallantly risked his life to protect her from "a fate worse than death." Later Arabella tells Willoughby of her disappointment that Blood has done "the unforgivable thing—to have put his revenge above everything else and to have destroyed himself," to which Willoughby responds: "Are you so much in love with him . . . that you care so much what he does?"

Like Arabella, the audience is meant to fall in love with Peter Blood, as indeed it did, elevating "a spirited and criminally good-looking Australian named Errol Flynn" (Sennwald 14) to immediate stardom. While viewers may enjoy a dangerous flirtation with Blood the rebel slave and Blood the pirate, they are instructed only to surrender fully to a Blood returned to respectability as first a physician and then as a cog of British colonialism when he becomes governor of Jamaica. Once purged of tyrants, the systems of both monarchy and imperialism receive the Warners seal of approval.

Mutiny on the Bounty, the year's top-grossing film, takes a slightly different stance on the relationship of oppressive social relations and tyranny. Here the rules of discipline governing the British Royal Navy are seen as needing at least minor adjustments. They are not corrupted by tyranny, but their weaknesses only become intolerably apparent when a tyrant is given the absolute power they assign to a ship's captain. The title card that begins the film advances the thesis that Captain William Bligh's abuses and the mutiny that came in response "helped bring about a new discipline," according to Greg Dening, "based upon mutual respect between officers and men, by which Britain's sea power is maintained as security for all who pass upon the seas." The film's message is that "the act of mutiny, wrong in itself, had had good effects. The reason was that institutions of power are ultimately responsive to men of good will" (350). History does not support such a cause–and-effect relation. "What does it matter," Dening continues sarcastically, "that the whole British fleet mutinied just ten years after the *Bounty* and thirty-six men were hanged? What did it matter that flogging went on in the navy for forty more years?"

Such double-think is necessary, however, for the film to bring off its portrayal of Bligh as a sadistic martinet, starving his men for his own profit, and at the same time to maintain that the institution that produced him— one that routinely pressed working-class Englishmen into what amounted to indentured servitude for years at a time, often in conditions worse than seen on Colonel Bishop's plantation in *Captain Blood*—must be protected from rebellions against even its most unworthy officers. The press-gang is legitimized early on when the film's hero, Fletcher Christian (Clark Gable), jauntily informs a tavern full of revelers that he is taking them aboard the *Bounty,* despite their protests, simply because "The King needs six men." Although Christian is ever the advocate of using humane treatment and persuasion to make those pressed into service embrace their duties to the Crown, he never once questions the morality of the press-gang itself.

Captain Bligh's (Charles Laughton, standing, right) obsession with having the whole crew witness his sadistic punishments causes the death of the ship's surgeon (Dudley Digges, bottom center) and arouses the hatred of Fletcher Christian (Clark Gable, seated, center) in *Mutiny on the Bounty* (Frank Lloyd, MGM). Collection Ina Rae Hark.

A similar contradiction occurs in an early sequence meant to establish Bligh's perverse enjoyment in subjecting rebellious sailors to physical punishment. (Christian will later remark that Bligh does not use punishment to enforce discipline; he does it because he enjoys making men crawl.) A sailor from another vessel has struck his commanding officer and is sentenced to be flogged through the fleet, which will inflict 300 lashes. Bligh rejoices that the *Bounty* has been included, telling the Royal Society naturalist who has sponsored the voyage, Sir Joseph Banks (Henry Stephenson again), that his bosun has mastered the "science of the use of the cat o' nine tails." But when the man is brought to the ship, he has already died from his punishment. Bligh insists that the corpse receive the mandated lashes anyway, inspiring shocked reactions from most of the onlookers. Yet is flogging a dead man that much more monstrous than flogging a living man until he is dead, an action agreed upon by the Royal Navy as totally appropriate to the crime of assault against a superior officer?

Even though the film is bracketed by assertions that the Navy needed to reform the relations between officers and men and the *Bounty* incident provided the stimulus for it to do so, there is a reluctance to equate the rebellion against Bligh, of which the film heartily approves, with a rebellion against government authority, of which it definitely does not approve. Complicating matters further is Bligh's feat in guiding the ship's launch to safe port in Timor, a voyage of more than 3,500 miles, with inadequate supplies for the eighteen loyal officers and men aboard. Here Bligh's insistence on adequate performance with reduced rations and sticking to ship's business no matter how rigorous the discipline starts to look less like sadism and more like heroic seamanship. The film gives Bligh his due in these scenes, but then it shows him engaging in an obsessive pursuit of the mutineers, abusing the loyal men who stayed behind because there was no more room in the launch, and wrecking the *Pandora*, the ship sent in pursuit of Christian and his companions. While drama as well as ideology make it a logical choice to have Bligh acting much as Colonel Bishop did in his obsessive pursuit of Peter Blood, in fact the *Pandora* had a different captain named Edwards. The real Bligh never attempted to chase down the mutineers at all. Publicity materials circulated ahead of the film's release excused this departure from historical fact, explaining that "the actions of Captains Courtney and Edwards were typical of the class of ship commanders to which Bligh belonged. The transference of these actions to Bligh allowed a closeknit, strong and more comprehensive study of Bligh's character and thus the exclusion of characters, who, having little or no part in the actual story, might have possibly confused the issue" (qtd. in Dening 358). As Dening observes, the film's "demonology" "needed the hyperbole reached by laying at Bligh's feet every violent and unjust happening in the early modern British navy" (346). (The historical Bligh was in fact less prone to doling out physical punishment than most of his peers. It was his volatile temper and verbal abuse of his men that earned their hatred.)

A similar departure from history undermines what might be seen as Bligh's vindication, the conviction and condemnation of the mutineers by a Royal Navy court-martial that does not dispute the facts of Bligh's behavior as a commander. Although the real Bligh was not present at these proceedings, in the film he extends his hand to congratulate the presiding officer, Lord Hood (David Torrence), on the just verdict. The officer looks down his nose at Bligh and declines to shake his hand as he departs, curtly remarking, "I must admire your seamanship and courage, but. . . ." And of course Laughton's scowling, supercilious performance with its trademark "Mister Christian" hissed as if through a cobra's fangs aligns the audience completely with the officer's disapproval.

Not only did the film have to vilify the ambiguous historical antagonist to make its point, but it had to deal with an ambiguous hero as well. Peter Blood may undertake an illegal career after he and his friends escape from slavery, but he does undertake a career, and the film makes a point of showing how his enlightened leadership works in contrast to the brutal methods of plantation owners like Bishop. Thus, once the king is deposed and he and his crew are offered a pardon, they are more than prepared to be productive members of the British Navy and Blood has demonstrated the qualities that will make him a just governor of Jamaica. Christian and the mutineers merely turn the *Bounty* around and head for the "Heaven" of Tahiti. Curtis Pew notes that this film, like subsequent Hollywood versions of the mutiny, concludes that "the *Bounty's* crew in general, and Fletcher Christian in particular, 'went native' once the vessel arrived in Tahiti. After a five-month stay in Tahiti, during which much of the crew remained ashore and developed a strong attachment to the native females, all of the movie versions 'agree' that Bligh, upon departing for Jamaica, sought to re-instill Royal Navy discipline by flogging, rationing of food and water, and attention to work" (Pew 612). (Writing in his journals, Bligh came to the same conclusion [Dening 8].) Thus we do not see Christian, a humane and admired first officer, turn into an exemplary captain who can run a ship on mutual respect instead of fear. His skills at command receive little attention because he immediately decrees a permanent vacation in the tropical paradise where food falls from trees and one can pass day after day swimming, sunbathing, and enjoying the company of nubile and willing maidens.

For this reason, the film, despite Gable's clear status as the star, has two protagonists. The second is Midshipman Roger Byam (Franchot Tone), an eager young officer on his first voyage. A scion of an aristocratic naval family and the protégé of Sir Joseph Banks, Byam has been given the task of compiling a treatise on the Tahitian language. He is immediately disgusted by Bligh's behavior, is a victim of one of his cruel punishments (being "masted," forced to stay for hours in the rigging during a violent storm), and becomes Christian's best friend and confidant onboard. Nevertheless, he actively resists the mutiny, then tries to talk Christian into restoring the ship to Bligh's command. Failing this, he pleads to be allowed to join Bligh in the launch, but by this time it has sailed and is too crowded to call back. Unable to prove his loyalty when the *Pandora* arrives (and by implication because he cannot help Bligh find Christian and the *Bounty*), Byam is court-martialed and condemned along with the three captured mutineers. At his trial, he articulates a new philosophy of leadership, one that he and Christian shared:

These men don't ask for comfort. They don't ask for safety. If they could speak to you they'd say: "Let us choose to do our duty willingly, not the choice of a slave, but the choice of free Englishmen. They ask only [for] the freedom that England expects for every man. If one man among you believed that—one man!—he could command the fleets of England. He could sweep the seas for England if he called his men to their duty, not by flaying their backs but by lifting their hearts.

With the intercession of Banks, Byam is pardoned (as was his historical counterpart); however, the film makes the strongest argument for his reprieve the fact that he has become identified with the movement to create "a new understanding between officers and men." In other words, he symbolizes the choice to reform the Royal Navy from within rather than to rebel against it. Except for a few brief scenes that show Christian and the mutineers searching for and settling on Pitcairn Island, the last movement of the film belongs to Byam, and it concludes with his being assigned to a ship where the entire crew works in harmony—literally, since the sailors are singing sea chanteys—and *everyone* wants to shake the hand of the man who inspired the "new understanding." As in all three of the year's rebellion films, *Mutiny on the Bounty* takes place within the context of British colonial expansion. The *Bounty*'s mission was to take breadfruit seedlings from Tahiti to be planted in the West Indies as "cheap food for slaves." While the morality of slavery for Africans imported to the Caribbean receives no more censure here than it does in *Captain Blood,* the film does contain an extended look at the interactions between the British and the indigenous Polynesians, whose complicated relations with Europeans during the previous 200 years are glossed over in favor of the usual "noble savage" tropes applied to South Pacific islanders. They are childlike, trusting, and eager to please their visitors, from Chief Hitihiti's (William Bambridge) assurance concerning the breadfruit that "all we have—for you" to the women's aggressive sexual pursuit of the Englishmen. Gaudy baubles and feathered hats enchant them. Byam describes the Tahitians as "simple and kind, yet somehow they're royal." Despite the condescension, however, the film does establish the community Hitihiti rules as a utopian alternative to the governance of Royal Navy vessels (and, by implication, of Great Britain itself).The chief may seem guileless and obliging, but he is quick to remind Bligh that his power ends at the water's edge: "*I* have authority on land." He is the only man in the film to whom the prickly Bligh ever defers.

If *Mutiny on the Bounty* disavows colonial oppression of non-Europeans, its plotline does offer an allegory of the rebellion of European colonists against the home country: the king whom everyone on the ship serves is George III, and Fletcher Christian's mutiny to start a new life in a new land cannot help but suggest the American Revolution that had ended less than a decade before the *Bounty* sailed. Indeed, as Christian tells his fellows how Pitcairn Island will allow them to live without fear of being flogged or starved and notes that the fire that burns the *Bounty* "makes quite a light," one practically expects to see an anachronistic Statue of Liberty super-imposed on the image. Yet even a rebellion that can be linked to the one that founded the nation is not immune from Hollywood's nervousness about endorsing such resistance this year. Pitcairn is chosen because it has no safe anchorage, and the *Bounty* is wrecked and burned upon arrival so that there will be no sign of the mutineers to attract the attention of those pursuing them. Thus the grand experiment in founding a new society in the wilderness is completely self-contained; no one can ever leave. This neatly symbolizes both the anxiety that the revolution which formed America might be replicated in America and the nation's ambivalence about engag-ing the forces of tyranny growing abroad. The film ends not on Pitcairn but with Byam's new ship sailing forth to "sweep the seas" as "Rule Britannia" plays on the sound track. Dening concludes that this is a film "in which the hero was not the mutineers at all, but the British Navy, and a British Navy that was a weapon of freedom in a threatened world" (349). Reflecting America's isolationist inclinations in this year, *Mutiny on the Bounty* leaves the resistance to fascism to our nation's European founders.

The Lives of a Bengal Lancer differs from the two preceding films in that it does not ignore imperialist domination of indigenous peoples. However, it characterizes the British colonial governance of India as "protection" rather than oppression and uses the colonialist context to justify what would otherwise look like an unjust command style practiced by Colonel Tom Stone (Sir Guy Standing) of the 41st Bengal Lancers. The challenge to Stone's authority comes from two sources that overlap as the film proceeds. Lt. Alan "Mac" McGregor (Gary Cooper), a "Scotch-Canadian" who joined the Lancers looking for action, chafes at "Old Ramrod's" rigid obsession with spit and polish military discipline and his defensive rather than offen-sive tactics in dealing with attacks from Indian rebels. Donald Stone (Richard Cromwell), son of the colonel and his estranged American wife, is devastated to discover, upon joining his father's command, that the old man treats him in the strict manner of the other officers and avoids any show of favoritism by scarcely acknowledging Donald as his son. McGregor becomes Donald's mentor and champion against the old man's perceived lack of paternal, indeed, merely human, feelings. But in aligning himself with the son, McGregor is not identifying with him. As the other new junior officer, Forsythe (Franchot Tone), points out through jibes about McGregor's "maternal instinct" and renditions of "Mother Machree" in which he substitutes "McGregor" for "Machree," Mac's position in this Oedipal struggle is that of Stone's ex-wife, like him a North American who could not understand how the colonel could put the regiment above everything else in his life. Forsythe, on the other hand, represents a son more suitable to the colonel's priorities. He has transferred to the 41st from the elite "Blues" and never questioned his destiny to continue in the footsteps of his own colonial officer father. Although he begins the film as snobbish and patronizing to the "old colonial" McGregor, and always rebuts Mac's arguments against regimental discipline, he becomes his good friend and co-protector of Donald, finally risking his life to rescue him from the clutches of rebel chieftain Mohammed Khan (Douglas Dumbrille). (Tone here plays much the same sort of mediating character as his Byam in *Mutiny on the Bounty*.) Symbolically, McGregor and Forsythe mend the fractured Stone marriage and act in concert as mother and father to set the petulant, erring Donald on the correct path to following in Colonel Stone's footsteps as a Bengal Lancer, the only reward available to the commander of the regiment as he faces a lonely and unproductive retirement two years hence.

The other two films on the surface advocate rebellion against tyranny, while then operating on the margins to contain it; *The Lives of a Bengal Lancer* works in the opposite way. The foregrounded narrative endorses Colonel Stone's methods even though Mac and Donald find them impossible to fathom. Lest a viewer miss the point, there is a pivotal scene in which Mac expresses his anger with Stone's refusal to save his son by having the regiment abandon its duty to keep a shipment of ammunition from falling into Khan's hands. He is then upbraided by Stone's longtime colleague Major Hamilton, portrayed by C. Aubrey Smith, whose star-image is inextricable from that of the "pukka sahib," variations upon which he played in nine films this year. When Mac lashes out, "If that's what you call being a man or a soldier, I don't want any part of it—not me. . . . Why can't he be a little less of a soldier and more of a man?" Hamilton replies:

> Have you never thought how for generation after generation here a handful of men have ordered the lives of 300 million people. It's because he's here and a few more like him. Men of his breed have made British India—men who put their jobs above everything. He wouldn't let death move him from it and he won't let love move him from it. When his breed of man dies out, that's the end, and it's a better breed of man than any of us will ever make.

Combined with Forsythe's feminizing rhetoric aimed at McGregor, the film suggests that Stone's type of unbending, duty-driven masculinity is the only kind upon which patriarchal and imperial power can rest.

If this is the overt message *The Lives of a Bengal Lancer* conveys, it is nearly undone by the film's delirious—if perhaps unconscious—Freudianism that is inscribed upon the visuals of most of the action sequences. These images place Mac's masculinity in contrast to Stone's as another configuration of phallic power, rather than pronouncing it a sign of effeminate lack. (This is, after all, Gary Cooper we're talking about.) Given that the colonel known as "Old Ramrod" commands a regiment of *lancers,* phallic symbolism is impossible to avoid. When we see the entire regiment assembled, they either charge with lances extended in front of them or stand at the ready with lances raised and pennons flying. The ceremonial contests traditional to the regiment also involve skill in handling the lance: there is "pulling pegs," in which the rider, while maintaining a full gallop, strives to spear a small wooden stake with the point of his lance and lift it out of the ground, and "pig-sticking," hunting aggressive wild pigs on horseback with only the lance as weapon.

McGregor's pegging contest with Forsythe results in his lance breaking and his being thrown from his horse. He holds pig-sticking in contempt. But when Forsythe's goofing around with a snake charmer's flute in order to annoy Mac puts him in deadly danger from a cobra, Mac pulls out his revolver and kills the snake with one shot. Like the well-named Colonel Stone, the virility of the lance is rigid, all about order, discipline, and self-control but short on action, on explosive release. At the beginning of the film, we see the first of many times that Mac disregard Colonel Stone's orders when the soldiers escorting a convoy under attack from snipers are supposed to hold their fire, so as to confuse the attackers about their strength and lure them in closer. When the officer in charge is killed, Mac immediately shoots back. Regimental discipline values just how long one can wait before firing; Mac is all about the climax.

This becomes abundantly clear in the actions that lead up to McGregor's heroic death in saving the regiment, as well as fellow captives Donald and Forsythe, from an ambush by Mohammed Khan and his followers. The Indians have gained the advantage by seizing a shipment of ammunition with the help of information Donald has disclosed under torture. It is stored in a tall stone tower. Mac and Forsythe manage to escape their cell and Mac seizes one of the rebels' machine guns. Carrying it as he storms the tower, he blasts all men in his way, then throws a torch onto the boxes of ammunition. The phallic tower explodes orgasmically, crushing McGregor

In this scene from *The Lives of a Bengal Lancer* (Henry Hathaway, Paramount) Lt. Alan McGregor (Gary Cooper, right) learns how to disguise himself as a native from the regiment's spy, Lt. Barrett (Colin Tapley, center). The lesson comes in handy when he goes against orders to infiltrate the camp of Mohammed Khan. Collection Ina Rae Hark.

underneath it but depriving Khan of the advantage. The film lingers on the moment. The tower's bricks propel themselves outward from the force of the blast while simultaneously collapsing downward. Smoke, fire, and falling debris are shot from several different angles, including the points of view of Donald and Forsythe. Because there is so much ammunition inside the tower, a number of further mini-explosions create more smoke and spew bullets everywhere.

McGregor's association with guns and ammunition and his "colonial" origins link his opposition to Stone not just with that of the colonel's American wife but with the rebellious Indians as well. It sits well with neither to have their lives, as part of the 300 million in the country, "ordered" by men of Stone's breed. Thus, even though he tries to assimilate what Hamilton has told him about his commanding officer, when he attempts to repeat it to Donald in order to reconcile the young man to his father's seeming heartlessness, he garbles the message and finally gives up: "How can I tell you what it's all about when I don't know myself?" But if an American audience's sympathies are bound to flow toward American-accented

Cooper/McGregor and his rebellion against Old Ramrod, as they would have done toward American-accented Gable/Christian and his mutiny against Bligh, the prevailing Hollywood ideology must nevertheless isolate them from any seeming victory and displacement of the breed of men who serve British colonial interests. As Taves says:

> The fact that alternatives to colonialism are inevitably posed in negative terms indicates there is no automatic predisposition on the part of audiences to accept the desirability of imperial policies. The effort necessary in each adventure to establish the need for a colonial presence indicates the pattern never became accepted in the way that the American Indian-as-savage was traditional in the western genre. Because of adventure's affinity for outlaws and rebels, it is almost obsessed with proving that imperialism is not oppressive. (194)

The colonial regime can handle the immature rebellions of Donald and of the ordinary Indian people, portrayed as childlike and superstitious in their Muslim beliefs, easily reduced to abject terror by the threat of being wrapped in an unclean pigskin as a burial shroud. Mohammed Khan is a real danger, however, because he claims an alternate patriarchal hegemony. Urbane and sophisticated, speaking British English without a hint of a "native" accent, the escort of Tanya, a Russian Mata Hari, Khan wants to usurp Stone's rule and substitute himself as father of the Indian people. As clearly as euphemisms demanded by the Production Code can do so, it is made clear that abuse of male genitals is part of the standard torture he enacts against British captives. Donald's Oedipal transition from dissolute and craven betrayer of the regiment to worthy successor of his father in the 41st therefore first requires his separation from "mother McGregor," achieved by Mac's heroic death, and then his killing of wicked father Mohammed Khan, suitably carried out by stabbing him with a sharp wooden stake.

Unlike *Blood* and *Bounty,* in which rebellions against stern taskmasters were given limited endorsement if the rebellion did not extend to murder and the men being oppressed were of European heritage, *The Lives of a Bengal Lancer* will tolerate no disrespect for the stern white father who is all that stands between a colonized nation and rule by its own indigenous leaders.

American Rebellions without Displacement: *The Littlest Rebel* and the Civil War Film

Extrapolating from the three films discussed above, one might almost assume that, if they could, Hollywood filmmakers would have rewritten history to have the American Revolution result in a negotiated peace, with the king more respectful of colonial rights, and the creation of a separate nation with ties to the Crown proceeding gradually. In other words, Alan McGregor would have behaved like the Canadian he is rather than the American he resembles. As I stated at the beginning of this essay, developments in labor-management relations this year made the issue of worker revolt a particularly vexing one and led to great care in the representation of rebellions of any sort. As for the particular stress on preserving British institutions despite their susceptibility to tyrant misbehavior, that too reflects the times: "With the growing fascist threat from the Continent, the affinity between the United States and England became more pronounced. . . . With the threat of war, American and British films frequently portrayed Englishmen as personifying the very type of Anglo-American morality and virtues—fair play, democracy, equality—that formed the values on which opposition to fascism and a new European War would be fought" (Taves 72).

Yet there are deeper and more long-standing ambiguities in U.S. culture's attitude to rebellion that become clear when Hollywood narratives of revolt take place on home soil rather than being displaced to far-flung outposts of empire. Although the descendants of the Englishmen who settled the thirteen colonies would seek independence from the nation that dispatched them, in their relation to the indigenous population, before and after the Revolution, they acted the part of the European colonialists who ordered the lives of nonwhite peoples from India to Africa to the South Seas. Indeed, the slippage in signification between (Native American) Indians and (South Asian) Indians particularly inflected the Empire films of the thirties during a period when westerns were not achieving A-picture status. Richard Slotkin in *Gunfighter Nation* devotes a whole section to "The World-Scale Western, 'Victorian Empire' Movies, 1935–1940," of which he remarks: "There is a striking and not fortuitous resemblance between this formula and the classic Indian-war scenarios of the Myth of the Frontier. In a sense, these movies merely flesh out in fiction the ideological implications of the [Theodore] Roosevelt thesis, which envisioned the transformation of the racial energies that won the West into the basis of an Anglo-Saxon alliance for the conquest and control of the undeveloped world" (266–67).

Still another layer of meaning occurs in the depiction of rebellion on American soil that Hollywood chose more frequently to represent than any other: the Civil War. Less than a century after its citizens threw off the yoke of British rule, the country was of course confronted with a subset of its own citizens of European ancestry attempting to throw off the yoke of federal rule. The schoolroom shorthand for the distinction is obvious: revolt against tyrannical king = good; revolt against a united United States for the sake of preserving slavery = bad. Yet one Civil War film of this year, Shirley Temple's *The Littlest Rebel,* demonstrates that Hollywood's take on the issue was anything but an obvious shorthand. And because the film is narrated from the viewpoint of a child, the ideological covers for a truly incoherent conception of that conflict are stripped away.

It has long been a truism in the American motion picture industry that films about the Revolutionary War will fail at the box office while those set during the War Between the States will do much better. The conservatism we have seen expressed in this year's films has less work to do when the forces that oppose rebellion can capture a good deal of immediate audience identification. And yet, as much as Americans love the rebel and outlaw, these Civil War films frequently adopt the viewpoint of the secessionist South. In another paradox, although Lincoln, far more than Washington, is the president invoked to represent core U.S. values in this year and through-out the decade, the enslavement of the Blacks he emancipated often receives tacit approval. *The Littlest Rebel* points up these contradictions quite clearly.

Temple plays Virginia "Virgie" Cary, the pampered daughter of planta-tion owner and Confederate scout Herbert Cary (John Boles). When the Cary land comes under Union control, their commander, Colonel Morrison (Jack Holt), bonds with Virgie but cannot keep the estate from falling into ruins. Virgie's mother dies and most of the slaves desert the family, but not loyal Uncle Billy (Bill Robinson), who cares for and protects the little girl. Morrison eventually agrees to give Cary a pass—and his spare Union uni-form—in order to take Virgie to safety at her aunt's house in Richmond, accepting Cary's word of honor that he will not take any intelligence he might gather back to his superior officers in the Confederate army. But Cary is apprehended by Union troops, and both he and Morrison are condemned to death, the former for spying, the latter for collaborating with the enemy. It is up to Virgie to appeal to President Lincoln to pardon them; this being a Shirley Temple film, he does.

If *The Lives of a Bengal Lancer* dealt with separating out the proper colo-nial father from various usurpers of that role, *The Littlest Rebel,* like so many of Temple's films, is about Shirley gathering as many adoring father figures as she can and then sitting them down to have a stern talking to about ridiculous things like war. (It is totally in consonance with her juvenile star persona that Ms. Temple worked with the diplomatic service as an adult.) "We grown-ups haven't as much sense as you children," Cary readily admits when Virgie asks him why Confederates and Yankees don't get along as well as she and the little girl of a pro-Union family.

What the film never provides is a clear answer to why the grown-ups are fighting. Here is the dialogue that ensues when Virgie and Uncle Billy discuss the onset of hostilities:

Virgie: What's a war?

Uncle Billy: Well, a war's a lot of soldiers and battles where men kill each other with guns. . . .

Virgie: Why?

Uncle Billy: Seemed like to me, honey, no one knows why. I heard a white gentleman say there's a man up North who wants to free the slaves.

Virgie: What does that mean, free the slaves?

Uncle Billy: I don't know what it means myself.

Furthermore, because the film follows the familiar pattern of embracing a rebel's point of view without condoning rebellion, a person ignorant of American history would never conclude that the South was anything but a victim of the "War of Northern Aggression." From the initial announcement that "Fort Sumter has been fired upon!" we only see southern troops and civilians on the defensive. Despite the film's title, taken from Morrison's playful nickname for Virgie, she insists that she is no rebel but a Confederate, because her "daddy said so." And never once does anyone mention that the South seceded from the Union to form the Confederacy. Even the Union's goal of freeing the slaves is treated as an intrusive attack upon a way of life that is working just fine for whites and Blacks. (The only whipping mentioned in the film is the twenty-five lashes ordered by Morrison for one of his sergeants [Guinn Williams] who has authorized looting at the Cary plantation and treated Mrs. Cary and Virgie abusively.)

Only one person seems to get what the conflict is all about, but his sentiments are discounted because of their source. He is slave James Henry, played by Willie Best in his usual function as Fox's second-string Stepin Fetchit. Called a "lazy jackass" by Uncle Billy and treated as the stereotypical mush-mouthed, shuffling, and dimwitted caricature of the southern Black, James Henry is nevertheless quite capable of noticing that things would go more quickly at Virgie's birthday party if she just passed the cake to the boy next to her rather than handing it to the slaves to be served. And when Uncle Billy insists that Virgie is in no danger from the Union soldiers, James Henry dares to disagree: "They won't hurt us because we slaves. They's fighting for us. But if you's white and southern, you's the enemy." His insight is quickly negated, however, when Uncle Billy notices how much James Henry is shaking: "For a man they ain't gonna hurt, you do a powerful lot of shiverin' every time the Yankees come around." James Henry must admit that whatever insights his mind comes up with, his body never quite believes them.

To give *The Littlest Rebel*'s creative staff credit, they do not ask us to believe that no African American is capable of translating intelligent thoughts into intelligent actions. Uncle Billy is smart, brave, resolute, and loyal, the only one of Virgie's three father figures who does not make a mess of efforts to protect her. He is also the one she is literally the most in sync with, as their matched steps and gestures in several delightful song and dance numbers attest. But the film finally treats Uncle Billy's affinity with Virgie as a sign of his placement as child rather than as a fully equal adult man, and he is excluded from the film's final shot in which Virgie is centered in the embrace of her Confederate and Yankee white fathers. Nor is it ever questioned that a man of Uncle Billy's abilities should fail to seek a life of his own after emancipation instead of continuing to play exactly the same subservient role he did as a house slave.

Conclusion

In a year that saw fascism grow ever stronger and freedoms threatened everywhere, Hollywood and most of America were far more concerned with discouraging the protests of workers (including the studios' own employees) against unfair labor practices (let alone their embrace of a full-scale, communist workers revolt) than encouraging an unstinting resistance to tyranny wherever it appeared (see Clark). The revolts of white people tyrannized by other white people were given considerable play, but only if they were somehow marginalized or defused in the end. As for tyrannies against nonwhites, few films focused on those injustices. Looking at the films of the year that focused on rebellions against oppressors, we can understand completely why America did not rise to the defense of the Abyssinians and why certain provisions of the film industry's exclusive seven-year contracts would one day be declared illegal because they violated California's anti-peonage laws (Balio 161). As much as Peter Blood or Fletcher Christian, Errol Flynn and Clark Gable were part of "a star serfdom. Glamour was its camouflage and fame its dazzling illusion. But behind the grandeur of being a movie star in these years lay all the gradations of servitude" (Alexander Walker, qtd. in Balio 143).

1936

Movies and the Possibility of Transcendence

SUSAN OHMER

Reflecting back on this year in American culture, writer Studs Terkel described it as a time of "great ideals and hope and trauma" (74). Since he was speaking retrospectively, Terkel knew that the ominous events unfolding in Germany, Italy, and Spain would eventually lead to World War II, but many at the time felt that the Depression was beginning to lift, that America would soon be back on its feet. Business was expanding; the economy was picking up steam; and Franklin Roosevelt's New Deal programs seemed to be working, despite fierce opposition from Republicans and the Supreme Court. Hollywood, too, enjoyed a banner year at the box office with many outstanding films that extended established genres, introduced new stars, and displayed the possibilities of new processes such as Technicolor.

Like other films of this decade, the ones made this year represent the Depression, sometimes directly, more often indirectly or symbolically. In live-action features and animated shorts, in genres ranging from screwball comedies to historical dramas to musicals, the characters, plots, and settings often speak of struggle, defeat, and continuing hope. Educator and sociologist Frederick Thrasher, writing in the *Journal of Educational Sociology* near the end of the year, argued that motion pictures "make a unique contribution to art that cannot be made in any other medium of human expression." Unrestricted by physical time and space, film can give viewers new perspectives, "transcend the material into realms of fantasy which other forms of art find it much more difficult to present" (130–31). The cinema's power to transport us has led many to think of Depression-era films as offering escape, but Thrasher's formulation offers another way to look at the films of this era. In them, we see how formal devices such as music, sound, camerawork, set design, and costumes incorporate elements of the material world but lift us beyond it into another realm. Five films in particular from this year demonstrate that the idea of "escape" is too simple. In *Show Boat, Swing Time, Mod-*

ern Times, and Disney's *The Country Cousin* and *Thru the Mirror,* we see characters who strive to move beyond their worlds, and appreciate how the medium of cinema conveys their struggles and aspirations.

■ "We Have Emerged"

During this year the economy improved so much that some executives thought the Depression might be ending. After years of deferred maintenance, businesses began to replace aging equipment and make other improvements, increasing overall manufacturing by 20 percent ("Economic Recovery"). The steel industry worked near capacity for much of the year, leading the head of U.S. Steel to assert, "We have emerged from the long and difficult struggle with adversity" ("Steel Faces"). Many businesses felt confident enough about the future to take on more debt, making this year's bond market one of the strongest in history ("1936"). And investors within the United States and from overseas put their money back into the stock market ("Indications").

The booming economy and expansion of government programs during the New Deal stimulated consumer spending as well. Then as now, the auto industry functioned as a bellwether. The number of cars manufactured this year increased to the highest level since 1928 and the combined net profits of the largest manufacturers rose 45 percent over 1935 ("Automobile Trade"). Department store sales increased 15 percent and demand grew for luxury items such as furs and jewelry ("Department Store"). The boom also pushed commodity prices higher, which helped farmers ("Commodities"). Consumers who could afford them enjoyed trips on the *Queen Mary* or the Santa Fe Super Chief, while those with simpler tastes or smaller incomes savored new items such as Mars candy bars and games of pick-up sticks (Young 119–45).

In the arts, *Gone with the Wind* became the first novel ever to sell a million copies in six months. Soon after its publication in June, David Selznick bought the film rights for $50,000. In November, the first issue of *Life* magazine appeared on the newsstands, with a cover photograph by Margaret Bourke-White celebrating the Fort Peck Dam. Playwright Eugene O'Neill won the Nobel Prize for Literature. In music, Eugene Ormandy replaced Leopold Stokowski as conductor of the Philadelphia Orchestra, and contralto Marian Anderson made her debut at Manhattan's Town Hall. *Billboard* released its first "Hit Parade" of songs, as Benny Goodman was becoming famous for a new kind of music called "swing" (Young 148–67). Visual artists sought ways to democratize art, to link painting, sculpture, and architecture to the everyday experiences of Americans. Many found work in the projects developed under Roosevelt's administration, including the Federal Arts Project that created murals for post offices, schools, and hospitals around the country (Saab 1–53). The Federal Theater Project toured the country with plays that included Sinclair Lewis's *It Can't Happen Here* and inaugurated the "Living Newspaper" series, designed to explore the causes and impact of current social problems (Bendiner 178–200).

Though business executives expressed cautious optimism, many Americans still struggled to attain basic necessities. The year is commemorated by some of the most searing photographs of the Farm Security Administration, among them Dorothea Lange's famous portrait of a migrant mother and her two children in the Dust Bowl (Yapp 65). Even beyond the Plains, the weather wreaked havoc on many lives. In March, floods ravaged thirteen eastern states, inundating Washington, D.C., with twenty-six feet of water and leaving Pittsburgh paralyzed, while in July a heat wave ravaged the Midwest (Allen 167–69). Unemployment remained high, at 17 percent, which was still lower than the 25 percent rate in the early part of the decade (Young xvi–xviii). Recognizing the improvement in business, and wanting to secure some of its benefits for workers, labor organizer John L. Lewis brought together miners, autoworkers, and others into the Committee for Industrial Organization (CIO). Instead of organizing by craft, like the American Federation of Labor (AFL), Lewis employed a "vertical union" strategy that united all the workers in an industry under one umbrella. This meant that an industry could be brought to a halt, thereby exerting more pressure on employers. The CIO inaugurated sit-down strikes this year, beginning with General Motors in November, and the action grew to involve 135,000 men in thirty-five cities ("Mass Industries"). GM eventually recognized the union and the strikes inspired workers in other industries to organize as well (Baulch).

This year also included a presidential election that many saw as a referendum on the New Deal and the profound changes it introduced. Democratic incumbent Franklin Roosevelt's resounding victory over Republican challenger Alfred Landon by a margin of eleven million votes served as a decided affirmation of his policies. The election witnessed the introduction of the first statistically based public opinion polls, by George Gallup and Elmo Roper. The election triggered an avalanche of articles ruminating about the nature of democracy and the will of the people that it expressed (Ohmer 51–75).

Though the United States enjoyed a peaceful election, the established democracies of Western Europe experienced much more tumult. In England, Edward VIII assumed the throne in January upon the death of his father,

George V, then abdicated in December to marry American divorcée Wallis
Simpson. In Italy, dictator Benito Mussolini annexed Abyssinia, forcing its
emperor, Haile Selassie, to flee, then struck an alliance with Germany. Hitler
remilitarized the Rhineland, throwing aside the Treaty of Versailles that had
ended World War I, and signed pacts with the Soviet Union and Japan. In
July General Francisco Franco launched a civil war against the elected Popular Front government of Spain. Many Americans joined the fight by forming Abraham Lincoln brigades; loyalist sympathizers included Ernest
Hemingway and George Orwell ("Foreign News"). The fierce battle for
Spain inspired lasting symbols of resistance such as Robert Capa's famous
photograph of a "Loyalist Militiaman at the Moment of Death, Cerro Muri-
ano, September 5, 1936" (PBS). The potential implications of these fascist
movements motivated William Cameron Menzies's cinematic interpretation
of H. G. Wells's *Things to Come*, which imagined life in England in the year
2036 and, from a different perspective, Leni Riefenstahl's *Olympia*. The
increasing international tensions led the *New York Times* to declare that
"war's alarms are louder and sound nearer than at any time since the guns
ceased to thunder in the last war. Diplomatically, dictatorships have drawn
together and democracies reluctantly are arming and looking to their own
defenses" (Birchall).

The political turmoil in Europe hurt the U.S. film industry. The civil war
in Spain cut off Hollywood's revenues from that country, and both Italy and
Germany severely restricted the amount of money studios could export
("Italy Penalizes," "Majors Quit"). Fascist governments banned films they
found offensive: Italy objected to any plots that praised English culture,
while Germany banned films whose stars were not Aryan—including Mae
West, Fred Astaire and Ginger Rogers, and Johnny Weissmuller ("Italy
Ban," "Nazis Go"). In Spain, Franco's forces executed three Paramount
newsreel employees ("Newsreel Man"). Besides these actions overseas, the
studios suffered much turmoil at home. William Fox declared bankruptcy
due to unpaid income taxes, and RKO's stockholders continued to argue
over reorganization ("Federal Lien," "RKO Reorg" 3). Even more secure
companies experienced significant management changes: Disney left United
Artists to distribute through RKO; Paramount reorganized with Joseph P.
Kennedy's help; and most dramatic of all, Universal's founder Carl
Laemmle sold his controlling interest to outside investors. Directors and
writers challenged the power of the majors by forming their own guilds,
and several stars, including James Cagney and Fred Astaire, sued over contract violations. In September Hollywood mourned the death of MGM producer Irving Thalberg; others who died this year included silent film actors

John Gilbert, Henry B. Walthall, and Radio City impresario S. L. "Roxy" Rothafel ("Industry Manpower" 6–7). And those enduring symbols of old Hollywood, Mary Pickford and Douglas Fairbanks, divorced.

Other changes offered hope for the future and new opportunities for profit. This was the year that Hollywood "went radio," as the networks expanded their operations on the West Coast and rushed to sign film stars for radio shows. Cecil B. DeMille became the host of "Lux Radio Theatre," a program that featured prominent stars in dramatizations of current films. Exhibitors in many cities charged that broadcasts with Hollywood stars cut into attendance ("Get Off the Air" 57). Though there was talk of an outright ban of film stars from the airwaves, studios and exhibitors decided to work together through strategic cross-promotions ("Exhibitors Now Taking" 13–16). Hollywood also kept an eye on another invention on the horizon— television. Audiences in London were beginning to enjoy regular daily broadcasts by the BBC, but in the United States, battles over patents hampered TV development, and experts predicted it would be several years before Americans had their own programs ("Practical Television" 5, "Films vs. Television" 3)

In other areas of technology, Hollywood renewed its interest in color films this year. The smashing success in February of Walter Wanger's *Trail of the Lonesome Pine,* the first Technicolor feature made outdoors, spurred studios to commit to making more films using this process. Color appeared this year in dramatizations of early California, such as *The Dancing Pirate* and *Ramona,* and enhanced the setting of David Selznick's *The Garden of Allah,* where Charles Boyer and Marlene Dietrich played out a story of frustrated love in the Sahara. Overall, the *Hollywood Reporter* wrote, "Color is here! Like the political talk of prosperity, the motion picture industry has long regarded color as being just around the corner. *The Trail of the Lonesome Pine* turns that corner" ("*Trail*").

For many observers, there was a sense that film had reached a point of maturity and cultural acceptance. As Ruth Suckow noted in *Harper's Magazine,* "the immense influence of Hollywood in our national life has lately passed the point where it was matter for comment (frequently for denunciation) and seems to be accepted as matter of fact" (189). The film education movement was in full swing and thousands of high-school students had taken film-appreciation courses (Dale 23). In January, the Museum of Modern Art's Film Library began circulating two programs designed to introduce students to the history of cinema; they included works by George Méliès, Edwin S. Porter, D. W. Griffith, and Walt Disney (Barry 14). Further evidence of the power of the cinema came in July, when Pope Pius XI issued an encyclical that praised the Legion of Decency and called for a worldwide ban on "immoral" films because, he wrote, "everyone knows what damage is done to the soul by bad motion pictures" ("Text" 67). Theaters did a booming business, however, and audiences continued to enjoy established genres and familiar stars.

Genres associated with the thirties, such as screwball comedies, flourished. William Powell and Myrna Loy appeared in *After the Thin Man* and with Spencer Tracy and Jean Harlow in *Libeled Lady*; Powell also paired with Carole Lombard in *My Man Godfrey*. Another Depression icon, eight-year-old Shirley Temple, appeared in four films: *Stowaway* and *Dimples* placed her in Shanghai and nineteenth-century New York, while *Poor Little Rich Girl* and *Captain January* explored various forms of family life. Katharine Hepburn challenged conventional notions of gender in *Mary of Scotland* and *A Woman Rebels,* but Greta Garbo sacrificed herself for love in George Cukor's *Camille. Desire* inspired Marlene Dietrich to give up a life of crime, and the lack of it ruined Rosalind Russell's marriage in Dorothy Arzner's *Craig's Wife*. Errol Flynn led *The Charge of the Light Brigade* and Fredric March adventured through several continents in *Anthony Adverse.* Jimmy Cagney took to the skies in the Howard Hawks's aviation drama *Ceiling Zero* and worked as a feisty government agent in *Great Guy.* Displaying contrasting motives, Gary Cooper played an American mercenary in China in Lewis Milestone's *The General Died at Dawn*; Warner Baxter took on the role of a stoic doctor in John Ford's *The Prisoner of Shark Island*; and Paul Muni enacted *The Story of Louis Pasteur.* Other dramas of masculinity and a search for ideals could be found in William Wyler's *Dodsworth,* Frank Capra's *Mr. Deeds Goes to Town,* and Fritz Lang's *Fury.* Broadway continued to serve as an important source of material, in films such as *Winterset, The Petrified Forest,* and *Anything Goes*.

Above all, musicals dominate the year. *The Great Ziegfeld* celebrated the work and life of the famous impresario, while Al Jolson displayed the style of more recent times in *The Singing Kid*. Jeannette MacDonald and Nelson Eddy sang their way through Canada in *Rose Marie*. Radio and stage stars also took their talents to the screen, as shown by Eddie Cantor and Ethel Merman in *Strike Me Pink* and Louis Armstrong and Bing Crosby in *Pennies from Heaven.* In animation, the Fleischer brothers' Popeye celebrated his second birthday. By creating worlds that escape the boundaries of daily existence both in form and intent, music and animation illustrate the transcendent possibilities of film in this year.

▬▬▬▬ Only Make Believe

In a year of great musicals, *Show Boat* stands out, not only for its immediate presence but also for its history, trailing back to the late 1920s and the transitional years of sound film. Edna Ferber published her novel about life aboard the Mississippi steamboat *Cotton Blossom* in 1926, the year after she won the Pulitzer Prize. It follows the troubled, decades-long romance between Magnolia "Nola" Hawks, daughter of the proprietor of the *Cotton Blossom,* and Gaylord Ravenal, a charming but irresponsible gambler recruited to star in the onboard variety show with Nola after the two leading players, Steve and Julie, must leave because they are discovered to be an interracial couple. Ferber sold both the stage and film rights to the book within a few days of each other, the first to Florenz Ziegfeld and the second to Carl Laemmle at Universal. In Ziegfeld's hands the play became a tremendous success and ran for eighteen months on Broadway, in large part because of its score, with music by Jerome Kern and lyrics by Oscar Hammerstein II. Although Universal had produced an earlier version in 1929, this year's full-length film with screen stars rather than a Broadway cast, featuring Irene Dunne as Magnolia, Allan Jones as Gaylord, and two major African American stars of the period, Hattie McDaniel as Queenie and Paul Robeson as Joe, immediately superseded it. By that time Robeson had performed in several stage versions of the play and, in the minds of many, was the only person to sing "Ol' Man River."

Many of the songs create a deep emotional resonance: we see Nola and Gaylord falling in love in "Only Make Believe" and "The Room Above Her" and feel the melancholy of disappointed love in "Bill" and "Can't Help Lovin.'" Though its music represents the essence of *Show Boat* to many, James Whale's direction highlights the cinematic possibilities of the story's river setting and romantic drama. The film's opening sequences illuminate a central tension of the narrative, between the characters' outward appearance and their private dramas. When the show boat docks, everyone turns out to greet the players, who put on a parade and offer previews of their acts. Intercut with their performances are revelations of the tensions among one of the actresses, Julie, her husband, Steve, and Pete, a man who has pursued her. The fight between the two men breaks out into the open, but the show boat captain assures the public that it is all part of the show. The encounter sets up a key subplot of the first part of the film, one that carries over from the novel, in which Julie, who appears white, is revealed to have a black mother. Knowing that she is about to be discovered, her husband Steve cuts her hand and drinks her blood, giving him the "one drop of

This scene from *Show Boat* (James Whale, Universal) vividly illustrates "the special world the stage creates." Collection Ina Rae Hark.

Negro blood" that qualifies him as black in Mississippi. Their obviously white skin, and the fact that he can become "black" on purpose, highlights the irrationality of southern racism and underscores the idea that seemingly fixed identities are in fact more fluid. The dialogue and action of this scene are nearly identical between the novel and the film—one of the few scenes that is—but Whale's intercutting and direction bring home the tension between public and private more forcefully. The film reveals the full depth and complexity of the world the characters inhabit and enables us as viewers literally to "see" beyond appearances.

Though Ferber's novel describes many of the *Cotton Blossom*'s productions, the film brings out more vividly the idea of performance and the special world the stage creates. Irene Dunne and the other members of the cast shift seamlessly from the exaggerated facial expressions and gestures of nineteenth-century melodrama, to blackface minstrel shows, to music hall nostalgia. While their performances in the plays-within-the-film are deliberately mediocre, their ability to switch immediately into their "real" screen selves proves the film actors' talents. The film's exploration of the line between performance and reality reaches its height in the scenes depicting Magnolia and Gaylord's growing attraction for each other. After Julie and Steve's departure, Nola steps into the female roles, but the troupe still needs a male lead. Her father and mother spot Gaylord lounging near the boat and invite him to join the group. Gaylord woos Magnolia with the song "Only Make Believe," in which two people begin by pretending to love each other and then reveal that they really do. After Gaylord decides to join the troupe, he and Magnolia become its stars because of the passion they feel for each other and can only express on stage. The audience can see that while they are "acting" love, they are in fact falling in love. In their romance, thematic contrasts between private/public and on-stage/off-stage disappear. The novel describes these changes, but the film's music and mise-en-scène bring them to life.

When Gaylord first appears, the other actors in the troupe debate whether he really is as well-off as he pretends to be or is in fact down on his luck, as his cracked shoes indicate. In the film as in the book, however, Magnolia loves him unreservedly, and leaves her family to follow him to Chicago. There Gaylord supports her and their daughter by gambling, and their fortunes rise and fall with his luck. Unlike the novel, however, the film traces one arc of movement, from wealth to destitution. Gaylord deserts his wife, prompting her to seek work on the stage, where she becomes a success. Their daughter follows in her footsteps to her own career in the theater and her father, not revealing his identity, takes a job watching the stage door so he can be near her. In the end the three are reunited, their identities and enduring love revealed. Performance is at once a family tradition, Magnolia's means of survival, Gaylord's strategy for concealing his presence, and, in the end, a way to enact continuing commitment.

In its treatment of both performance and music, the film illustrates the conflicted relation between black music and white musical culture. Scholars praise Ferber's critique of 1920s racism in the miscegenation subplot, and note the prominence of black music in the stage production, which was unusual for a Broadway show of the period (Campbell 32–33, Bordman 470). As on Huck Finn's raft, black and white characters live together on the show boat, sharing their experiences and learning from each other (Mast, *Can't Help* 62). Magnolia's warmth and sensitivity is shown in the book, play, and films by her ability to absorb and imitate black dance and music; her unique interpretations of black songs become one of her hallmarks. Yet more recent critics have pointed out the inherent racism of this situation: it is whites that carry on black musical traditions, rather than talented black performers (Knight 22).

While the novel and play bear the traces of the conflicted racial politics of 1920s America, Whale's film provides a stronger critique of racism and opens up a space where at least one black musician, Paul Robeson, dominates the screen. Though the film contains many of the stereotypes of its time, such as shuffling "pickaninnies" and lazy men, it also creates a strong subplot about the love between Hattie McDaniel's Queenie and Robeson's Joe, a plot that parallels the white women's attachments to men who do them wrong. Their song "I Still Suits Me" was especially composed for the film and affords both performers their own scene and extended screen time. In the original Broadway play, a white actress in blackface performed McDaniel's role (Breon 90–91). Whale's direction offers further critiques of racism in shots that draw attention to the separate entrances for whites and Blacks at the Show Boat's theater, and that pan across the backs of the black audiences in the balcony, reminding us of their presence.

Most memorable, however, is the film's presentation of Robeson's performance of "Ol' Man River," on stage and on screen one of *Show Boat*'s most memorable moments. Whale devotes four and a half minutes to the song, and includes multiple verses and a full chorus. Robeson sits on a bale of cotton and whittles as he begins singing, and during the first verse he takes on the role of the suffering Blacks described by the lyrics: the camera intercuts scenes of him lifting the bales as he sings about "sweat and strain." In the second verse, other black men are shown lifting the loads and their voices join him in the chorus. The scene thus depicts Robeson as an individual, then as a representative of a larger group, then expands to include the larger group itself, linking him and the song with the wider history of slavery and oppression. Whale frames him as a star: the camera pans around him in a 360-degree movement and emphasizes his size and importance through repeated low angle shots and close-ups. Robeson's intensity and the painful history described in the song mark a break from the tone of the rest of the film; in contrast to the world of performance the other characters inhabit, one senses that Robeson speaks of a deeper truth. Ferber wrote that when he first performed the song on stage, audiences "stood up and howled" (quoted in Duberman 159), and the visceral feeling in his voice ignites a similar reaction today. Robeson also changed the lyrics of the song from those of the stage production: Hammerstein's "Niggers all work on the Mississippi" became "There's an ol' man called the Mississippi," despite Kern's protests (Breon). For both Magnolia and Joe, music becomes the means of transcending the harsh realities of their present, a way of taking themselves out of their surroundings to another place.

In contrast to the deliberate evocation of past musical traditions in *Show Boat,* the Astaire-Rogers hit *Swing Time* represents the essence of Art Deco modernity. Jerome Kern wrote the score for this film as well, and it includes such hits as "The Way You Look Tonight," "Let's Face the Music and Dance," and "Bojangles of Harlem," Astaire's tribute, in blackface, to the great Harlem dancer. *Swing Time* is, for many, the most memorable Astaire-Rogers film and the one that lifts the integrated musical to new heights. The film met with immediate box office success: it set an all-time record for opening day ticket sales on its debut at Radio City Music Hall and was held over at every theater it played during its first run ("*Swing Time,*" "Hold Over"). In its narrative and musical numbers, the film sets the gritty realities of the Depression next to spaces of fantasy and luxury, yet shows that they are always connected.

As Arlene Croce notes in her study of the Astaire-Rogers cycle, *Swing Time* is a world of "top hats and empty pockets," one where Fred hops a freight car while wearing a morning coat, and has to win an orchestra's contract by gambling in order to dance. Performance, romance, and finance are linked in the convoluted plot. Astaire's "Lucky" Garnett misses his wedding to Margaret Watson (Betty Furness), and she'll only give him a second chance if he proves his dancing talents are enough to earn him $25,000. Once he falls in love with dance instructor Penny Carroll (Rogers), he's not so eager to obtain the money, and the film is bookended by another abortive wedding, as Lucky persuades Penny not to go through with her own marriage to bandleader Ricky Romero (Georges Metaxa). *Swing Time* proceeds through antithesis, "contrariwise," as Croce puts it, in songs that deliberately undercut the romance promised by Kern's lyrical music (*Fred Astaire* 101). The lyrics of "A Fine Romance" complain about how theirs is not; after Astaire sings "The Way You Look Tonight" to an off-screen Ginger, he turns to see her standing before him in a bathrobe with her hair full of shampoo. This song is heard again in the following scene, where the orchestra leader who pursues Ginger despite her lack of interest sings it to her. At the end of the film, we hear the plaintive notes of "A Fine Romance" as Ginger tells Fred she is going to marry someone else. Several dance numbers in the film also function in a contrariwise manner by playing against the famous couple's image: in their first number together, "Pick Yourself Up," Fred pretends that Ginger has just taught him to dance, in order to save her job, and displays a seasoned performer's skill while pretending to be a neophyte. In the last number of the film, "Never Gonna Dance," the narrative posits that they will never be together again, when audiences know they are an enduring team. "In this way," as Celestino Deleyto writes,

Ginger Rogers and Fred Astaire look ready to transcend gravity as they dance on the "big white set" of *Swing Time* (George Stevens, RKO Radio). Collection Steven Cohan.

the film "proposes an alternative layer of meaning to that of the action, which sometimes confirms our first impressions but which at other times anticipates, frustrates, openly contradicts them" (24).

In *Follow the Fleet*, the pair's other film of this year, Astaire broke from his prior screen image in top hat and tails to appear in sailor costume as a man who joins the navy after he is rejected by his dancing partner, played by Rogers. In that film, the machinery, decks, portholes, and stairways of the ship form the stage and props of their dances, illustrating the principle of "bricolage," or dances that make use of available materials, that Jane Feuer has described. In *Swing Time*, however, many of the musical numbers take place in Van Nest Polglase's "big white set," with its white on white décor, curved staircases, gleaming floors, floor to ceiling glass windows, and repeated geometric patterns (Speigel). Besides Polglase, John Harkrider, who created the costumes for the stage production of *Show Boat*, designed the Silver Sandal nightclub set that evokes the skyscrapers of Radio City. As historians William and Nancy Young note, the chromed tubular steel, Bakelite bars, glass curtain walls, and miles of dance floor embody modernism in its most visible and fantastic form and create "dream clubs" that have "no real-life equivalent" (67).

This world of nightclubs and rooftop cafés forms the backdrop for many of the dance scenes, and the rest of the film often consists of Penny (Ginger) and Lucky (Fred) scheming to return to that world. The plot demonstrates over and over how hard it is to enter and stay in the realm of glamour and luxury: it requires professional contacts, the right clothes, unsurpassed talent, and a great deal of luck. Yet while the film never lets us forget that money matters, it is not the most important thing in life. The opening sequence makes fun of people who judge others by their financial worth. When Lucky fails to appear for his wedding, his potential father-in-law is furious until he hears that the almost-groom made $200 that afternoon. "Well, that's different," the father says. He agrees that Lucky can return to marry his daughter when he has amassed $25,000 and the almost-bride seems content to wait. The mise-en-scène here makes fun of this bourgeois preoccupation: the ancestral paintings on the wall look angry at Lucky when he arrives, then smile when they hear he made money. Yet he never does make enough money to return; in fact, each time he comes near to the magic $25,000, he stops himself from reaching it. In this case, money would prevent him from achieving his dream, which is to be with Ginger.

Astaire-Rogers films remain some of the finest examples of the integrated musical, in which songs and dances emerge "naturally" from the rest of the narrative and serve to reveal characters' emotions and changing relationships. *Swing Time* displays these qualities even more obviously that Kern's earlier *Show Boat,* to many the original integrated musical. The singing often emerges from conversation, and the dances may begin as walking before they take off into a waltz. Several dances enact the rituals of courtship and the couple's changing feelings toward each other. In "Pick Yourself Up," Penny is angry that Lucky keeps falling over his feet during their lesson. When he reveals his talent to save her job, her emotions shift from anger to surprise to delight to gratitude as she realizes what he is doing. Their last number, "Never Gonna Dance," embodies their despair at parting; the angles of and curves of their torsos literally embody sadness. Their courtship proceeds through fits and starts and these shifts are visualized in the movements of their dances.

Historians credit Astaire for many of the dance innovations in his films: it was he who changed the "Bojangles" number to a faster swing beat and requested that the "Waltz in Swing Time" be a jazz waltz with brassy orchestration (Croce, *Fred Astaire* 112). Astaire mixed genres of dances and incorporated stops and starts, sudden shifts in tempo, hesitations, and bursts of speed. The stop-and-start tempo of "Pick Yourself Up" both illuminates John and Penny's changing views of each other and continually reenergizes the dance. Astaire also changed the way dance numbers were captured on film because he insisted on keeping the dancers' full bodies on camera and minimized the number of reaction shots (Delameter 64–68). Many of the numbers are even more amazing when one realizes that they were done in one take.

Promotional tie-ins with the film suggested that, through Astaire and Rogers, audiences could achieve their own dreams of romance. In many cities theaters invited audiences to fill out an entry form describing what they liked about the new models of Packard cars. Thirteen lucky viewers won one for attending the film ("Simplified Rules"). Similarly, associations of dance teachers saw an opportunity to promote ballroom dancing and published brochures that explained how to do various numbers ("Dance Conventions"). Yet, as Delameter points out, while the musical numbers draw on the movements of ballroom dancing, Astaire and Rogers elevate waltzes and tangos to an athletic and balletic level beyond the reach of ordinary mortals. While audiences may remember their own efforts at dancing, the skill these stars demonstrate elevates their performances into another world (Delameter 50, 63–64).

■ The Pursuit of Happiness

Using movement as a means to comment on or transcend one's environment characterizes Charlie Chaplin's *Modern Times* as well, though the environments are very different from the rooftop cafés that Fred and Ginger inhabit. In *My Autobiography* Chaplin describes how he was inspired by stories of the assembly lines in Detroit, "a harrowing story of big industry luring healthy young men off the farms, who, after four or five years at the belt system, became nervous wrecks" (Chaplin 383). The description of factory workers as healthy young farm boys highlights the way that bodies are emphasized in the film, and the ways in which the narrative contrasts human pleasures and appetites with the cold steel of machines. *Modern Times* is also the first film in which Chaplin spoke, and his performance of garbled speech reflects his cautiousness toward the new technology. In explaining his reluctance, Chaplin argued that talking limits a film's reach to "the particular tongue of particular races," whereas pantomime is the "universal means of communication" (Chaplin, "Rejection" 63). Sound does not have to be dialogue, though, and *Modern Times* demonstrates that music and sound effects can be used in place of words. Both within and between shots and sequences, sound operates contrapuntally to comment on the characters, action, and situations.

The film's famous opening presents a clock on which are superimposed the words "'Modern Times' A story of industry, of individual enterprise—humanity crusading in the pursuit of happiness." This uplifting paean to the rising hopes of the mid-1930s is abruptly undercut by the following sequence of shots, in which an image of a herd of workers emerging into the street dissolves into a herd of sheep moving in exactly the same way. As the workers force their way into the factory, any idea of individuality or the pursuit of happiness is left in the dust. Inside the factory, shots of gleaming metal machines fill the space of the screen, machines that dwarf the people who seem to serve them.

The assembly line where Chaplin's tramp works at turning bolts puts the relationship between man and machine into material form. The tramp's small body and quick movements distinguish him from the lumbering giants who work beside him. Unlike them, the Tramp cannot control his body; he needs to scratch himself, to swat a fly, and falls behind in his work. When he goes to the bathroom, he is told to get back to work by a boss who surveils him through a mirror/screen. Unable to keep up, he eventually gets entangled in the gears of the big machine, in what has become one of the most widely known images from the film. The Tramp surrenders to the machine, and by giving himself up to it, turns it into a toy.

The conflict between the needs of the body and the demands of machines drives the first part of the film. In the famous feeding machine sequence, the Tramp is held hostage by a device that shoves food into his mouth. At one point the machine begins to spew fire. When the demonstrator fixes it, he absent-mindedly puts some bolts up on top of the revolving circle that contains the food. As the circle revolves, it keeps pushing food at Charlie, then at one point shoves the bolts into his mouth as well. It is a key moment that is accentuated with a pause and a close-up; the objects he tried to escape earlier are literally forced inside of him. In this scene as in the first one, spoken words are associated with tyranny and inhumanity: the first words we hear in the film are the boss's, as he orders the workers to speed up the pace, and the feeding machine is introduced by a recorded sales pitch. Words are tools of deception and cannot be trusted, but movements speak the truth.

After the Tramp is removed from the factory, several sequences in the film illustrate the haphazardness that governs his life. When he picks up a flag that has fallen in the street, others think he is leading a protest march and join in. He is arrested and taken to jail. In jail he thwarts an escape by fellow inmates, but only by mistake while under the influence of "nose powder." He does not want to leave his comfortable quarters in jail when

The Tramp (Charlie Chaplin) and the Gamin (Paulette Goddard) live out a fantasy of wealth when he gets a job as night watchman in a department store in *Modern Times* (Charlie Chaplin, Charles Chaplin Productions–United Artists). Collection Ina Rae Hark.

headlines scream of "Strikes and Riots!" When he does, he encounters "the gamin" (Paulette Goddard), a "child of the waterfront" whose innocence inspires a desire to protect her.

It is in the scenes between the gamin and the Tramp where *Modern Times* makes its most poignant commentary. Continuing the theme of the body that began in the early part of the film, later sequences show the gamin and the Tramp's efforts to imagine and construct a home for themselves. In one sequence the two sit on the grass outside a small suburban home and watch the man leave for work and his wife skip happily back into their house. The Tramp describes to the gamin a vision that we see, of a living room smothered in chintz, oranges ready to be plucked outside the window, and a cow standing by to provide milk for breakfast. The vision dissolves into a shot of the Tramp cutting his meat, in pantomime, then the camera pans left, to reveal the gamin with desperate eyes, complaining that she is hungry. The stark contrasts between the images he evokes and their ongoing struggle to feed themselves underscore the limited nourishment that fantasy can provide.

When the Tramp does find a job, as the night watchman in a department store, he immediately brings the gamin in and feeds her at the store café, where the counter is piled with sandwiches and a layer cake has already been sliced. This time they act out their fantasies in real space: they roller skate in the toy department and the gamin tries on fur coats before falling asleep in a thick pile of blankets. The Tramp loses this job as well, when he fails to stop a group of burglars that includes one of his factory buddies. "We ain't burglars—we're hungry," they tell him. Again he goes off to jail, and again the gamin is waiting for him when he gets out. This time she has found a real home—of sorts—a rundown shack near what might or might not be a river. Though the roof and walls are literally falling down around them, the two settle in for a cozy meal. And the cycle begins again: he gets another job in a factory, but the workers strike, and once more he is unemployed.

Near the end of the film, hope awakens again. The gamin finds a job dancing in a café and gets a position for the Tramp as well, as a singing waiter. The sequence marks Chaplin's speaking debut, and he uses it to mock the idea of speech: the Tramp delivers his song in gibberish, but his comic gestures make it humorous, and the audience shows they "get it" by their laughter. Though Chaplin gives in to the expectation of speech, he thwarts it at the same time, and the Tramp continues to communicate in pantomime.

But here againthe authorities intervene, and the gamin is arrested for a past charge of vagrancy, even though she is now gainfully employed. They both lose their jobs and escape to the open road once more. When the gamin feels she cannot go on, the Tramp convinces her to "smile" and we hear the music Chaplin himself wrote for the film. Though they set off arm in arm into the sunset, the cycle of hope and loss, happiness and despair, has begun again. Unlike in *Swing Time* or *Show Boat*, we see their fantasies as fantasies and are reminded of the ongoing struggle that makes up their daily lives. Made in the middle of the Depression and representing its struggles so clearly, *Modern Times* feels almost heartbreaking today.

Thru the Mirror

Disney's films of this year mark the apogee of the studio's art. Disney was the first Hollywood studio to commit to Technicolor, and all its cartoons this year used that process. Color enabled Disney's animators to craft more subtle backgrounds and use shading to create more rounded figures. The studio had introduced a greater degree of complexity in animation through a process of divided labor that involved animators who created key drawings, in-betweeners who drew the intervening movements in more detailed sketches, and an ink and paint department that translated the animators' sketches into colored paint on celluloid. Disney's work process resulted in more rounded, three-dimensional characters that moved in fluid and expressive ways that illustrated their personalities (Barrier 136–51).

Humor in Disney films resulted less from gags and slapstick and more from the comic possibilities of the situations in which characters found themselves. Animators watched live-action shorts for inspiration, and one can imagine the characteristic movements of Charlie Chaplin and Buster Keaton in the cartoons of this period. Disney sought to develop characters through animation itself, in movements that revealed their personalities and reactions, much as the relationship between Astaire and Rogers in *Swing Time* develops through dance. *The Country Cousin* and Mickey Mouse's *Thru the Mirror* exemplify the artistry for which the studio had become famous.

In *Country Cousin,* Monty Citymouse invites his cousin Abner Country-mouse to leave his home in Podunk and live in the big city. Abner walks there, in patched overalls and carrying a hobo bag, and is met by his cousin, in top hat and dinner coat, at his residence at 66 and 1/8 ParkRitz Row. The following scenes portray the hazards of the good life, such as mousetraps, but also its pleasures: a beautifully drawn and painted tabletop scene reveals sliced ham, a silver tray with mouth-watering deserts, and a round of Swiss cheese twice the size of the mice. While Monty sniffs each morsel and dabs at his cheeks with a silk napkin, Abner happily stuffs his mouth with cheese and cleans his ears with the same cloth he uses to wipe his face. Abner's delight in this land of plenty is conveyed through his large, expressive eyes and mobile facial reactions.

When Abner munches celery and gets the hiccups from drinking too much champagne, Monty reprimands him again for making noise. The film makes brilliant use of subjective shots when Abner sees Monty in triplicate, and tries to box with his own reflection in a block of gelatin. His tipsy attempts to twirl an umbrella recall Chaplin's performances in similar situations. After gorging himself, Abner discovers the reason why his cousin insists on silence: they share their home with a large and ferocious cat. In his drunken state Abner has no fear, however, and kicks their nemesis in the behind, rousing its fury. Abner is forced to escape by jumping onto the roof and sliding through a drainpipe, and winds up in a tin can that rolls through the streets. The medium of animation makes it possible to convey the overwhelming noise and speed of the city through dramatic shifts in perspective and changes in the size and scale of cars and buildings. Car horns take on angry faces, and their cacophony finally drives Abner out of town and back to his sleepy Podunk. The contrast between the noise of the city and the quieter pleasures of small town life recalls the dynamics of *Modern Times,* and Abner's unabashed joy in eating and childlike lack of manners offer points of identification for audiences of all ages and backgrounds. Like Chaplin's film, Disney's award-winning cartoon celebrates the simple pleasures.

Mickey Mouse also experiences altered states of consciousness in *Thru the Mirror.* Mickey appeared in nine cartoons this year, all in color, but he is rarely the central protagonist. Instead, he shares the screen and action with Pluto, Goofy, and Disney's most recent creation, Donald Duck. In these ensemble films it is often Mickey who sets a good example for the others, while Donald acts up. In *Mickey's Circus,* for example, Donald gets to juggle and fight with the sea lions, while Mickey struggles to keep some semblance of order. The humor in these films derives from the characters' comic interactions with objects that often take on lives of their own. The piano in *Moving Day,* for instance, plays hide and seek with Goofy while emitting spooky noises, while household items such as a toilet plunger and an aquarium attach themselves to Donald, who is forced into humorous contortions to get rid of them. In these films Mickey rarely changes his shape or his disposition, but in *Thru the Mirror* he enters another world.

In the film Mickey falls asleep in bed while reading Lewis Carroll's *Alice in Wonderland,* and through a doubling effect we see his "spirit" leave his sleeping body. The spirit of Mickey climbs onto the mantelpiece and pokes his hand through the mirror as if it were toffee. Soon his whole body has crossed through the mirror and, like Alice, he has entered another world. In contrast to the living room he left behind, the chairs and couches in this other room have eyes and mouths and react angrily when he jumps on them. A nutcracker eats the walnuts it opens, but when Mickey tries one his body expands and enlarges as Alice's did when she drank from the bottle labeled "drink me." For Mickey, the effect is only temporary, however, but it affords an opportunity to display the stretch and squash techniques of animation.

After Mickey changes shape and returns to normal again, the other objects in the room take on lives of their own. A phone rings and answers itself, then asks to talk to Mickey, and uses its cord to play jump rope with him. The sounds of his jumping become a tap dance that starts up the radio; the jazz music it produces launches Mickey into a dance that recalls Astaire's performances with top hats and walking sticks. In contrast to

Astaire's live-action surroundings, however, Mickey's environment is more malleable: through animation, he is able to dance with a miniature hat and stick while at the same time dancing in tandem with a human-size pair of the same objects. The hat on which he dances shifts to become his partner, in a doubling effect that evokes comparisons with the "Bojangles" number in *Swing Time*.

After leaping from the hat top to a tabletop, Mickey disrupts a deck of cards that begins to march behind him in a tap dance of their own. Mickey shuffles himself into the deck and then taps the cards into piles that he arranges in a fan around himself. Soon the cards, too, take on a life of their own, forming abstract patterns that are shown in an overhead shot that recalls Busby Berkeley's distinctive style. The illustrations on the cards come to life: Mickey dances with the queen of hearts, until the king attacks him with both his heads and swords. The other cards rush to his defense, their hearts, diamonds, spades, and clubs turning into flying bullets. Mickey is forced to escape back through the mirror, as the ringing of the telephone behind him melds into the sound of sleeping Mickey's alarm clock. Though Disney had in the past parodied Hollywood and its stars in other cartoons, in this one he celebrates the possibilities of animation to create identities, movements, and worlds not found in live-action films.

The films of this year incorporate and comment on the harsh realities of the Depression. Yet when we look back on them, it is their transcendent qualities we remember, the way they lift us out of material existence into another realm.

1937

Movies and New Constructions
of the American Star

ALLEN LARSON

When Franklin Delano Roosevelt delivered his second inaugural address on 20 January, he envisioned himself as the leader of a nation fundamentally transformed by the brutal lessons of economic devastation. As the federal judiciary, conservative legislators, and industry leaders emboldened by the slow tide of economic recovery threatened to unmake the "New Deal" wherever they could, Roosevelt sought to canonize the victories of his administration's first one hundred days as the refurbished philosophical foundations of U.S. society (*Inaugural* 148–49). "Our progress out of the depression," he told the nation, "is obvious. But that is not all that you and I mean by the new order of things . . . the greatest change we have witnessed has been the change in the moral climate of America" (*Inaugural* 149–50). Ostensible recovery still left "one-third of a nation ill-housed, ill-clad, ill-nourished," and Roosevelt promised another four years of work "to bring private autocratic powers into their proper subordination to the public's government" and to make manifest a new national moral vision that had undermined "old admiration of worldly success as such" and abandoned "tolerance of the abuse of power by those who betray for profit the elementary decencies of life."

Four months after Roosevelt's address, the horrific bombing of Guernica, Spain's civilian population, memorialized in Pablo Picasso's great painting, would draw the world's attention more intently to the escalating turmoil in Europe. As speculation about the merits and arguable inevitability of U.S. military involvement in the turmoil abroad continued to grow, Amelia Earhart's shocking disappearance in the South Pacific turned a news media sensation designed to celebrate American individualism and technological idealism into a sobering occasion for collective grief, and another drastic economic downturn in autumn further polarized debate about the virtues of Roosevelt's economic policy agenda. The opening of the A&P supermarket chain, featuring on its shelves new products like Spam, Pepperidge Farm bread, and Kix cereal; the initial marketing of home freezers to keep other foods from the grocery store fresh over extended periods; and the first Howard Johnson's motel-restaurant were small consolations to workers with empty pockets. Nor would the wealthier clientele that attended Broadway theaters be particularly cheered up by the stage adaptation of John Steinbeck's *Of Mice and Men* or Clifford Odets's *Golden Boy*.

Many of the year's most expensively budgeted and high-profile Hollywood films evinced the uncertainties and contradictions of this shifting moral and economic climate. As the final entry in producer Irving Thalberg's legacy, MGM's adaptation of Pearl S. Buck's Pulitzer Prize–winning tale of Chinese peasants and epic class struggle, *The Good Earth,* explored themes that resonated deeply with American social experience of the era. Minor studio Columbia Pictures' bold jump into the deep end of prestige production with director Frank Capra's lavish adaptation of James Hilton's *Lost Horizon* offered up the mythic land of Shangri-La as a canvas for contemplating the nature of utopia, private property, and individualism. Warner Bros.' *The Life of Emile Zola* confronted antisemitism, institutional corruption, and the pitfalls of nationalist loyalty, and Samuel Goldwyn/United Artists' gorgeous adaptation of the social-realist stage hit *Dead End* explored a stark cityscape of poverty and despair. Although none of the source material escaped tampering or Hollywood simplification in the adaptation process, as a whole the year's top-shelf product was remarkable for its tentative embrace of commercial cinema's capacity to pose meaningful questions about complex political issues.

As an industry that had itself been widely accused of betraying the "elementary decencies of life" for profit, Hollywood's ongoing endeavors into "important" filmmaking of course served more than artistic ambitions. Eric Smoodin has shown how *Lost Horizon* was, for instance, immersed within a discourse of "film quality" as Capra's own status as star director "entered directly into the era's discussions about Hollywood and the moral, intellectual, and emotional uplift" of audiences (77). Although prestige films comprised only a small percentage of the films made each year, massive promotional efforts sought to make them the focal point of Hollywood's cultural articulation. Effective as those publicity efforts may have been in eliciting a vastly disproportionate amount of movie press attention and commentary, however, the merits of big budget production as a business model remained unclear. *Lost Horizon* was considered a box office failure, and even *The Good Earth* strained to recover costs.

Artistic ambitions aside, the movie business still depended as much as ever upon the rapid flow of economically manufactured, programmatic fare through the distribution pipeline in order to turn reliable profits. Collectively, the films released by Hollywood this year reveal the industry's continuing struggle to discover the right recipe for blending quantity and quality while wisely negotiating a variety of internal and external pressures. The volatility of those struggles is especially apparent in the array of films featuring actresses whose star images had been intrinsic to the iconicity and very idea of "Hollywood" in the first half of the decade. Amidst much publicity surrounding her rogue walkout to protest chronic placement in mediocre material, Bette Davis graced screens in four Warner Bros. films that arguably proved her point: *Marked Woman, Kid Galahad, That Certain Woman*, and *It's Love I'm After*. At MGM, Joan Crawford persevered by working opposite William Powell and Robert Montgomery in *The Last of Mrs. Cheney*, with director Dorthy Arzner in *The Bride Wore Red*, and opposite Spencer Tracy in *Mannequin*, only the latter of which was considered a hit for the perennial audience favorite. A lukewarm reception greeted films starring some of MGM's other top female stars as well. Although Greta Garbo began the year triumphant after the 1936 Christmas day release of *Camille*—more than enough to sustain the Garbo mystique—that luminosity didn't carry over to *Conquest*. The Jean Harlow vehicle *Personal Property* performed perfunctorily, but did not quite provide the boost needed to revitalize the star's languishing career. At RKO, Katharine Hepburn hit a low point with *Quality Street*, and Paramount's Marlene Dietrich and trailblazing director Ernst Lubitsch stumbled with the commercial failure *Angel*. The Mae West vehicle *Every Day's a Holiday* provided Paramount with satisfying box office returns, despite audience and critical responses that were decidedly mixed.

Although Twentieth Century Fox had nothing to complain about in its biggest female star (as Shirley Temple's *Heidi* and *Wee Willie Winkie* delivered on cue), when it came to effectively managing the careers of full-grown women stars, Hollywood was clearly not at the top of its game. With the exception of *The Good Earth* star Luise Rainer's meteoric rise to the pinnacles of acclaim and fame for MGM—followed by a plummet back into obscurity by the end of the decade—the year's greatest successes for actresses emanated from the margins of the big five studio system and outside the parameters of the exclusive option contracts through which studios mechanistically cultivated and mined stars' commodity value. Columbia Pictures' sleeper hit *The Awful Truth* gave Irene Dunne some luster and reinvigorated the screwball comedy genre, while maverick producers Samuel L. Goldwyn and David O. Selznick scored big by featuring veteran female stars in high-end product released through the semi-independent United Artists umbrella. Nobody benefited more from Goldwyn's initiative than Barbara Stanwyck, whose performance as *Stella Dallas* indelibly molded her star image and endured as one of the year's most beloved classics. Meanwhile, Selznick had been swift to engage Janet Gaynor and Carole Lombard after both were liberated from soured relationships with their respective home studios. Gaynor's turn as Esther Blodgett in *A Star Is Born* was avidly hailed as a major comeback, while Lombard's starring role in *Nothing Sacred* solidified her status as one of the industry's most sophisticated and bankable comediennes.

The unpredictable results yielded by efforts to refine generic recipes for the widest possible appeal and to balance stars' brand value against potential dissipation from overexploitation were never problems unique to the major studios' female stars. But female stars had also been distinctly and disproportionately implicated in some of the wider shifts in mid-decade production strategies influenced partly by political pressures. Despite Roosevelt's blithe appropriation of the term "morality" to refer to the means by which the public might compel government to close the vast divide between rich and poor, in the daily business of moviemaking concerns about morality were the domain of administrators newly charged with the task of policing cinema's representational field for proper modulation of social codes of individual virtue and vice. In varying ways, each of the four films examined in this chapter—*A Star Is Born, Stage Door, Saratoga,* and *Nothing Sacred*—directly engages the peculiar fact of female stardom's entanglement in efforts to gauge, define, and control "the moral climate of America," further illuminating the cultural and industrial pressures that molded the manufacture of female stardom, and thus classical Hollywood cinema as a whole, in the second half of the decade.

It Happened in Hollywood

Conversations about a germinating "Hollywood picture" that would portray the trials and tribulations of a rising female star began to appear regularly in the production correspondence of Selznick International Pictures (SIP) in the early summer of 1936. In one teletype between the fledgling studio's East and West Coast offices, executive Lowell Calvert chimed in with some thoughts on how to develop the concept into a sure-fire hit movie:

FOR YOUR GIRL, GET A BEAUTIFUL ONE. HAVE A HELL OF A TIME GETTING HER, HAVE HER KIDNAPPED SEVERAL TIMES IF NECESSARY—OF COURSE, IN A LAW-FUL MANNER—DURING THE COURSE OF THE PRODUCTION HAVE HER MIXED UP

IN ONE ESCAPADE AFTER ANOTHER AT CATALINA, MALIBU, PALM SPRINGS, ETC.
BRING IN A NUMBER OF LOVE AFFAIRS. THIS WHOLE THING CAN BE CARRIED TO
A POINT WHERE SHE IS FRONT PAGE NEWS TWO OR THREE TIMES A WEEK. IT'S
A LOT OF HOKUM, BUT LEGITIMATE AND HAS NOT BEEN DONE FOR A NUMBER
OF YEARS, AND THE PICTURE AS I VIEW IT LENDS ITSELF ADMIRABLY TO SUCH
EXPLOITATION. YOU WILL COME OUT WITH A MILLION DOLLARS WORTH OF
PUBLICITY FOR THE PICTURE AND MAYBE A NEW HARLOW.[1]

As SIP's New York manager of sales and distribution, Calvert first envisioned a full-throttle promotional launch for the project, proposing an exploitation treatment of manipulated glitz, glamour, and intrigue that would draw upon a preexisting mythology of "tinsel town" as a fantastical space unrestrained by social convention or provincial law. He could not have known that a year later, the iconic figure he aspired to emulate—Jean Harlow—would suffer an early tragic death, helping to demarcate the end of an era; nor could he necessarily have foreseen that the prevailing sentiment within this young, "independent" studio would evolve to conceptualize the film that became *A Star Is Born* as an antidote to the image of Hollywood evoked in his teletype musings. "I believed," producer David O. Selznick would later write, "that the whole world was interested in Hollywood and that the trouble with most films about Hollywood was that they gave a false picture, that they burlesqued it, or they over sentimentalized it, but that they were not true reflections of what happened in Hollywood" (Behlmer 96). Described by film historian Robert Sklar as the first wholly "self-conscious" image of Hollywood as a "cultural institution" (*Movie-Made* 192), Selznick's *A Star Is Born* ultimately aspired to shed the more sensationalistic flavor of its source material, *What Price Hollywood?* (1932), and shroud its fictional movie star protagonists in an aura of classical tragedy, not farce.

Decisive as Selznick might have been from the outset about wanting to make an elegant and dignified "Cinderella story" staged across the landmarks of Hollywood, decisiveness about how to best realize that ambition remained elusive throughout all phases of the production process. An early story summary based upon William Wellman's first pass at a full script, under the working title *It Happened in Hollywood,* shows that the basic plot trajectory was relatively fixed from the start, describing the planned film as

> the story of a Canadian girl whose pioneering spirit, inherited from her great-grandmother, brings her to Hollywood where, by sheer determination, she begins to rise to stardom. On her way to the top she meets and marries another star, Norman Maine, whose career is on the down grade. She is a famous, world renowned star when he commits suicide. Heartbroken, she

returns to her family home, where her great-grandmother points out her obligation to her public and instills in her the re-determination to go back to Hollywood and 'carry on' gallantly.

A pained and defensive three-page memo from Wellman to Selznick after the first production team conference reveals, however, that the director's first script was not initially well received, and archival records show that the script development process was especially protracted and volatile as Selznick, Wellman, and a rapid succession of other writers endeavored to concoct the right mix of dramatic plot, comedic spice, and atmospheric Technicolor spectacle while remaining cognizant of budget constraints. Some issues were resolved immediately—for instance, the unsurprising relocation of Esther's origins from Canada to Montana—while other elements, such as the question of how to portray Esther's final re-ascent from grief and despair, remained in flux throughout the shooting of retakes only four weeks before the film's scheduled April opening.

At particular issue right from the beginning and in every version of the script, however, was the question of how to best represent the nature of Esther's rise to stardom. Uncredited story editors Budd Schulberg and Ring Lardner criticized "the total weakness of Esther's character" in a report to Selznick: "She is entirely a negative character, acted upon in every scene. We do not think that an audience can sympathize with her when she shows neither the determination, imagination, originality or talent to make her a potential screen star." When Dorothy Parker and Alan Campbell were brought in next to work on dialogue, their directives from Selznick thus also included "the possible necessity" of creating additional scenes that would show "more pathos in Esther's search for work" and "something to get over Esther's struggle for a break after she is in the studio." Wellman, on the other hand, had defended his original characterization, arguing that it was unnecessary to show "the girl going through all the heartbreaks to accomplish success" and that his version was just as true to the random twists of fate that defined life in Hollywood. "There are many examples," Wellman wrote, "of girls who have suddenly had opportunities literally jammed down their throats—out of which have come great success."

But providing an accurate reflection of the inner workings of the film business was obviously never the genuine goal or an operative measure for assessing script quality. "You cannot tell the truth about Hollywood," one SIP executive had bluntly noted when objecting to *The Truth About Hollywood* as a proposed titled because it would have been "misleading" and sure to "disappoint [the] audience." Indecision about how to best ensure that the female protagonist would sufficiently solicit and hold the audience's emotional investment was fueled less by concerns over capturing the "truth" than by fundamental contradictions in the very idea of female stardom itself. Discourses of Hollywood stardom had, since their advent two decades earlier, always played upon a range of types and themes, some of which were more closely tied to their antecedents in the traditions of legitimate theater and a discourse on acting as artistic vocation, and some of which articulated female stardom as a simple state of being that would, of its own volition, carry someone to the heights of stardom. Because these two poles pulled against each other—the discourse on stardom as performative skill versus the discourse of "star quality" as a set of preexisting traits simply "discovered" by the cinematic machine and carried to the masses— the female star emerged as an inherently contradictory construct insofar as her active, performative labor, so often manifested in highly sexualized terms, threatened to unsettle the symbolic foundations of a patriarchal culture organized by the sexual division of labor and gendered assignment of economic roles. Reflecting upon the popularity among women fans of strong female stars of the early studio era, Molly Haskell wrote that these figures functioned as such compelling sites of fan identification precisely because they offered alternatives to restrictive codes of normative middle class femininity. In its circumvention of sanctioned modes of social mobility, female stardom registered far more, in other words, than only aspirations for wealth and its attendant consumptive pleasures. To the contrary, female stars gave expression to aspirations for autonomy in the social world, self-definition, and the greater possibilities of female identities neither restricted to nor dependent upon the private, consumptive realm. "In no more than one out of a thousand movies was a woman allowed to sacrifice love for a career," observed Haskell, but, "in real life," women knew, "the stars did it all the time" (5).

The farmhouse scene that opens *A Star Is Born* thus speaks directly to the intimations of transgression that always hovered around female stars while also rendering apparent the writing team's desire to seize upon this story of female stardom as an opportunity to refute accusations of Hollywood "immorality." Returning home from an evening at the picture show, farm girl Esther Blodgett is confronted in the family living room by the scorn of her Aunt Mattie: "You and your movies, that's all that you think about. . . . You'd better be getting yourself a good husband and stop mooning about Hollywood!" With her moralizing condemnations of the movies' capacity to warp a young girl's mind, Aunt Mattie personifies the copiously recited complaints of religious leaders and women's groups inclined to blame the movies for societal ills of every variety. The script soon refutes Aunt Mattie's self-assumed role as the guardian of America's moral fiber, however, by appealing to a higher symbolic ground. Later that night, Esther's Blodgett's grandmother (May Robson) counsels her star-struck progeny: "You know, Esther, there'll always be a wilderness to conquer; maybe Hollywood's *your* wilderness now." Shortly thereafter, Granny bestows her life savings upon Esther to fund a westward journey, confiding, "When *I* wanted something better I traveled across the plains in a prairie-schooner with your grandfather."

Endowing Esther's desire for Hollywood stardom with a pioneering spirit inherited through the rights of "American" providence ("if you got one drop of blood in you," says Granny, "you won't let [them] stop you!"), this intimate conversation with the ancestor further foreshadows the imminent, impending tragedy, extending the frontier metaphor across the film's entire plot. Before she escorts Esther to the station—where she rejoices, "there's *your* prairie-schooner now!" upon sight of the train—Granny issues a sober warning: "For every dream of yours that may come true, you'll pay the price in heartbreak." "I was in love with your grandfather," she recounts, "and when some injun-devil put a bullet through him, I felt as if it had gone right straight through my heart too." Even in the face of heartbreak, though, Granny "kept right on going." Cost and other considerations eventually led SIP to replace Esther's originally planned venture back to her hometown with Granny's more efficient trip to the coast, where she reappears after Norman's death to remind Esther that she, too, must "keep right on going" and return to work and her adoring fans. Through these conversations, Granny transforms Esther's ambition for stardom from a derided media effect into the ultimate personification of the truly pioneering "American Way," reimagining the apparent "wild(er)ness" of Hollywood as exemplary, rather than transgressive, of true American values.

The active drive and determination that *A Star Is Born* ascribes to Esther through the pioneering spirit theme also finds counterbalance, however, in the equally potent invocation of innate "star quality" as a passive state of being. Concerns that Esther should be shown struggling to get work led to the creation of her discouraging visit to the Central Casting Bureau and other exposition scenes designed to set up her desperate acceptance of a one-night waitressing gig at a private Hollywood party in hopes that she will catch the eye of one of the movie producers or directors sure to be in attendance. In an effort to vie for guests' attention as she offers them her tray, Esther tries to affect the persona of a female movie star. She begins by imitating Marlene Dietrich. When that fails, she moves on to Katharine

Waitress and aspiring actress Esther Blodgett (Janet Gaynor) hopes to impress some Hollywood power brokers (Eddie Kane, left, and Dennis O'Keefe) with her Mae West imitation in *A Star Is Born* (William A. Wellman, Selznick International–United Artists). Photofest New York.

Hepburn. Lastly, she tries her hand at Mae West. Ultimately, this misbegotten effort serves as the basis for turning the traditional logic of the cinematic discovery scene inside out. When Esther works to imitate the most famous and glamorous female stars she appears silly and remains virtually ignored. It is only when she is "being herself"—when she is *not* performing—that her star quality shines through, allowing her to capture the attention of her matinee idol and future husband Norman Maine (Fredric March) and to become the movie star Vicki Lester.

Like the double-inflection of the film's long debated title, which intimates that true stars are "born" that way rather than manufactured by the machinery of modern culture industries, the ascription of an essential passivity to the nature of Esther's stardom also works to exonerate her from the infraction committed by her original flight from the heartland and a life of domestic containment. Earnest as the efforts may have been to write sufficient pathos into the story of Esther's desire for a public career, it is ultimately the problems that such a desire poses to the "natural" order of bourgeois domesticity that provide the film's primary dramatic tension. After a delivery boy addresses the newly sober but unemployed Norman as "Mr. Lester" when he answers the doorbell, Norman's emasculation at the hands of Esther's career success triggers a return to the bottle. When Esther informs studio boss Oliver Niles (Adolphe Menjou) of her decision to leave Hollywood in hopes of saving Norman from self-destruction, the patriarchal figurehead reiterates the cultural language that divides Esther into mutually exclusive private/public selves: "Goodbye Vicki Lester. You were a grand girl. Good luck Mrs. Norman Maine." And it is only when Esther expresses her willingness and desire to sacrifice her public selfhood on Norman's behalf that she fully redeems herself, and female stardom, from the gender role betrayal enacted in the film's opening scene. When Norman preempts Esther's intentioned self-sacrifice with his fatal daybreak swim in the Pacific, the film rejects outright any inclination to resort to the pretext of a morality tale and concedes nothing in the culture wars that cast Hollywood as antithetical to the sanctity of virtuous middle-class domesticity. In the memorable concluding moment, farm girl Esther Blodgett, renamed movie star Vicki Lester, renames herself once again—"this is Mrs. Norman Maine"—as the actress and wife merge in an asserted synthesis of Esther's public and private selves in defiance of the cultural language that claimed she could never be both a "true woman" and a true star.

Acting and Stardom in *Stage Door*

The choice to use Dietrich, West, and Hepburn as the foils for positing an authentic ordinariness as the root of Esther Blodgett's rise to stardom bespeaks the difficulties that all three stars faced during this period, as their names became embroiled in wider efforts to refashion Hollywood's institutional identity. But if it was convenient, in certain contexts, to eschew the glamour and artifice associated with these stars and profess that female Hollywood stars were just "nice girls" rather than strong, independent career women at least partially in control of their own manufacture as sexualized commodities, the larger explanatory chores to which discourses of stardom were compelled to attend rendered this conceit impossible to sustain. As they continued to relocate popular notions of film craft from the actor to the director and producer, discourses of film quality were nevertheless still tied to constructions of the movie actor as artisan and consummate performer, and few female stars embodied this ethos more forcefully than Katharine Hepburn. RKO producers struggled, however, to find potentially crowd-pleasing material that could accommodate Hepburn's formidable presence, and her career was considered to be in crisis at the time when Janet Gaynor invoked her as the antithesis of authenticity by imitating her on the screen. In purchasing the rights to Edna Ferber and George S. Kaufman's *Stage Door*, RKO turned out to be another innovator in rethinking the prestige apparatus as a strategy for reinvigorating its major female contract stars while rearticulating female stardom at the same time.

Stage Door endeavors to mediate the Hepburn star image by tossing her into a community of female characters maneuvered to explore the range of cultural connotations attached to the figure of "the actress" and the female star. On one level, this involves a few terse meditations on the nature of "the life of the theater" and acting itself. But the women that Hepburn's eccentric debutante Terry Randall finds in the Footlights Club theatrical boarding house when she arrives to make her mark on the New York stage are, as a whole, not much predisposed to salon-style conversation. They volley one-line zingers at Terry's pretentious efforts to impart the wisdom of the serious classics upon a decidedly uninterested school of pupils: "After you've sat around for a year trying to get a job, you won't take anything seriously either," warns Judy Canfield (Lucille Ball). And, while Judy isn't exactly correct (Terry will remain, if nothing else, serious), the sentiment provides a cogent enough synopsis of the story trajectory sure to unfold. Handicapped by the blinders of her own privilege (her grandfather, it turns out, "crossed the country in a covered wagon" too, and somehow this is tied to the importance of properly appreciating the works of William Shakespeare), Terry must of course "learn something" from the women who will, we know, fast become her new friends before she can become the great actress she imagines herself to be. Thus, the language of aesthetic value and artistic tradition in crisis will find itself intertwined, as it nearly always does, with a bigger crisis of class conflict, mirroring the ways in which the decade's morality wars were themselves a function of struggles for power

Terry Randall (Katharine Hepburn, left) finds that her artistic and class pretensions do not fit in very well with the more down-to-earth concerns of her fellow lodgers at the Footlights Club, such as Jean Maitland (Ginger Rogers), in *Stage Door* (Gregory La Cava, RKO Radio). Collection Allen Larson.

between social groups whose concerns about the nature of cinema were often only a convenient forum for the expression of more expansive political agendas.

Although the scenario for *Stage Door* seems quaint enough on the surface, the Depression-era context saturates the story. The Footlights Club is crammed full of a beautifully dressed and made-up pool of underemployed itinerant labor struggling to survive in noisy, crowded urban conditions. ("Let's all go on relief and get it over with," says one of the girls as news spreads through the parlor that two more plays have closed.) Simple food, itself, serves as the primary object of most of the women's daily scheming as they hover hungrily at the margins of the theater industry and try to change their fortunes however they can: by dating men simply to get a good dinner, by putting a flirtatious squeeze on the butcher's helper to throw in a little extra meat in the next day's order, by succumbing to the inevitable temptation to become a wealthy man's mistress, or, in the case of Lucille Ball's Judy, by giving up for good and marrying one of the "hicks" from back home. Throughout, there is never any question raised that their world is dominated and controlled by men who treat women and female sexuality as a form of property to be owned, consumed, and traded. And, despite all of Hepburn/ Randall's eloquent protestations in the name of dignity and integrity, there is a notable absence of decisively rendered moral judgment regarding the various choices the women make to secure their own survival as best they can, except insofar as we learn to recognize clearly the difference between a serious actress and a chorus girl gold-digger.

The commingling of members of different social classes ostensibly serves to edify everyone involved: the boarding house girls learn that Terry isn't so bad, and Terry learns to appreciate the wisdom of their uncouth ways and the severity of the circumstances in which they live. For her agricultural magnate father, however, Terry's career ambitions are a smear on the family name, so he hatches a deal with the lecherous manager-producer-nightclub owner Anthony Powell (Adolphe Menjou) designed to bring his foolish daughter home. As a result, Terry is given the part that another of the boarding house guests, a gifted young actress named Kay Hamilton (Andrea Leeds), should rightfully have had. Starving to the point of collapse because she can't find work and has too much pride to ask for help, Kay goes mad with grief and kills herself after she learns the part has gone to Terry. This twist will provide Terry with the genuine experience of heartbreak that she needs to become a great actress. As news of her friend's death travels backstage on opening night, Terry flutters in distress in her dressing room, unable to embark upon her journey into the limelight. But the aged actress who has anointed herself Terry's coach (Constance Collier) calls Terry to the true meaning of her vocation: "There are fifty living people dependent upon you . . . the ushers, the property men, the old women who clean out the theater. Each one of them has the right to demand that you give as good a performance as you can. That's the tradition of the theater!"

Now that she knows heartbreak, she can, in Kay's honor, give a star-making performance: "The calla lilies are in bloom again . . ."

The idealized female star ultimately posited by *Stage Door* is a remarkable amalgamation that binds together, in the figure of Hepburn, a set of ideas about both "acting" and the movies that had otherwise worked, for much of Hollywood's history, as distinctly oppositional terms. That film acting was believed to be entirely and inherently inferior to its theatrical counterpart had been a sore point for decades. But, overall, Hollywood cinema benefited much more than it suffered from its positioning as a popular form antagonistic to the tastes and conventions of bourgeois culture. Even as it hungrily appropriated respectable culture toward its own legitimation, Hollywood cinema reveled in the mocking of official institutions at every turn and was generally content to assert the supremacy of popular entertainment over the rarified criteria used to delineate aesthetic importance or superiority. *Stage Door* uses characters representative of these competing traditions to create an appearance of compatibility as they arrive at a mutual understanding of each other. More importantly, though, the film unabashedly claims, in the figure of its star, to be the conduit of the thing Hepburn/Randall embodies, the discourse on acting as transcendent human endeavor, while recasting, at the same time, the idea of what is "important" about acting in populist terms. The audience's presumed need for some higher level of human consciousness acquired through consumption of great art is not, it turns out, the rationale for the "show must go on" speech that Terry receives from her backstage coach. Instead, the speech resorts to a decidedly non-aesthetic rationale: the ushers and housekeepers and fifty other "living" workers involved are counting on her so they can keep their jobs. In the meantime, the meaning of what constitutes great art is changed as well. Terry's ultimate star turn is predicated upon the fact that she rewrites the lines of the play during her opening night performance because she has now "seen," first hand, a starker, more compelling truth about the world in which she lives, drawn from the life experience of the economically disenfranchised. In a concise rendering of the New Deal wisdom and sentiment she has newly acquired, Terry rewrites her lines on the spot and proclaims, rather plainly: "Help should come to people when they need it."

The Bombshell Vanishes

While producers clearly hoped that, with *Stage Door*, Hepburn's persona might be tempered to better fit within the programmatic formulas that dominated the era, other more overtly sexualized female star images that developed in a pre-Code cinema context—most notably Jean Harlow's and Mae West's—also had to be inventively adapted to a more circumscribed production environment. Nearly thirty years after the fact, movie critic Gerald Weales reminisced that with Jean Harlow's death, "a point of reference disappeared; a part of everyone's vocabulary—the word 'Harlow,' which had been used casually, often obscenely—was pushed suddenly into the past. A fact of daily life, as accessible as the neighborhood moviehouse, was transmuted into myth" (39). Describing the star as "a kind of combination of Mae West and Shirley Temple," Weales attributed Harlow's appeal to the way her image "kept seduction from becoming ludicrous by suggesting that sex was not all that serious"; Harlow "took the softhearted, hard-boiled, good-bad girl . . . glamorized her slightly, kidded her a little, and planted her squarely in the popular imagination" (39).

Harlow's sudden, untimely death from misdiagnosed kidney disease at the age of twenty-six forced MGM to make a difficult decision regarding a film titled *Saratoga* that was mostly done shooting, but not quite done enough. They either had to scrap the project entirely, reshoot most of the film with a different female lead, or, as they ultimately chose, revise the overall script and use stand-ins to shoot remaining scenes vital to story continuity. Louis B. Mayer would insist that his decision to pursue the last option was not financial in nature but rather a response to the outcries of fans who desperately wanted to see the star's final performance. Whatever the motivation for going forward, the result stands as a fascinating testament to the logic of the industrial machine over which Mayer presided. The efforts undertaken to disguise Harlow's absence instead rip the text apart, as the stand-in who dons her pastel designer dresses, who steals her seat in the racetrack grandstand with counterfeit platinum hair tucked inside a wide-brimmed hat, can only signal the disruptive fact of the missing body—some actual, laboring, human being upon whom this particular cinematic utterance was built—and renders all the more conspicuous both the perfectly slick and exemplary studio product that *Saratoga* might have been and the new "Harlow" it might have helped to create.

The racetrack and horse farm setting that veteran scriptwriter Anita Loos and co-writer Robert Hopkins developed for *Saratoga* was adeptly concocted to accommodate the thematic and stylistic hallmarks of glossy, romantic comedies of the moment, allowing for pastoral imagery and opulent, sparkling interiors, folksy atmosphere and glamorous couture fashion, exterior action elements and dialogue-driven wit. Combining gambling, spectator sports, and the amenities of bourgeois leisure, the scenario provided a full palette for the epoch's predominant preoccupation with narratives centered upon the negotiation of social identity and assimilation, class loyalty and class mobility. As *Saratoga* began filming, a somewhat different kind of thirties star named Seabiscuit was beginning to get a lot of attention at the nearby Santa Anita Racetrack, and would arguably become the year's biggest celebrity. Like the movies themselves, professional horse racing and other spectator sports brought together working- and middle-class fans in an avidly articulated national culture based upon narratives of individual will and self-determination metaphorically invested in spectacles of virtuoso, bodily performance.

Virtuosity in performative femininity was, on the other hand, a far more divisive cultural lightning rod. Loos's own fictional *Gentleman Prefer Blondes* (1925) heroine Lorelei Lee became a common reference point for the cultural archetype of the gold digger embodied in throngs of ambitious female characters seeking to better their fortunes by trading upon sex—whether delivered or withheld until marriage, and whether as literal prostitutes, showgirls, mannered social climbers, or female stars. However cleaned-up their roles became via the intervention of the Hays Office, figures like Harlow carried the connotation of entrepreneurially managed female sexuality across the Production Code divide, and continued to allegorize social anxieties about the breakdown of class hierarchies and racial and ethnic miscegenation in stories of heterosexual intrigue and romance. As the heiress to a bankrupt racehorse breeding farm, Harlow's *Saratoga* character Carol Clayton inhabits the position of a Depression-ravaged white "middle" class. The anachronistic sign of a lost agrarian tradition, Grandpa Clayton (Lionel Barrymore) still has his feet firmly planted in the land, artfully tending and cultivating the prize stock upon which the family's livelihood was built. His relationship to the stuff of production is personal and passionate, an embodied identity deeply rooted in the fulfillment of dirty, honest work. But Grandpa's way of life on Brookvale Farm has been imperiled by the financial speculations of his own modern, business suit–wearing son. Like the millions who had gambled in an economy of abstracted property only to see their hard-won savings wiped away in an instant with the swipe of an accountant's eraser, Frank Clayton (Jonathan Hale) has lost all his money betting at the track and must pass the deed to the family farm to bookmaker Duke Bradley (Clark Gable) to cover his debts. The conflict between old and new economies of labor, property, and class invested in the generational divide between patriarchs will be played out across the figure of their inheritor, Carol, as she must find her way, after her father dies of heart failure, to save the family farm (and thus, Grandpa) while keeping her viability as a Hollywood heroine intact.

Before Harlow ever appears on screen, *Saratoga* defines Carol as a problem of class identity. Told that she is on the phone from London, Grandpa
retorts: "I can't talk to her. She's got so high and mighty since she's been in
Europe that she won't talk to nobody but kings!" Later, he complains that he
can no longer understand a word she says. Still under the mistaken impression that she is wealthy, Carol eschews her social origins as, in father Clayton's own words, "a dressed-up gypsy" and uses her family's money to don
the mannerisms of an Anglophile socialite. Performed as comedy by Harlow,
the "respectable" accent that Carol affects grates the ear with every word,
betraying the fiction its bodily source intends to create even as the story
works to redeem Carol's motivations in putting on airs. Having returned from
London engaged to a wealthy New York banker named Hartley Madison
(Walter Pidgeon), Carol visits Duke after her father's death to buy back (with
Hartley's money) the family farm. Duke makes it clear that he is no heartless
banker and would never displace his good friend Grandpa Clayton. Whether
one can, or should, ever leave behind the home community in pursuit of
"something better" has been, for many, the driving dilemma of American
social experience. Together with a cast of atmospheric supporting players,
Duke lives happily in the place Carol means to reject, a subcultural community bound together by its own economy, outsider identity, and shared way
of life even as its members travel within open public spaces.

Because the early-twentieth-century logic of class assimilation is, itself,
entirely contradictory—as discourses of heredity, "breeding," and predesti-
nation clash with the ideological precepts of egalitarian possibility based
upon effort, talent, and emulation—the textual figure Carol Clayton/Jean
Harlow has more than a little work to do in *Saratoga*. As she moves between
cramped train cars and luxurious club rooms, she must simultaneously
anchor a sentimental affirmation of authentic folk community while also
sanctifying the logic of the institutionalized capitalist property relations
against which her home community has been defined. "Don't try to pretend
to me that me Frank Clayton's daughter has fallen for a Wall Street chump,"
objects Duke Bradley. "From where I sit, a gal that puts the bite on a bride
groom for sixty thousand smackers [the price of the Brookvale deed] before
she even gets him to the altar is awfully full of larceny." Gable's Duke gets
the task of articulating the inference of deceit and transgression that cannot
help but hover around Harlow's blond ingénue (although Duke by no
means disapproves: "If I had a kimono I'd marry him myself," he tells her).
And, because the contradictions she must transcend are not hers but rather
the substance of the cultural discourses she inhabits, only the acrobatic
shenanigans of Hollywood plot contrivances can—in the fashion of a street

huckster's shell game—make this story roll. Carol is not, we soon learn, a mere gold digger. Her loyalty to Hartley Madison is repeatedly tested as Duke and his cohorts call upon her to help them soak the guy with "a bankroll like the U.S. treasury" for some spare change. Offended by Duke's accusation that her romantic entanglement is economic in motive, she returns to her father's vocation of race track handicapping and betting— "Luck, is it?" she will later protest, "I call it hard work!"—in an effort to pay off the debt on her own. Drawn back into "the life," she nonetheless keeps her distance from her family's gang of pals and puts forth an impassioned defense of the fineries of bourgeois culture. But sincere or not, something bigger—something stored deeply, mysteriously, within her body—will take her back where she belongs.

In his quest to maneuver everyone into place so he can finally make some money, Duke Bradley convinces Madison that his fiancée has developed a "nervous condition" as a result of her work and traveling from track to track. Outraged at the suggestion that she should be examined by Madison's physician, Carol gets so furious she betrays herself, as her funny accent momentarily disappears inside Harlow's brassy shouts until Duke reminds her, "Haven't you forgotten something?" But she eventually submits and, even though she has not actually been sick, the doctor ascertains that she suffers from something that "can't be cured with pills" called "love." The problem is the ongoing deferment of her wedding to Madison; her symptoms will not subside until she is "married" and "cooing contentedly in [her] own little nest." But we also know from assorted glances, sighs, and tears that the doctor has misunderstood the source of Carol's disease: she is in love with Duke, and vice versa. As Carol Clayton/Jean Harlow manifests the hysterical symptoms resulting from her unmet sexual desire in later scenes, she becomes a striking—and funny—indexical marker of the regulation and codification of active female sexuality in Hollywood cinema. Forced beneath the surface of the representational field, female sexual desire speaks ever more obtrusively through the body in codes. Carol's "chest cold" disappears as soon as she confesses her feelings to Duke, but comes back immediately when she again believes she cannot be with him. Articulated here as a joke that mocks its own textual conceit, Harlow's hystericized feminine sexuality nevertheless testifies to her own subjection to harsh institutional scrutiny and regulation, and to the longer legacy of examined and interrogated female ciphers and femmes fatale that Hollywood cinema would render through this lens.

As the plot structure lurches forward to deliver Carol to her "cure," the intrusion of the tragic Harlow biography (again like our heroine's mis-

The frequent Clark Gable–Jean Harlow romantic pairing is seen for the last time in *Saratoga* (Jack Conway, MGM). Harlow died before the picture was completed, and the finished product is haunted by her absence and the attempts to disguise it. Collection Allen Larson.

diagnosed hysterical symptoms) materializes on the screen. Released only seven weeks after her death, *Saratoga* never had any other kind of life— the collective public gaze could only scrutinize her, too, for signs of the mortal peril she was in. Director Jack Conway's seasoned technical command of the commercial group style renders, for most of the first hour, a relatively seamless diversion: dazzlingly chic interiors, Harlow's shimmering sequined gowns and smooth silk negligees, a horse race here and there, and what's more fun than a sing-a-long on a train? One can overlook, without much effort, the traces of the last-minute alterations designed to conceal the film's circumstances and in this way, too, *Saratoga* stands as a shining example of the system that delivered it for our pleasure: the proficient continuity editing and sound looping invisibly do their work in exactly the way spectators had been trained to expect and complacently ignore over a period of decades. But as the bulk of the replacement scenes done with stand-ins unfold, *Saratoga* compels us to lunge forward into the obliteration of our own cinematic illusions. While we should be enjoying the journey toward some climactic, implausible unification of everything our real lives make entirely irreconcilable—the idea of the absurdly appealing Harlow and Gable living happily with Grandpa on Brookvale farm, freed of the otherwise mutually exclusive values imposed upon them throughout the film—the fact that we are being duped becomes impossible to repress. Just as Carol's affected voice sometimes slipped into something else—the "real" beneath the image she meant to present—Harlow's own supple send-up of the patrician elocution in which MGM's aspiring starlets were relentlessly drilled disappears, as some other voice tries to convince us that the woman beneath the bonnet or behind the binoculars, shot from afar, is really her. When the story takes us, in the final scene, to a screening room where a slow-motion film will reveal which horse won the fate-making race, the insult stings. There, in some fictional world, they look to the filmic apparatus as the arbiter of truth; but for us there is only that imposter, that woman whose face we cannot see, who dares to reach out her hand to Gable in the end. Although she is there to ease the burden, a mere pawn in the conspiracy of the cinematic scenario, she does not provide relief or allow us to forget but instead makes viscerally present the structuring absence, as Jean Harlow vanishes before our eyes.

Reinventing Realism

If one believed the musings of the movie press, Harlow's actual death only preempted a more figurative but imminent career death at the hands of unfolding changes in cinema technology. Prepackaged "stories" fed from the offices of Russell Birdwell, SIP's press agent for both *A Star Is Born* and its next release, *Nothing Sacred* (which again teamed Wellman and Fredric March), avowed that the age of "the peroxide blonde" would surely wane with the perfection of the new Technicolor process. One widely picked-up press release offered extensive quotes attributed to Wellman in which the director opined: "You can't pull the wool over the eye of a Technicolor camera. . . . Stars without fine natural complexions or with unreal general coloring cannot make the grade. . . . Bleach blondes will never find success in the new medium."

The outpouring of publicity items about Technicolor that accompanied both *A Star Is Born* and *Nothing Sacred* attests to the somewhat peculiar industrial circumstances that helped bring both films to the screen in order to demonstrate that color could be used for making more than just musicals, fantasy films, or period costume dramas. The biggest obstacle to adopting color was the additional production and screening costs involved, but another hurdle was the widespread belief that only black and white conformed to classical realist conventions. To undermine this roadblock, John Hay "Jock" Whitney, a major shareholder in Technicolor, Inc., merged his Pioneer Pictures (whose sole purpose was to produce films in color and thereby promote industry adoption of the company's proprietary technology) with Selznick International Pictures. One of the new studio's stated tasks was to prove that quality films of any genre could be made profitably in Technicolor. Thus, the creative flair of David O. Selznick was now passionately devoted toward counteracting the prevailing mindset that color photography was inherently antithetical to the codes of Hollywood realism, as *A Star Is Born* and *Nothing Sacred* aptly proved.

As the second film produced under the auspices of the Whitney/Selznick partnership, *Nothing Sacred* thus shared with *A Star Is Born* the general premise that it would offer audiences an equally captivating behind-the-scenes glimpse inside a dominant modern media institution. This time, the setting was the newspaper industry, presented in a far less flattering light than was reserved for Hollywood's own self-portrait, beginning with the opening graphic text announcement of the film's urban setting: "This is New York, Skyscraper Champion of the World, Where the Slickers and Know-It-Alls peddle gold bricks to each other . . . And where Truth, crushed to earth, rises again more phony than a glass eye." From that acerbic Ben Hecht introduction, *Nothing Sacred* tells the story of a newspaper hoax perpetrated by a Vermont watch factory worker named Hazel Flagg (Carole Lombard) who has been misdiagnosed by her incompetent doctor as a victim of terminal radium poisoning. Getting wind of the story, Wally Cook (Fredric March), a reporter for New York's *Morning Star* newspaper, heads to the young woman's hometown, Warsaw, with the intention of turning the tragic story into a newsstand sensation. By the time he arrives, Hazel has already been informed that the diagnosis was false and that she will live, but she can't refuse Wally's offer of free passage and room and board for a visit to the big city, so she conceals her reversed diagnosis. Once she is there, the newspaper turns Hazel into a sensational, sentimental hero, venerated for her bravery and cheerfulness in the face of adversity and imminent death. She is wined, dined, dressed, and coifed in the highest style, enjoying all the enviable privileges and luxuries of celebrity.

Although Hazel's deception provides the central dilemma of the film's plot, it is nevertheless not the subject of *Nothing Sacred*'s moral scorn. That honor is reserved for the newspaper industry, which is portrayed as exploitative, heartless, and fundamentally dishonest. When Hazel collapses while being honored at a nightclub (not, as it is perceived by the attendees, due to her "illness" but from indulging too liberally in the tasty champagne), a newspaper photographer coldly snaps a shot of her lying on the ground but makes no gesture to help. *Morning Star* editor Oliver Stone (Walter Connolly) rushes over to ask the attending doctor for his assessment and says: "Doctor, I want to know the worst. I don't want you to spare our feelings. We go to press in fifteen minutes." Indeed, Wally Cook and Oliver Stone make it clear at the outset that their intention is to milk Hazel's story for all it's worth, and when they discover that Hazel is a hoax, they take immediate action to further perpetuate the fraud. Final plot resolution comes not in the form of revelation and punishment, but escape. The *Morning Star* announces that Hazel has left New York so that she might die in peace alone and we last see Hazel and Wally aboard an ocean liner heading off, presumably, to live "happily ever after."

Despite differences in setting, generic formula, and tone, *A Star Is Born* and *Nothing Sacred* readily appear, stylistically and thematically, to be the veritable twins that they are in terms of their productive origins. Both films strain to produce the overall feel of an up-to-the-minute present-tense setting in which the workings of modern institutions are revealed and scrutinized, thereby assigning the status of "truth-teller" to the cinematic apparatus itself while working to more effectively associate Technicolor with "realism." And, even though the film is not literally set in Hollywood, *Nothing Sacred* is equally engaged in the way discourses of stardom anchored fantasies of class mobility within the transition to post-Fordist society. The story portrays, like that of *A Star Is Born*, a protagonist's flight from life in small-town or rural America, only in this case there is a very different type of symbolic weight attributed to the place of Hazel's origins. When Wally first visits Warsaw, he finds among the townsfolk overt hostility and pervasive fear of speaking out in a way that would displease the owners of the watch factory where Hazel has ostensibly been exposed to radium. ("Paragon Watch factory owns this town," the train station attendant tells Wally. "You better take the next train back.") Here, small-town America is not the pastoral home of a pioneering spirit but the most dystopic envisioning of the "company town," a violently repressive community ruthlessly dominated by industrialists who, among other things, might carelessly poison their workers. In a historical moment when much of the nation's agrarian tradition and roots literally turned to dust, these twin films each present a narrative of flight from the "heartland" to a modern world wholly defined by the transformative powers of mass cultural production. Rendered in state-of-the-art color film technology imbued, contrary to most of its prior uses, with the signifying connotations of a "present day" realist aesthetic, the modern cultural apparatus of mass media enables the protagonist's escape from class oppression. Through clever manipulation of a productive system based upon a shrewd understanding of her own status as commodity, Hazel secures her freedom from Warsaw.

Conclusion

In a publicity card mailed directly to patrons, Radio City Music Hall promoted the premiere of *Nothing Sacred* by promising a "brilliant satire" of America's "gullible throngs creating popular idols of people and things . . . heaping hero worship upon the celebrity of the hour . . . idols that are here only for today, gone tomorrow." The stark contrast between that impulse to mock the artificial manufacture of "celebrity" by the modern media versus the sentimental sanctification of Hollywood stardom offered by nearly the exact same production team in *A Star Is Born* a few months earlier bespeaks the duplicity of stardom as both an industrial production strategy and cultural imaginary. SIP's extended struggle to properly calibrate *A Star Is Born* as both a box office commodity and self-representational articulation of institutional identity, RKO's efforts to refashion Katharine Hepburn in a more populist mold in *Stage Door,* and the more polished post-Code version of the quintessential bombshell Jean Harlow seen in MGM's *Saratoga* all reveal how Hollywood took the textual construction of idealized femininities as a forum for managing its own industrial image. Female stars of the period were never merely "reflections" of the era's dominant gender ideology, but rather the peculiar products of one institution's unique situation within a complex web of power relations, consigned to pull double duty as both compelling sites of audience identification and pleasure on movie screens while also serving as the symbolic ambassadors through which Hollywood sought to define itself as the authentic locus of a "new" America.

NOTE

1. All referenced archival materials are quoted from the David O. Selznick and John Hay Whitney collections housed in the Harry Ransom Center for Humanities Research at the University of Texas at Austin.

1938

Movies and Whistling in the Dark

SAM B. GIRGUS

Still in the midst of the Great Depression and suffering from accumulated woes of poverty, unemployment, poor housing, economic inequality, Jim Crow racism, and social injustice, most Americans probably hoped and thought they had survived the worst of times and could look forward to change for the better. In fact, the country stood at the gates of hell. Such an image provides an appropriate metaphor for the country's and the world's place at that moment in history. Even the experience of World War I could not prepare people for the devastation to come. Who could foresee how the world would come through on the other side of this journey to hell, let alone imagine the journey of horrors itself—the tens of millions dead, the Holocaust, the death camps, the massive displacement, the total destruction of life as it was known? This year started the fulfillment of the implied prediction by Freud in his book that opened the decade, *Civilization and Its Discontents*. The death instinct, the irrational, and the incurable division of the Western psyche started to bud in its preparation for a full flowering of death and destruction.

The signs of this destruction were there to be seen and interpreted this year, but few could imagine the future from the seemingly fragmented and distant events. In March, Germany easily annexed its neighbor Austria to the chagrin even of Italian dictator Benito Mussolini, who chafed at his friend Adolf Hitler's conquest of the country at Italy's border. Like America during those months and weeks, Europe was preoccupied elsewhere. Mussolini himself was dealing with the problems of his own aggressiveness in the Mediterranean, Spain, and Africa. Britain busily worked to make peace agreements with the Italian dictator, including acceptance of Italy's defeat of Abyssinia, while also acquiescing to Germany's takeover of Austria. French concern focused primarily on its own internal political problems with a new cabinet crisis.

Not content to stop with the incorporation of Austria, Hitler through the winter and spring increased the tensions of the German-Czech crisis.

Early in the year, he had promised to protect German minorities outside of Germany, a direct insinuation about conditions for Germans in the Sudetenland of Czechoslovakia. This implicit threat prompted a response in early March by Czech premier Milan Hodza. His proud declaration that he intended to defend his nation's borders dissipated in May when the annexation of Austria meant his republic was now surrounded on three of its borders by the Reich. September brought Western democracies' appeasement to Hitler's aggression. After initial meetings at Berchtesgaden and Godesberg came the famous Munich conference when, without Czech representation, British prime minister Neville Chamberlain and French premier Edouard Daladier negotiated the surrender of the Sudetenland to Germany. Chamberlain's infamous declaration at the conclusion of this acquiescence to force—that he had negotiated "peace in our time"—captured the mood for many of the peoples in the rest of Europe and in the United States who desperately blinded themselves to the portentous implications of their failure to resist conquest and violence.

To the Jews of Germany, the year as a gateway to hell grew more apparent every day with the increasing tempo of systematic persecution and state-sponsored and -organized violence and destruction. After several years of instituting legalized racial discrimination and persecution involving intermarriage and citizenship, the Nazis on 16 June ordered German Jews to register all property, a restriction that had been imposed on the Austrians. For Jews, fears and anxieties were fulfilled on the horrific night of 9 November, the date known as *Kristallnacht*, an evening of historic violence, destruction, and persecution. At the time, however, much of the rest of the world simply prepared for the Christmas season, apparently oblivious to what would soon engulf Europe and the world at large.

The impending catastrophe achieved only surface recognition in Hollywood films of the year. Two films, William Dieterle's *Blockade* and Frank Borzage's *Three Comrades,* allude to the situation in Europe but so vaguely and indirectly as to guarantee a level of skepticism for some about their validity. Disjointed and fragmented, *Blockade,* starring Henry Fonda and Madeleine Carroll, attempts to describe the injustices of the Spanish Civil War but actually functions more as a heavy-handed means for broadcasting the left-wing sympathies of the screenwriter, John Howard Lawson, in its overheated rhetorical speeches. *Three Comrades,* the film version of Erich Maria Remarque's novel, begins at the end of World War I and proceeds quickly to the year 1920. It shows the comrades and veterans of the title valiantly enmeshed in a different kind of war as they attempt to build lives for themselves in the midst of the growing chaos and violence of Germany in the early days of the Nazi era. In an early scene, two of the main characters, played by Robert Young and Franchot Tone, come across a wild scene of mob violence with German thugs and bullies taking control of the streets. Observing the mayhem with steadily increasing dismay and agitation, Tone expresses his anger over the way people have acquiesced to mob violence. Young says that people "close their doors and windows and keep whistling in the dark." Radically rewriting F. Scott Fitzgerald's only credited screenplay, producers and censors deleted any strong language about the rise of Nazism out of fear of hurting the potential German market. Thus, Young's words speak for not only this film but many of the major films of the year.

In the midst of continuing economic crisis and on the verge of another world war, several films hid in the darkness of their own timidity and uncertainty and peeked from behind closed doors and windows at signs of the emerging calamity. In terms of individual and collective psychic behavior, such films demonstrate Freud's fundamental insight that efforts to repress and hide dangerous impulses from consciousness ultimately must fail. Instead of fading away and dying, such impulses, Freud said, "proliferate in the dark" of the unconscious only to emerge in distorted forms ("Repression" 570). Thus, close examination of the films of this year suggests that recognition of the threat to life and freedom remained hidden and tended to manifest itself primarily through indirection in various narrative styles, dramatic structures, and rhetorical forms.

Sadly for Hollywood, intimations of Americans' still untapped potential for resilience, courage, and fortitude in the face of historically unprecedented challenge could be found more readily and powerfully in sports and popular culture than in the films of the year. One event involved the unlikeliest of horses, Seabiscuit, and the other, of course, concerned Joe Louis in his triumphant second fight with Hitler's boxer, Max Schmeling. In her excellent social and cultural history of the meaning and achievement of Seabiscuit to Depression-era Americans, Laura Hillenbrand writes, "In 1938, near the end of a decade of monumental turmoil, the year's number-one newsmaker was not Franklin Delano Roosevelt, Hitler, or Mussolini. It wasn't Pope Pius XI, nor was it Lou Gehrig, Howard Hughes, or Clark Gable. The subject of the most newspaper column inches in 1938 wasn't even a person. It was an undersized, crooked-legged racehorse named Seabiscuit" (xvii). Describing Seabiscuit as "nothing short of a cultural icon in America," Hillenbrand goes on to detail how this "smallish, mud-colored animal with forelegs that didn't straighten all the way" in combination with its jockey, trainer, and owner came to epitomize an American spirit of the triumph through adversity of the underdog—or in this case, to repeat an obvious pun, the underhorse (xvii, xviii). On 1 November, forty million Americans, reportedly including President Franklin D. Roosevelt, listened to their radios for what many still regard as "the greatest horse race in history" and a miracle of a victory for the ultimate outsider, as Seabiscuit triumphed over War Admiral at Pimlico in Maryland.

Several months earlier, on 22 June, another sporting event, ultimately of even greater significance, ended with Joe Louis knocking out Max Schmeling at 2:04 in the first round before 70,000 spectators at Yankee Stadium in New York, the same site where the unthinkable had happened two years earlier when Schmeling had knocked out the seemingly invincible "Brown Bomber." The sadness and shock at Louis's earlier defeat only added to the near-mythic quality of the importance of his victory in the second bout. Nowhere was the celebration of this victory greater than in New York's Harlem. One account describes the jubilation. "In Harlem, empty streets turned into a multicolored carnival at 10:03 P.M. Impromptu parades, with revelers marching with a goose step and salutes mocking the Nazi regime, started throughout the city of New York—and the rejoicing was echoed in towns and urban centers throughout the country" (Barrow and Munder 101). Civil rights leader Andrew Young, later the U.S. ambassador to the United Nations and mayor of Atlanta, noted, "You could almost say that Joe Louis fought the war in advance. He helped to defeat the Hitlerian concept of a master race with his victory over Max Schmeling" (qtd. in Barrow and Munder 101). In a year in which the U.S. Supreme Court ruled that the University of Missouri Law School would have to either admit African American students or build a separate but equal facility for them, Louis's victory seemed like a landmark event for equality and civil rights for black people in America.

The uncertain world situation led to an upsurge in American nationalism and attempts to minimize internal divisions. The House Committee on Un-American Activities was formed to test all Americans on whether they deserved to be called American. Not too far from this zone of protection at the nation's capitol, President Roosevelt presided over the groundbreaking ceremonies for the Jefferson Memorial. On Broadway, *Hellzapoppin* premiered and Mary Martin sang "My Heart Belongs to Daddy." On Armistice Day, Kate Smith told the country where to place its heart when she sang Irving Berlin's new song designed to bring everyone together as Americans, "God Bless America." Superman first appeared in comics to fight for "truth, justice, and the American way." For security not provided by the Deity or a superhero, the Navy began a billion-dollar expansion in two oceans with expanded bases and ports and sixty-nine new ships with bigger carriers. Nonetheless, even with Europe on the verge of starting the worst war in human history, the war that frightened Americans the most was the one Orson Welles started and finished on the radio Halloween night with the broadcast of his version of H. G. Wells's *War of the Worlds*.

As noted, with a few unsuccessful exceptions, Hollywood took pains to avoid directly confronting the forces of darkness overseas and the economic and political troubles at home. Instead it offered the vaudeville nostalgia of *Alexander's Ragtime Band*, the Viennese balls of *The Great Waltz*, the disaster melodrama of *In Old Chicago*, the triumph of colonialist ambitions in *Suez*, the redemptive uplift of *The Citadel* and *Of Human Hearts*, and the romance of *Holiday, Shopworn Angel, Vivacious Lady, Bluebeard's Eighth Wife*, and, on the juvenile level, *Love Finds Andy Hardy*. Merely touching on the imminence of hostilities were the remake of the World War I aerial combat drama *The Dawn Patrol* and Clark Gable's heroics as a *Test Pilot*. However, close readings and analysis of many of the year's successful and popular films suggest these films can be divided into three general categories of response to conditions both at home and abroad: melodramas of history and romance that reveal fear of change and the concomitant desire for maintaining social order through social and class hierarchy; comedies that in turn can be divided between films of comic containment, in which detachment through humor establishes distance from economic and social conditions, and insanity comedies that include the traditional screwball form but that also imply deep, underlying incoherence and uncertainty regarding the meaning, significance, and organization of life and events; and finally, films of entrapment and oppression.

Historical Melodramas and Conservative Social Maintenance

The first category of romantic history and melodramas of social maintenance represents an obvious and immediate response to the changes and turmoil at home and abroad. This group of films seeks stability, order, and hierarchy. Two films in this group are *The Adventures of Robin Hood* and *Marie Antoinette*. Both suggest sympathy for established institutions, even in the face of blatant economic and social inequality and the deprivation of the populace in general. Another film in this category is *Boys Town*, the biopic of Father Edward Flanagan.

Robert Osborne has described *The Adventures of Robin Hood* as one of the best examples of Hollywood classic cinema that deserves highest recognition and awards in all categories of consideration, an opinion apparently shared by the editors of several movie guides. Of course any film directed by Michael Curtiz demands attention, especially with a cast that includes Errol Flynn, Olivia de Havilland, Claude Rains, and Basil Rathbone, a score by Erich Wolfgang Korngold, and art direction by Carl Jules Weyl. As James C. Robertson says, "A peerless cast is in top form in every case, and Flynn and de Havilland have some of their best love scenes together, showing Curtiz's unerring instinct for balance between pace and character development. The climatic fencing duel between Flynn and Rathbone in the castle is unlikely ever to be bettered" (44). As its excuse for what Robertson terms the film's "fairytale, romantic and virile content," the plot focuses on Robin Hood's (Flynn) defeat of the corrupt Prince John (Rains) and Sir Guy of Gisbourne (Rathbone) in order to pay for a ransom to free King Richard the Lion Hearted (Ian Hunter), who has been captured by Austrians while on the Crusades. The thoroughly unrealistic dramatic situations, combined with the religiosity of the devotion to Richard by his followers when his reign is ultimately restored, no doubt would make a modern-day Mark Twain laugh at the gullibility of popular audiences and their desire for a return to the certitude of absolute political and religious authority. At the end, following the example of Robin and Maid Marian (de Havilland), all bow in total reverential devotion to the king.

While Robin and lovely Maid Marian apparently continue to please audiences and critics alike with the film's romanticization of the glories of medieval kingship and courtliness, *Marie Antoinette* also sympathizes with royal order but actually deserves closer critical attention than it has received because of a remarkable performance by Norma Shearer. In the public mind, Shearer's reputation suffers from the belief that her career succeeded through her marriage to the "boy genius" of Hollywood, Irving Thalberg. Thalberg had promised to make her "the first lady of Hollywood" but died in 1936 before completely fulfilling the promise, so that writers such as David Thomson now regard her somewhat dismissively (Thomson 801). However, her performance in *Marie Antoinette* deserves recognition for its depth and range. In a comparably conservative film, *Boys Town,* Spencer Tracy remains stolid, stern, stable, sound, and steadfastly one-dimensional and thrives as a national icon. In *Robin Hood,* Flynn smiles and smirks and conquers hearts. But Shearer, from the beginning to the sad and emotional climax, grows and grows in her increasingly complex characterization of a multi-dimensional Marie Antoinette. She takes her portrayal well beyond the cartoon caricature that history and popular culture have made of the actual person.

Norma Shearer may be dressed to say "Let them eat cake," but her performance in the title role of *Marie Antoinette* (W. S. Van Dyke, MGM) is multi-faceted and poignant. Collection Ina Rae Hark.

No doubt, Shearer gains enormous support from an outstanding cast. Her portrayal of Marie Antoinette intensifies through successive encounters with other performers. First, as the young princess she must face the disappointment of her marriage to the prince, brilliantly played by Robert Morley as a thoroughly inept and incompetent but ultimately sympathetic and brave husband and father. John Barrymore's ferocity and power as

King Louis XV further tests and challenges her growth, as does her betrayal by a false ally, the Duke of Orleans (Joseph Schildkraut). Each of these encounters involves a stage in her development. Shearer combines vulnerability, innocence, ambition, charm, and humor in her portrayal.

By the time Marie meets her ultimate romantic partner in the film, Count Axel de Fersen (Tyrone Power), she becomes thoroughly convincing in being both supremely powerful as a beautiful, brilliant, and charming woman of passion and conviction and thoroughly defenseless in an impossible personal and political situation. When she first meets de Fersen, she already has become alienated from and disenchanted with her situation in the court. However, in the scene she triumphs as a genuine charmer and flirt, a royal party girl of her era. There is with Shearer here none of the anguished self-absorption of Greta Garbo or the demonic glaring of Marlene Dietrich, only a quality of giddy laughter with a compelling suggestion of deeper desperation and sadness as she plays and teases with Power. At the end, her portrayal of the horror of the destruction of her family and her own life achieves a real operatic quality of emotional catastrophe.

As part of its construction of sympathy for Marie Antoinette and her royal family, the film only vaguely relates the actual nightmare existence for the vast majority of people who lived and suffered under the rule of this French tyranny. As Barrymore's Louis proclaims (reading the line as if it were entirely his own idea and no one had ever heard it before), "Apres moi, le deluge!"

In one of *Marie Antoinette*'s few attempts to describe the underlying conditions that helped cause the revolution that Louis XV predicts, the film conflates the history of its own time of production during America's Great Depression and the historical period it portrays in late-eighteenth-century France. In an accelerated montage of shots, it renders close-ups and group shots of the misery, deprivation, and starvation of the masses. The editing technique reflects a kind of Russian montage sensibility with all its political implications, using sequences of images to convey powerful political facts and realities for the purpose of influencing ideas and emotions. It was a familiar cinematic style that clearly commented upon current conditions in Depression-era America but offered little enlightenment about the realities of Marie Antoinette's France that led to a plague of decapitations.

Comedies of Containment and Insanity

Among the year's many comedies, the category of the comedy of containment demonstrates something of a response to economic conditions but employs a process of irony and humor that provides distance and detachment from any expression of general rebellion and opposition to the rich and powerful. The films in this grouping recognize the economic crisis of the Depression in America but blunt criticism of the rich by treating them as figures who in general are not to be taken seriously. Two films in this category are *The Mad Miss Manton* and *A Slight Case of Murder*. Like the romantic and historical melodramas of maintenance and hierarchy *Robin Hood* and *Marie Antoinette,* the comedies of containment are thoroughly conservative in absorbing and assimilating into the existing social order any potential criticism of the economic system and the upper class. The films use the devices of humor, emotion, and sentiment in their narrative structures and characterizations to achieve their conservative ends.

A second form of comedy in this category of comedic films—the insanity comedy—involves a more complex comedic involvement with reality and events of the times by dramatizing a level of incoherence and incongruity that literally borders on the insane. A classic representative of the genre is the screwball comedy *Bringing Up Baby*. Coupled with another major film of the year, *You Can't Take It with You,* the conventional and accepted epithet for this form of comedy as screwball probably fails to do justice to the extent of the break from reality these films exhibit. Both *Bringing Up Baby* and *You Can't Take It with You* represent an extreme form of escapism.

In the films of comic containment, the only people who lose their heads tend to do so figuratively through excessive emotions involving such matters as love, ambition, or greed. In *A Slight Case of Murder,* Edward G. Robinson parodies the criminal stereotype he helped create by portraying Remy Marco, a reformed gangster in the post-Prohibition era who turns legitimate by distilling a gross-tasting beer, as opposed to upscale Remy cognac. The film continues a subgenre of gangster comedy that Robinson also helped to create and perpetuate, as in this year's *The Amazing Dr. Clitterhouse*. In this example of such a comedy, the poor quality of Marco's beer becomes a synecdoche for his attempt to move his whole family and his gang into respectable society. The film stays true in language and tone to the original Damon Runyon/Howard Lindsay play. The film, however, strikes a special chord in its insinuation of the Jewish origins of the character, not unlike Robinson himself, who was born Emmanuel Goldenberg in Bucharest, Romania, and became, like Paul Muni (a Jew originally from Austria), one of Hollywood's most celebrated actors. The comedy here contrasts with the classic gangster seriousness of the year's *Angels with Dirty Faces* starring James Cagney and Pat O'Brien.

Gangster Remy Marco (Edward G. Robinson, right) goes legit after the end of Prohibition, but the straight and narrow proves much more complicated than a straightforward life of crime. Here he seeks advice from henchman Mike (Allen Jenkins) and his wife Nora (Ruth Donnelly) in *A Slight Case of Murder* (Lloyd Bacon, Warner Bros.). Collection Ina Rae Hark.

Early in the film, Remy takes his wife, Mora (Ruth Donnelly), and daughter, Mary (Jane Bryan), to the "Star of Good Hope Orphanage" and recalls his own past there, clearly connecting the orphanage to historic Jewish settlement houses and orphanages of New York's Lower East Side, such as the Grand Street Settlement House and the Educational Alliance. He gives a speech to the assembled youth, including one prominently positioned African American boy, that begins, "Look here you mugs!" and then insists upon assuming responsibility for the most difficult juvenile delinquent there. He says to the matron, "I don't want the best. I want the worst. You know some little mutt that nobody else wants. I wanna give him a chance, see. . . . I wanna mold him, see!" The boy he gets is Douglas Fairbanks Rosenbloom (Bobby Jordan). As with his own name, this name also symbolizes change, an attempt to suggest through humor the potential of overcoming differences and inequality through classic American melding and transformation. As the plot unravels, Remy and his family and his gang overcome all obstacles. His gracious and educated daughter marries the rich man's son, Dick Whitewood (Willard Parker), who has fallen in love with her, and both families become reconciled to each other. Robinson's grandiosity as an actor incorporates religious, economic, and social differences. Humor, fed and energized by American optimism, ameliorates all serious differences and antagonisms.

Similarly, in *The Mad Miss Manton*, Peter Ames (Henry Fonda) and Melsa Manton (Barbara Stanwyck) find that romantic comedy also can triumph over class and economic differences. Peter is a newspaper editor who attacks and belittles the public behavior of Melsa, an heiress known for her antics with her similarly rich and prominent girlfriends. The pretense for action involves Melsa's discovery of a body that then disappears to the extreme annoyance of the detective in charge, Lieutenant Brent, played with typical style and exuberance by Sam Levene. More important than the murder mystery, the real plot focuses, of course, on teaching Peter to overcome his prejudices against the rich. In fact, he succeeds so well in overcoming his disdain for the leisure class that at the end of the movie when the mystery is solved, he speaks the film's funniest lines. He proposes to Melsa, suggesting they go to South America for six months, maybe more. "Can you afford it?" she asks, to which he answers, "No, but you can!" Melsa responds with emphatic speech and physical gestures: "Isn't there a drop of red blood in your veins?" Professing a sentimental, old-fashioned attitude toward marriage, she says, "I want to live on your income." Peter realizes the ludicrousness of that idea: "That's foolish. Who's going to live on yours?"

While the film repeatedly acknowledges the realities of economic differences and the deprivations of poverty in the era of the Depression, comedy and attitude form a bridge to contain the potential for violence and radical change. Peter's concluding lines in the film signify his conversion to a confident, uninhibited, unapologetic acceptance of privilege, class, leisure, luxury, and self-indulgence—all the things he opposed at the beginning. The police serve as a protection not against injustice and real crime but against things getting too ponderously and boringly serious. Humor also attempts to bridge racial difference here but ultimately fails. Hattie McDaniel, in her role as Melsa's maid, Hilda, operates with some degree of at least temperamental independence, so that Melsa says, "In my home, the revolution is here."

The second category of comedy films insinuates a deeper, more complex relationship to reality and experience by seeming to question the capacity and perhaps even the value of any attempt to deal rationally and coherently with the most ordinary and accessible kinds of daily and immediate experience. Interestingly, widely celebrated at the time and still treated with serious regard and respect by historians and critics, Capra's *You Can't Take It with You* departs significantly from strict screwball comedy, a form Capra helped invent and pioneer. Screwball comedy involves a hyperactive romantic relationship between a woman, who is usually notoriously independent for her time and place, and a male counterpart who tries to deal with her independence. The Great Depression provides a background for the zany antics and pungent dialogue that characterize the romantic relationship. In *You Can't Take It with You*, Capra takes this comedic form in another (and extreme) direction to argue that spontaneity, creativity, impulsive gratification, and self-indulgent expressionism help achieve happiness and even mental and physical health. As James Harvey indicates, in this Capra movie, the dramatic tension shifts from the lovers, Alice Sycamore (Jean Arthur), the secretary, and Tony Kirby (James Stewart), the boss's son, to the boss and father, Anthony P. Kirby (Edward Arnold), a stereotypical Capra villain, the very personification of the evils of capitalistic greed and masculine domination (148). Attention also focuses on the differences between both families, the eminently respectable and prominent Kirby family of Stewart and Arnold and the completely chaotic and madcap Sycamores, as inspired and guided by the insouciant leader of the family, the grandfather Martin Vanderhof (Lionel Barrymore).

Beneath Barrymore's benign and paternalistic visage of approval and Arthur's charmingly gracious smile of tolerance and acceptance, the supporting cast of outstanding veteran character actors engage in activities that exceed mere eccentricity to verge on the appearance of genuine lunacy. Harvey describes them as "the happy loony Sycamore family" (148). While some still find real humor and fun in the antics and shenanigans of the Sycamores that go on throughout the entire film, a split in the psyche of the film compares to the psychological divisions of the characters themselves. In other words, even Tony's true love of Alice could not blind him to the madness of her family. Alice herself worries about how the family would present itself to the rest of the world, especially her would-be in-laws, the Kirbys. In this household, grown men set off fireworks that explode indoors and rockets soar from the basement. A grown daughter, Essie (Ann Miller), dances around the house with repetitious enthusiasm, endlessly entertaining herself like a crazy person moving through an asylum, while her husband, Ed (Dub Taylor), hammers out his newest tune on his xylophone. Persistent intrusions occur throughout the film, dissimulating madness and hysteria as eccentric, free-spirited humor, what Harvey terms "happy bedlam" (150), stretching to an unreasonable degree the bounds of credulity. Capra tries to present the Sycamore household as an exaggerated version of real-life values and attitudes that can offer an alternative to the predatory business ethic of Kirby. As Charles Maland says, "Capra aptly described the conflict between Grandpa Vanderhof and Kirby as a clash of two philosophies: 'Devour thy neighbor versus love thy neighbor'" (*Capra* 103). However, it can be argued that the attempt to impose this kind of ideological material on such a weak structure as the insanity and absurdity of the Sycamore household dooms both the message of positive, humanistic values and the strained effort at humor. In contrast to other Capra triumphs of moral renewal, the attempt here to persuade the viewer that Kirby has undergone a transformation from ill-tempered, ruthless businessman to joyful benefactor fails. Aesthetic incoherence in the portrayal of the characters and in narrative development in Robert Riskin's screenplay and Capra's direction weakens and cripples the moral argument.

In contrast, absolute coherence of tone, voice, language, and intention make the insanity thoroughly believable, charming, and workable in Howard Hawks's prototypical screwball comedy, *Bringing Up Baby*. The film shows how a naive and stuffy paleontologist's involvement with a daffy socialite, her pet leopard (the baby of the title), and the search for the intercostal clavicle bone necessary to complete his dinosaur skeleton leaves his career in ruins but his heart and soul liberated. Structural tightness and efficiency enable it to achieve and fulfill its artistic promise. Hawks's refusal to apologize for the insanity, incongruity, and incoherence of the dialogue, as well as the relationships, events, actions, and characters, maintains the consistency of the comedic form. Hawks could, as he said, make "all the characters crazy" largely because his two stars, Cary Grant and Katharine Hepburn, were geniuses as actors who suffused the screen with so much charm, charisma, energy, and authenticity that they were able to sweep up in the insanity the rest of their outstanding cast as well as generations of audiences (McCarthy 285). Ironically, they turned the situation inside out and normalized insanity. Although *Bringing Up Baby* was only one of a popular new genre of screwball film comedies, its genuinely insane quality distinguishes it from the others. Hawks, Hepburn, and Grant took the genre to an extreme that even Hawks hesitated to repeat. Moreover, it would be hard to exaggerate the power of the legendary chemistry between Hepburn and Grant. With them the ludicrousness of singing to leopards, of a man dressing in a negligee and calling himself "gay" without elaboration, of tearing the backside of an evening gown to expose underwear, of innumerable goofy reactions to thoroughly incongruous female verbal and physical attacks, of executing startling physical moves for laughs all make this film form of insanity a perfect means for escape.

■■■■■■■■■■ **Dramas of Entrapment and Oppression**

Escape also occupies the concerns of many films in the final category of entrapment and oppression, which includes those with stories and situations of various forms of imprisonment, enclosure, and danger. In these films, diverse internal and external forces subdue, control, and dominate the characters. Two exemplary films in this group are *Jezebel* and *Algiers,* but others include *The Sisters, Four Daughters, Angels with Dirty Faces,* and the two films already noted as being concerned about the situation in Europe, *Blockade* and *Three Comrades.* The films vary as to the causes of confinement from crime and justice, to internal psychological dynamics, to war and public violence, to repressive forces of race, gender, ethnicity, and sexuality, but they all radically differ in mood from the films of comedic containment.

Bette Davis triumphs in *Jezebel,* whose drama of entrapment concerns New Orleans under siege by a yellow fever epidemic that decimates the city's population. The fever obviously symbolizes the deeper social and psychological trauma of racial, sexual, and social values and institutions that become another form of suffocating imprisonment through their crippling incapacity to deal with change and reform. *Jezebel* has become a Hollywood legend for being offered to Davis as compensation for not getting to play Scarlett O'Hara, the heroine of *Gone with the Wind.* Like Scarlett, Davis's Julie Marsden is a spoiled, inconsiderate, and rebellious young woman whose selfish actions manage to alienate her two suitors. It is only when the fever sickens the man she truly loves, Preston Dillard (Henry Fonda), that Julie's pride and willfulness are broken, and she risks infection herself in a redemptive gesture that has her accompanying Pres to quarantine in order to nurse him. In spite of its extravagant melodrama and stylistic excesses, scene after scene deserves detailed attention and respect for the awesome performances of the stars, Davis as the quintessential southern belle and Fonda as the southerner (or, perhaps more accurately, the archetypal "New" southerner) with Yankee values and business instinct. Also excellent are the performances of the supporting cast, including George Brent as a thoroughly convincing personification of Buck Cantrell, a blend of southern pride and manhood, arrogance and courtliness, gentility and brutality, and the charming Fay Bainter, playing Julie's Aunt Belle Massey, who watches helplessly as Julie's destructive pattern of pride and anger destroys her happiness. Toward the end, Aunt Belle seems to gain insight at last into a similar pattern of blind self-destruction for her native region of the South and appears equally helpless and lost. As an indication of his

Julie Marsden (Bette Davis, center) likes to be the center of attention, but her Aunt Belle (Fay Bainter, left) and suitor Buck Cantrell (George Brent, right) are not totally charmed by her headstrong ways in *Jezebel* (William Wyler, Warner Bros.). Collection Ina Rae Hark.

affection and regard for Davis, William Wyler's brilliant direction helps the performances triumph over the film's self-indulgence and excesses.

On the face of it, the most famous scene in the film would seem impossible to execute because so much personal and family disaster must result from what appears to be a trivial action. In the scene at the Olympus Ball, Davis wears a gorgeous but outrageous red dress to a ball when only pure white gowns are acceptable for virginal southern belles. However, as Wyler shoots and directs and organizes the scene with Davis and Fonda, it becomes an unforgettable and historic Hollywood event. As Jan Herman writes, "Were it not for Wyler's creative imagination, however, *Jezebel* would not have the sweep, the size or grandeur that make it so impressive even today. A case in point is the movie's pivotal Olympus ball sequence, which launches Julie on her headlong rush to destruction. It not only highlights Davis's formidable performance but underscores the movie's themes about Southern chivalry and male honor, social convention and the price of defiance" (180). Davis graciously acknowledged the importance of Wyler to her success in the role and her development as an actress: "He made my performance. It was all Wyler. I had known all the horrors of no direction and bad direction. I now knew what a great director was and what he could mean to an actress. . . . Willy really is responsible for the fact that I became a box-office star" (182).

At first, the reaction of offended guests to Davis and the dress seems predictable, but then the scene becomes Fonda's and Davis's special moment. Fueled by his anger and frustration over Julie's own behavior, Pres refuses to back down, while Julie suffers unspeakable public humiliation. The scene becomes an in-depth study of both characters. Wyler engineers the shots from close-ups to long shots to make the extraordinary performances powerful. In addition, Wyler achieves a kind of double vision and staging in the scene as the people at the ball become an audience to Julie's and Pres's battle of wills. Their look upon the couple also increases the tension of the scene. The multiplicity of looks and perspectives help generate the emotional energy and social friction that make the scene so legendary in film history. Interactions between Buck and Pres over southern values and standards and Julie's perverse manipulations of people's lives achieve comparable authenticity and intensity throughout the film.

At the very heart of the film, *Jezebel* exposes the complexity of the representation and situation of Blacks in film. In this film about the collapse of southern culture because of its resistance to change and its prejudices, Blacks appear on the screen replicating to a certain degree the humiliation and dehumanization of the characters they portray. This representation constitutes a powerful comment on both antebellum southern society and contemporary America. Thus, Eddie Anderson plays Julie's slave, who devotedly takes her through an infested swamp to find Pres; Theresa Harris plays the ineffective maid for Julie, just as McDaniel plays the maid for Melsa in *The Mad Miss Manton* (Bogle 79, 81). Stymie Beard, one of Hollywood's often seen black children, simply occupies space to create amusement in the film.

However, in one scene an amazing visual interaction occurs. As internecine hostility intensifies to the point of duels and other disastrous discord among the whites, Bainter's face, reaction, and body movement indicate Aunt Belle's growing understanding of the situation of chaos and impending disaster for her family and the South. On the verge of a duel to be fought between Pres's brother Ted (Richard Cromwell) and Buck that was precipitated by Julie's rash behavior, Julie moves toward celebrating black children and adults to lead them in their singing "Raise a Ruckus." The singing gets louder and the physical action grows more animated as Julie herself becomes louder and more frenetic. Belle looks on the scene of near madness with helpless sadness. Her look establishes a connection between herself and the black singers, signaling an awareness at some level of the gap between reality and behavior both races share in the scene. Belle proffers a prophetic glance of recognition that slaves and masters are caught in a common madness that can lead only to disaster.

To add to the complexity of the significance of such portrayals of Blacks in Hollywood film, Wyler was considered a liberal and sympathetic to the mistreatment of African Americans. At one point, after Pres has returned from the North with his new wife, Wyler has him attempt the unthinkable act of sharing a drink with the totally devoted house slave, Uncle Cato (Lou Payton). Because of the special occasion of his return, Pres holds up a glass and asks Cato if he will join him in "one" and the slave awkwardly responds, "It ain't hardly proper." He then adds, "I will kindly take one out in the pantry and bless you and Miss Julie." As Herman writes,

> The picture's idealization of the South cannot help but seem a Hollywood cliché. Also, there are blatant examples of racist stereotyping characteristic of movies in the thirties. *Jezebel* features a large contingent of happy plantation "pickaninnies." But if the picture can hardly be said to escape the era's paternalistic racism toward Blacks, Wyler went out of his way to humanize them. In addition, he bolsters the political themes of North vs. South and abolition vs. slavery with a debate of ideas during a powerfully staged dinner sequence. The scene illuminates the psychology of individual characters and spells out why Southern society as a whole was doomed to crumble with or without the Civil War. (179)

The amazing scene of the attempt at human conversation between Cato the servant and Pres precedes another one when Julie, not realizing Pres has married, appears in a remarkable white dress and kneels to beg Pres's forgiveness and love: "Pres, I'm kneeling to you, to ask you to forgive me, and to love me as I love you." Failing to win him back, Julie later corners him alone outside the house and proclaims their shared entrapment in the South. She insists that Pres returned because both she and the South are in his blood and cannot be escaped. Such fatalism offers little chance for escape or redemption in the film, so that even Julie's heroics at the end to sacrifice herself to help Pres, who has been stricken with fever, seem false and motivated more by her own inescapable self-obsession than her professed desire to redeem herself.

While *Jezebel* constitutes a look backward on a dying culture, *Algiers* anticipates the advent of a future society of rebels, strangers, and internal adversaries. An American remake of Julien Duvivier's *Pepe Le Moko* (1937), which starred Jean Gabin, *Algiers,* directed by John Cromwell, constitutes a significant turn and development in the popular cult of the criminal in Hollywood film, a kind Europeanized version of the gangster hero. It tells of a master jewel thief, Pepe (Charles Boyer), who eludes capture by North African police by hiding out in the notorious Casbah district of the city of Algiers, until his love for a beautiful Parisian woman, Gaby (Hedy Lamarr), spells his undoing. In this film, the criminal as outsider turns into the ultimate insider. When Hollywood makes the criminal a film's protagonist, such as Cagney in *Angels with Dirty Faces,* he often acts as an extension and extreme version of the society as a whole, a kind of perverted exaggeration of the elements in respectable and legal society. Robert Sklar opines on the significance of the figure of the gangster in American film and culture:

> In 1929, the gangster for the first time surpassed the cowboy as a subject for Hollywood filmmakers. This may be one of the overlooked watersheds of American cultural history. In commercial popular culture, this ranks with— and perhaps completes—the historian Frederick Jackson Turner's declaration at the end of the previous century that the time of the frontier had passed. The concept of frontier remains perhaps the strongest and most enduring of American national metaphors, but by the end of the 1920s a rapidly urbanizing society had begun to assert its distinctive qualities fully, perhaps predominantly, into imaginative life.   (*City Boys* 8)

Sklar adds that "the gangster came to represent the city even more than such other urban figures as the corporate businessman, the socialite, or the cop and the private eye" (*City Boys* 9). Sklar's linkage of the criminal and gangster with these other prototypes of modern American character indicates the centrality of this personality type to understanding American film and culture. Thus, even as an antihero, the criminal figure remains part of the larger society and interacts with it. At times, as an oppositional figure, the criminal in his negativity helps define respectable and conventional culture. He often simply wants to be bigger and better than his adversaries on the other side of the law, implying that he is a metaphor for the capitalism, violence, and aggressiveness of the dominant society. Sometimes portrayed as an actual underdog, the criminal in Hollywood wants a piece of the action, what everyone else in society seems to have and enjoy. In this sense, Robinson's comic gangster in *A Slight Case of Murder* really personifies in a humorous fashion the serious aspect of the idea in gangster films of the wish to belong and be part of society as a whole. Such sentiment also encourages the treatment of the gangster, even when truly violent and dangerous, as himself a victim of the society that excludes him or of his own uncontrollable inner needs and urges.

In this history and understanding of the gangster, the emergence of Pepe le Moko as a gangster hero represents a change perhaps of comparable importance to the transition that Sklar describes. In the most inner of inner cities in the Casbah, Pepe also operates as a truly inner man. He has isolated and imprisoned himself to escape capture by the police. But he also remains his own authority and law within his domain, an untouchable for the French and Algerian authorities, who consequently obsess on seeking him out in order to arrest him and devalue his legendary successes that occur at the expense of their own authority and reputation. However, Pepe cannot be caught. He only can surrender to his own emotions and needs.

Accordingly, Pepe's physical separation constitutes an external representation of an inner, spiritual, and ultimately philosophical and religious separation from the dominant society. This difference puts Pepe out of reach not only physically but temporally as well, at least in terms of America. He actually exists in a time that had not yet come to America. He anticipates a later generation of American outsiders, "beats" or cultural "refuseniks" who live and think in something like an internal country with a counterculture of values and ambitions. The classic American gangsters that Sklar and others study are city heroes in the true sense of wanting to be out and to be seen as tough and prominent as any American who was given privilege, success, and power through birth. Pepe le Moko only laughs at such dependence upon social acceptance and approval. He yearns for Paris as a return to the primary source of alienated energy, not as an arena for entertainment and exhibitionism. Both as the gangster figure and as the comic version of that personality, Robinson's search for recognition and assimilation are foreign to Boyer's character. Pepe personifies a hero of modernism in his embodiment of internal resistance to corporate, social, elitist values of the dominant society. He seemed strange and exotic in the Casbah with his friends and a variety of women even more exotic and fascinating than himself. But a generation later, he would become a movement of rebellion and dissidence.

The freedom that Pepe represents also includes its own contradictions that undermine it. As much as he maintains his independence, he also faces the crisis of modern man's freedom. As Emmanuel Levinas writes, "The modern is constituted by the consciousness of a certain definitively acquired freedom. Everything is possible and everything is permitted, for nothing, absolutely speaking, precedes this freedom. It is a freedom that does not bow before any factual state, thus negating the 'already done' and living only from the new. But it is a freedom with which no memory interferes, a freedom upon which no past weighs" (124). Such freedom Pepe enjoys. In his freedom, he exhibits a certain kind of modern soullessness that leaves him vulnerable and without inner resources when truly challenged.

Ultimately, Pepe succumbs to Gaby, a woman from the outside, the consort of rich men she disdains; she appropriately and ironically represents a female counter-image and counterpart to Pepe's isolation. She carries her own internal Casbah of detachment and distance that makes her as emotionally and morally independent and autonomous as Pepe but equally vulnerable. Significantly, his betrayal also comes at the hands of the Algerian woman, Ines (Sigrid Gurie), who loves him enough to destroy him out of jealousy, passion, and possessiveness. Her values and love are instinctive, tribal, vital, and irrational. Ultimately, such love of clinging dependence proves as destructive as Pepe's independence. He is also betrayed by Slimane (Joseph Calleia), the native policeman who acts as a friendly adversary but lies to tempt him from his secure domain in the Casbah.

The cruelty, dishonesty, and injustice of the world outside the Casbah make that world no better or more moral than Pepe's. In fact, like a true Hemingway hero of the night, the boxing ring, or the bullring, Pepe would retain his autonomy without ever betraying a friend. Survival in the Casbah necessitates such loyalty beyond the law. At one point, Pepe advises a young man, Pierrot (Johnny Downs), not to "hang around so much with your friend Regis" (Gene Lockhart), an untrustworthy character. To Pepe, young Pierrot is like the classic Hemingway apprentice figure in need of training and guidance from an older, more experienced man. Pepe explains, "Did you ever see a clock that pointed to two but struck four when it is really quarter past twelve? Well your friend Regis is like that. He doesn't ring true." As Pepe expatiates upon true friends, the detective Slimane sits behind him in the background perfectly aware of the accuracy of Pepe's words and Regis's readiness to join in any plan to deceive and capture both Pierrot and Pepe. Equally memorable is the criminal examination and trial of Regis by Pepe and his friends after Pierrot has been deceived and betrayed. It is the Casbah's version of criminal justice from the inside without the pretense of legal guarantees and rights that dissimulate the actual inequality and injustice of the system. A world hidden within the streets and alleys of the Casbah has its makeshift trials and impulsive justice that compare to the chaos of its relationships and beliefs and values.

Of course, the physical magnetism, sensuality, and emotional compatibility between Boyer and Lamarr create the film's greatest tension and attraction. While Ines and her friends from the Casbah belong there, ultimately Pepe and Gaby really belong nowhere and therefore, ironically, have no place to go for each other in their perverse freedom. The betrayal of Pepe by those closest to him only accelerates the inevitable catastrophe. Knowing to distrust all truths and beliefs including his own, Pepe nevertheless decides he must believe in something beside himself and goes to his doom, chasing Gaby who also has been deceived to think he is dead. Gaby neither hears nor sees Pepe cry out to her as a policeman shoots him, mistakenly thinking he is trying to flee. His final words declare his ultimate escape through death.

Free of his entrapment in the Casbah, Pepe's journey through hell ends on an Algerian dock. For many in America and the world, the journey was just beginning.

1939

Movies and American Culture in the *Annus Mirabilis*

CHARLES MALAND

Conventional wisdom says that this was the *annus mirabilis*—the year of wonder, a time of remarkable achievement—in Hollywood movies. The industry itself initiated the claim even before the fact. Responding partly to an antitrust suit filed against five studios, the Academy launched a campaign called "Motion Pictures' Greatest Year" for the 1938–39 release schedule. Over 150 mayors and governors issued proclamations recognizing the campaign (Thorp 50). Later commentators have shifted a half-year to fix on the movies of 1939. In 1975, in just the third issue of *American Film,* Larry Swindell observed that the supremacy of the year's movies was "common knowledge" (24). A book on movies from "Scarface to Scarlett" said that the movies of this year "reached a fabulous zenith it was never again to attain" (Dooley 611). A historian of the era agreed: "There are good reasons for selecting 1939 as the greatest year in Hollywood history" (Bolino 109). When the assessment even makes it to the reference shelves, we know it is deeply embedded: a recent reference book on American movies asserted that in this year the studio system reached "its peak year of artistic success, as Hollywood release[d] a record number of critically acclaimed films" (Corey and Ochoa 59).

While it is tempting to get swept up in all the praise, in this chapter we look more closely at American culture, the Hollywood film business, and the movies from other perspectives. We can call this year the *annus mirabilis,* but more accurately if we use that term as *The American Heritage Dictionary* defines it, as a "year of wonders or disasters; a fateful year." The year was one of achievement and crisis, both in the movie industry and the broader culture, and the sense of crisis shook Hollywood loose, however tentatively, from its public position that its sole commitment was to entertain moviegoers by suggesting that movies might also serve a larger social purpose. Following an overview that will help us understand how in this year the tension between entertainment and social engagement came about, and how the studios responded to it, this chapter will focus on six films that draw on some of the year's key genres and stars and that indicate a variety of ways that movies during that year sought to engage (or not) with some of the central social concerns of the era.

American Culture and Crisis

As a decade of economic distress and domestic social reform moved toward its conclusion, many Americans became more concerned about international affairs. In Richard Pells's words, "Inexorably, the crisis in Europe and the Far East supplanted the depression as the decade's major concern" (293). Certainly the zeal for New Deal reform had diminished by this year. One historian of the era puts it simply: "By 1939 the New Deal as a source of innovation was through" (McElvaine 307). Several legislative actions in this year emphasized the decline. After considerable controversy, the Federal Theatre Project lost its funding because of what Republicans (and some Democrats) perceived as its partisan activity. The Hatch Act, which forbade all political activities by federal employees, was in some ways a response to political activism by members of government programs like the Federal Theatre Project. Another sign of the times was the Relief Act of 1939, which required that all WPA workers employed for eighteen or more consecutive months be fired. Even though unemployment remained at 17 percent at the end of the year, more than 775,000 WPA workers were dismissed in July and August (McElvaine 308).

When Americans wanted to turn away from their troubles, they could read everything from the new Batman comic books or impressive modernist novels such as *Finnegan's Wake, The Day of the Locust, Tropic of Capricorn,* or *The Grapes of Wrath.* Theatergoers could attend *The Little Foxes, The Philadelphia Story, The Man Who Came to Dinner,* or *Key Largo.* The radio provided Edward R. Murrow's broadcasts from London and Frank Sinatra singing with the Harry James Band. And if one really wanted to get away from it all, commercial transatlantic passenger air service was inaugurated, although that sort of trip was leaving the frying pan for the fire.

The thirty-two-month Spanish Civil War ended in late March when the Loyalists surrendered to forces led by Generalissimo Francisco Franco and aided by Hitler and Mussolini, after deaths in the hundreds of thousands had occurred (Bolino 223–26). Even more troubling to many Americans was German expansionism. In March German soldiers goose-stepped into Czechoslovakia after Hitler offered the Czech president a choice between surrender and annihilation. Despite a letter of protest from President

Franklin D. Roosevelt in April calling Germany and Italy to agree to a ten-year guarantee of peace, and despite the efforts of British diplomats throughout the summer to work out a peace agreement with Germany, Hitler formalized a military alliance with Mussolini in May, then shockingly signed a non-aggression pact with the Soviet Union on 23 August. On 1 September, German forces invaded Poland and quickly overran the country, splitting it with the Soviet Union. In response to the German invasion, England and France declared war on the Axis powers, and World War II began (Barone 129–31). For much of the rest of the year, an "eerie lull" characterized the conflict—Senator William Borah of Idaho went so far as to mock it as a "phony war"—until Russia invaded Finland at the end of November (Kennedy 434–35). Hitler's fearsome European *blitzkrieg* would follow months later.

The American response split between the isolationists and the internationalists. Despite warning the American people about the rising fascist threat and urging military preparedness, FDR was confronted with isolationist sentiment, strongest in the German American Upper Midwest, that hindered his desire to provide military support for England and France. As the events of the year moved forward, a vigorous national debate ensued; many internationalists held strong antifascist beliefs and believed that it could well become necessary for the United States to enter the war in support of England and France (Leuchtenberg 290–98). In addition, as the perceived threat of Nazi Germany grew, challenge from outside led to internal self-definition: Americans found themselves in the midst of a resurgent nationalism and a concerted effort to define the essence of American democratic traditions (Alexander). By the end of the year, Americans were uneasily balanced between hope and fear: "hope that with American help the Allies could defeat Hitler, and fear that events might yet suck the United States into the conflict" (Kennedy 434).

Movies and the "Genius of the System"

How did Hollywood fare during this year of crisis? On one hand, the studio system was a well-oiled machine by the end of the decade. Sound technology, including musical scoring, had been fully integrated into classical Hollywood filmmaking. Film music had become "the glue that joins scenes, the polish that brightens a point" (Bordwell et al. 303). Faster black-and-white film stocks like Eastman Plus X had become available, making a crisper image and deep-focus cinematography more possible, and Technicolor stock was beginning to be used in some genres like musicals and historical epics. Finally, by this year the large studios had separate special effects departments capable of working with miniature sets, process cinematography, full-size composites, matte paintings, and other optical effects (Bordwell et al. 343, 353–57, 324), leading to memorable scenes like the tornado in *The Wizard of Oz* or the siege of Atlanta in *Gone with the Wind*. Commenting on the American film industry during this period, André Bazin urged cineastes to "admire in it what is most admirable, i.e., not only the talent of this or that filmmaker but the genius of the system" (154).

Marketing films by genre, star, and sometimes director or producer, Hollywood's output in this year was remarkable by almost any standard. Two big films set in the American past were based on popular novels: *Gone with the Wind* (GWTW) and *Drums Along the Mohawk*. Crime, gangster, and action films included *The Roaring Twenties, Each Dawn I Die, They Made Me a Criminal, Golden Boy*, and Howard Hawks's *Only Angels Have Wings*. Musicals appeared: *The Wizard of Oz*, the Rooney-Garland *Babes in Arms*, the Astaire-Rogers *Story of Vernon and Irene Castle*, and *Hollywood Cavalcade*. "A" westerns experienced a resurgence in *Stagecoach, Jesse James, Dodge City, Union Pacific, Destry Rides Again*, and *Oklahoma Kid* (starring Jimmy Cagney!). Women's melodramas included *Dark Victory, The Old Maid* (both Bette Davis vehicles), Leo McCarey's *Love Affair, Midnight*, and *The Women*. Adaptations of classic or modern literature were issued: *Wuthering Heights, The Hunchback of Notre Dame, Huckleberry Finn, Of Mice and Men*, and *Goodbye Mr. Chips*. Screwball comedies included *Ninotchka, Made for Each Other*, and Frank Capra's *Mr. Smith Goes to Washington*. Colonialist dramas did well: *Stanley and Livingstone, Gunga Din*, and *Beau Geste*. Biopics included *Juarez, Young Mr. Lincoln*, and *The Story of Alexander Graham Bell*. Two of the most profitable lower-budget series featured Sherlock Holmes (Basil Rathbone) and Andy Hardy (Mickey Rooney).

Variety reported that the three stars whose films made the most money this year were Mickey Rooney, Jimmy Stewart, and Bette Davis (Ungar 1, 28–29), although Clark Gable would certainly have been on the list if *GWTW* had not been released in late December. To give a sense of what films the trade press admired, we can note that *Film Daily* named these to its Ten Best List: *Goodbye, Mr. Chips, Stanley and Livingstone, Mr. Smith Goes to Washington, The Wizard of Oz, Dark Victory, Wuthering Heights, Pygmalion* (released in December 1938), *The Women, Juarez*, and *The Old Maid*.

Despite the output, however, the year was also a trying one for the industry. Summing it up in *Variety*, Roy Chartier wrote, "As another year is left behind, the clouds of war hang menacingly over the entire world, and the picture industry, a world enterprise of fabulous stature, prepares to steel itself, not only against the threats of disturbance originating abroad but also against the blows that are being struck it at home" ("Year" 5). Hollywood counted on foreign income for 40–45 percent of its revenues, and the loss of much European revenue because of the war was forcing the industry to try to make up those losses by belt-tightening, increasing domestic ticket prices, and expanding South American revenues. Chartier wrote that the Justice Department's antitrust suit against the majors, filed the previous year, is "No. 1 on the list of current nightmares" but that producers and distributors were also losing sleep over the Neely Bill, a bill before Congress that proposed to ban block-booking, and also over the expansion of union power in the industry (5).

Thus, despite impressive film output, the year was not as successful financially as it was aesthetically. Box office receipts were almost identical to the year before at $660 million, but combined corporate profits actually declined 13 percent from the previous year, to $19.4 million (Finler 32). Chartier's analysis of the year's box office results noted that even though "the quality of the product has been better than the same period last year," for various reasons "business has not jumped in recognition of the improvement shown" ("1939" 8). As we shall see, budgets for a number of prestige films like *Juarez* and *The Wizard of Oz* were so high that even though they generated considerable rentals, they were not especially profitable. War anxiety certainly contributed: according to Chartier, when the war broke out, attendance suffered because people "stayed at home glued to the radios to keep in touch with world events" (8).

"Harmless Entertainment" versus "The Social Import of the Art"

Hollywood industry spokesmen had long adhered to an ethic of "pure entertainment" and a view that Western Union—not movies—should deliver messages. Yet evidence suggests that this was a watershed year for Hollywood, one in which the industry became more receptive to films that dealt with topical social concerns. Leo Rosten, who was conducting a sociological study in Hollywood, sensed "an increased seriousness in the movie colony" during this time and, while admitting that "Hollywood still boasts an abundance of egomaniacs, buffoons, semi-literates, and persons of surpassing obnoxiousness," he also found filmmakers who felt "an urgency to put their visions on the screen" (28–29).

This change seems evident in President Will Hays's Annual Report to the Motion Picture Producers and Distributors of America. In the previous year's report Hays wrote that "in a period in which propaganda has largely reduced the artistic and entertainment validity of the screen in many other countries . . . American motion pictures continue to be free from any but the highest possible entertainment purpose." Just a year later, though, Hays reported that "the past year has been notable for the rising tide of discussion as to the social function of the screen. In a period of great tension in world affairs, the conflict of opinion, however, as between those who would preserve the motion picture theatre as a center of popular recreation and those who would emphasize the social import of the art was more often apparent than real" (qtd. in Thorp 274–75). Hays spoke approvingly of films "which dramatized present-day social conditions"; by doing so, according to Margaret Thorp, "the motion picture industry extended an official welcome to ideas" (276, 271). Thorp may have overstated the case, but such factors as growing anti-fascist political activism in Hollywood (Ceplair and Englund chap. 4), pressure from the left for movies to address real social concerns, the growing sense of foreign threat, and a resurgent American nationalism combined to put cracks in the wall of "pure entertainment" and offer opportunities for some filmmakers to explore more directly the "social function of the screen."

A useful way to see how this tension between pure entertainment and "social import" worked itself out in Hollywood is to look more closely at six films. Selecting the titles has been difficult, because choosing six means rejecting around 370 major studio features from the same year, including many that would be interesting to examine and some that may be among the favorites of many viewers. However, six films can give us a sense of the range and quality of the year's output in Hollywood. Discussed chronologically by date of release, they are *Stagecoach* (United Artists, released 15 March), a western directed by John Ford and produced by Walter Wanger; *Juarez* (Warner Bros., 26 April), a biopic featuring Paul Muni in the title role and Bette Davis as the Empress Carlotta; *Confessions of a Nazi Spy* (also Warner Bros., 27 April) , a topical story about the exposure of a Nazi spy ring in the United States, framed as a G-man story starring Edward G. Robinson; *The Wizard of Oz* (MGM, 17 August), the big budget Judy Garland musical based on the L. Frank Baum novel; *Mr. Smith Goes to Washington* (Columbia, 19 October), Frank Capra's signature blend of screwball comedy and social problem film, starring Jimmy Stewart; and *Gone with the Wind* (Selznick International, 19 December), the highly publicized adaptation of Margaret Mitchell's best-selling novel that also became the biggest grossing film of the decade. If we placed these six films on a spectrum from socially engaged films on one side and pure entertainment on the other, *Confessions of a Nazi Spy* would be toward the socially engaged side of the spectrum, followed by *Mr. Smith Goes to Washington*. *Juarez* and *Stagecoach,* as we shall see, are two historical genre films whose makers sought to comment directly on contemporary concerns through the filter of the past. *The Wizard of Oz* and *Gone with the Wind* depend more on spectacle and fall more toward the entertainment end of the spectrum.

■ A Closer Look: *Stagecoach* and *Juarez*

Stagecoach played a key role in resurrecting the "A" western, which in turn, according to Richard Slotkin, inaugurated a thirty-year period in which the genre offered the central popular forum "for the making of public myths and the symbolization of public ideology" (278). Besides its importance in the history of the genre, *Stagecoach* is the work of an auteur. Director John Ford—with the help of his frequent screenwriting collaborator, Dudley Nichols, cinematographer Bert Glennon, and others—was given creative control by independent producer Walter Wanger, who released the film through United Artists (Bernstein 147). Ford had directed many westerns during the silent era, but *Stagecoach* was his first in the sound era. Based on a short story by Ernest Haycox, the film contributed to the revitalization of American cultural mythology and the resurgent American nationalism so evident at the time. (Ford, indeed, worked overtime in searching for a usable American past this year. Besides the western, the Irish American director added two other such films: *Young Mr. Lincoln* and *Drums Along the Mohawk*.)

Ford was justly famous for narrative economy, his ability to tell stories with images and a minimum of dialogue, and the combination of complexity and clarity in *Stagecoach* offers an outstanding example of this. Three plot lines intersect: 1) a diverse group of people travel in a stagecoach from Tonto to Lordsburg during a time of Apache raids, eventually forming a temporary democratic community because of the external threat; 2) a "good/badman," the Ringo Kid (John Wayne, in his first A-film starring role), escapes from prison to confront three Plummer brothers and avenge the murders of his father and brother; and 3) a romance develops during the course of the journey between two social outcasts, Ringo and the prostitute Dallas (Claire Trevor). Each plot has its resolution: the group makes it safely to Lordsburg, although class difference and status distinctions reemerge upon arrival there; Ringo has a shootout with the three Plummers at night on the main street of Lordsburg; and, finally, the sheriff frees Ringo, enabling him to depart with Dallas to his ranch across the border.

In *Stagecoach* (John Ford, United Artists) the banker Gatewood (Berton Churchill, seated) and the gambler Hatfield (John Carradine) stare disapprovingly at Ringo and Dallas, while the pregnant Lucy Mallory (Louise Platt) looks down. These elitist "respectables" soon move to the opposite end of the table. Digital frame enlargement.

Besides the stagecoach driver, Buck (Andy Devine), and the shotgun-riding sheriff, Curly (George Bancroft), stagecoach riders include four "respectables"—Lucy Mallory (Louise Platt), a pregnant Virginian traveling to reunite with her cavalry officer husband; the Virginia aristocrat/gambler Hatfield (John Carradine); the blustery banker Gatewood (Berton Churchill); and Peacock (Donald Meek), a whiskey drummer—joined by three social outcasts—Ringo, Dallas, and the endearing drunken Doc Boone (Thomas Mitchell). In an oft-analyzed early scene, the first three respectables refuse to sit at a breakfast table near Dallas and Ringo. Yet Ford and screenwriter Dudley Nichols depict the outcasts (victims, says Doc, of "a foul disease called social prejudice") with consistent sympathy. Only after the respectables shed their prejudices, which happens, significantly, after Doc Boone sobers up and delivers Mrs. Mallory's baby, does a democratic community temporarily form.

The film's narrative is quick moving and suspenseful, the characterizations rich and diverse, but *Stagecoach* also has a social function: to affirm a public ideology best labeled progressive liberalism. A form of American liberalism most widely held between 1936 and the decade's end, it emerged largely through the popularity of FDR's "second New Deal" legislation (like the Social Security Act, the Wagner Act, and the WPA), designed to provide government support for those who were suffering most from the Depression.

Nichols was a progressive actively involved as president of the Screen Writers Guild, which was struggling to win studio recognition when he was working on the screenplay of the film, and Ford—often thought of as a patriotic conservative later in his life—probably was more sympathetic to leftist ideas around the time that he made it than at any other time of his life (Maland, "Ford" 49–58). Nichols invented two characters not found in the short story—Doc Boone and the banker Gatewood—who underpin the film's ideological perspective. Doc Boone, the humane intellectual, shows consistent support for Dallas and Ringo: he understands and analyzes the mean-spirited prejudice of the Ladies of the Law and Order League who banish Dallas from Tonto, and he sees beyond the lower social status of Dallas and Ringo to perceive their basic decency.

Gatewood, on the other hand, is the film's key antagonist: early in the film Ford includes two close-ups of him scowling, predisposing viewers to dislike him. On the stagecoach he blusters a Republican ideology that recalls Herbert Hoover ("What's good for the banks is good for the country") while carefully guarding a valise filled with money stolen from his depositors. In one of the film's most satisfying moments, Gatewood is arrested when the stagecoach reaches Lordsburg. In a long shot Ford shows Ringo sitting at the front of the stagecoach, looking down at and talking to Curly. The Lordsburg sheriff enters from screen left. We see him carrying handcuffs—apparently meant for Ringo—and he asks Curly if he should take the prisoner. Curly says he doesn't need the handcuffs, but Gatewood, also entering screen left, sticks his nose in and insists, "If you don't want to lose your prisoner, Sheriff, you better take care of him yourself." In an unexpected reversal, the sheriff learns that the speaker is Gatewood. He turns left and tells Gatewood, "You didn't think they'd have the telegraph lines fixed, did you?" As he reaches forward to handcuff Gatewood, Ford matches the action by cutting to a straight-on medium close-up of Gatewood struggling when the sheriff and his deputies secure the handcuffs and lead him off, surrounded by an approving crowd. The greedy antagonist invented by Dudley Nichols goes to his just reward.

Gatewood's arrest is balanced by the film's conclusion. Doc Boone figures prominently in the final shots, in which Ford again uses framing to defy our expectations. In a medium shot Ringo is sitting on a buckboard with Curly, back to the camera, in the foreground, and Doc Boone and Dallas on the far side of the wagon. Just before, Ringo had told Dallas she could go to his ranch across the border and wait for him to finish his prison term. As he reaches down to shake her hand and say goodbye, we expect Curly to jump on the buckboard and take Ringo back to prison. But Curly invites Dallas to step up and ride a bit with Ringo. Ford cuts to a long shot of Doc and Curly stepping left and behind the wagon, picking up rocks and throwing them at the horses. As the buckboard darts forward and exits screen right, Ford cuts to a two-shot of Curly and Doc smiling approvingly as they move forward into a medium shot. Doc gets the film's final ironic comment: "Well, they're saved from the blessings of civilization." When Curly turns and offers to buy a drink, Doc says, "Just one," and Ford cuts to the film's final shot: in an extreme long shot, Dallas and Ringo are heading toward his ranch, the beautiful and rugged landscape of Monument Valley in the background. Nondiegetic music swells, and "The End" zooms from the distance to fill the width of the screen. The generosity of Curly and Doc contrasts to Gatewood's acquisitive individualism.

One might add, however, that the celebration of marginal men and women in *Stagecoach* does not extend to Native Americans. The Apaches (played by Navaho living in Monument Valley, where the film was shot) are the film's group antagonists, and the film shows no sympathy for the plight of Native Americans in the western frontier. In fact, when Hatfield nearly shoots Mrs. Mallory as the Apaches seem poised to subdue the stagecoach, his racist assumptions about Native Americans are expressed most clearly (Telotte 115–27). Civil rights for racial minorities were no higher on the cinematic agenda in this year than they were on the American political agenda.

If *Stagecoach* embedded progressive liberalism within the western, *Juarez* expressed the international conflict between democracy and dictatorship within a biopic. Paul Muni was one of Warner Bros.' leading actors following the success of his two previous starring roles, *The Story of Louis Pasteur* (1936) and *The Life of Emile Zola* (1937)—both directed by William Dieterle—and the company was looking for a third. *Juarez* came about in part because of a 1938 inter-America conference held in Lima, Peru, to promote FDR's "Good Neighbor" policy. Studio head Jack Warner traveled with the official delegation, and discussions led to several film projects designed to encourage positive relations between the United States and Latin America.

Juarez did so through telling the story of Mexico's struggle against European occupation between 1863 and 1868 and giving that story contemporary relevance. Directed by Dieterle, it was scripted by John Huston, Aeneas MacKenzie, and Wolfgang Reinhardt, and based on Franz Werfel's play *Juarez and Maximilian* and Bertita Harding's best-selling novel, *The Phantom Crown*. Although the play celebrated Juarez, the novel focused on the doomed relationship between Austrian Maximilian and his Belgian wife Carlotta, and the film's narrative somewhat uneasily combines both concerns. The film has two protagonists—the deposed Mexican president Benito Juarez (Muni), a self-made man of Indian descent, and the imposed Mexican monarch, Maximilian of Hapsburg (Brian Ahern). Maximilian and Carlotta (Bette Davis) are duped by the film's antagonist, Louis Napoleon (Claude Rains), into believing that a legitimate plebiscite in Mexico has urged them to ascend the throne. After a time Napoleon decides to withdraw his troops from Mexico, which will surely doom Maximilian's rule. Maximilian refuses to leave the country, is captured when Mexican forces return Juarez to power, and is executed. In the film's final scene, Juarez attends the funeral and, standing over Maximilian's casket, asks for his forgiveness.

The film aimed in part to foster good Mexican-American relations and to support FDR's Good Neighbor policy by celebrating a Mexican hero. Yet Reinhardt also intended explicit contemporary relevance in the story, as he wrote in an explanatory note on the screenplay: "Every child must recognize that Napoleon in his intervention in Mexico is no one other than Mussolini plus Hitler in their adventure in Spain" (qtd. in Vasey 156). Like the Loyalists in Spain, the democratically elected Juarez and his supporters are ousted from power. In his opening scene, Napoleon, echoing Hitler's expansionism, says that the conquest of Mexico "is only the beginning of the fulfillment of our holy mission." Learning of the Union victory at Gettysburg, Napoleon is contemptuous: "Democracy—rule of the cattle, by the cattle, for the cattle—Abraham Lincoln, parliaments, plebiscites, proletarians. . . . Am I to be destroyed by such filth?" Rains plays Napoleon as cynical, ruthless, and—in a scene where he poses for a portrait sitting on a wooden horse—ridiculously vain. His manipulation of Maximilian to get him onto the throne, combined with his impulsive withdrawal of French troops from Mexico, leading to a certain defeat for the monarch, emphasizes his complete lack of principle.

In contrast, Juarez embodies democratic values, emphasized by the multiple links between Juarez and Abraham Lincoln. In Carl Sandburg's biography of Lincoln, Robert Sherwood's play *Abe Lincoln in Illinois,* and other Depression-era works, Americans found in Lincoln the essence of democratic leadership, and *Juarez* does, too. Like Lincoln, Juarez came from humble beginnings, was self-educated, turned first to law, then to politics, and eventually was elected president. In some scenes Juarez wears a stovepipe hat that recalls Lincoln, and he is frequently framed with a portrait of Lincoln in the background. Indeed, in the first scene Juarez is reading a letter from Lincoln that praises Juarez and his supporters for the way they "have defended the democratic principle." Later in the film, Maximilian, sensing Juarez's popular support, releases Porfirio Diaz (John Garfield) from prison to ask Juarez if he will join his government as prime minister. Juarez refuses because a single word—democracy—separates him from the monarch. As Juarez tells Diaz (with the portrait of Lincoln framed over Juarez's shoulder), that one word "is an unbridgeable gulf. . . . When a monarch misrules, he changes the people. When a president misrules, the people change him."

Maximilian is initially presented as an enlightened monarch, unwilling to return to elite landowners the farmland that Juarez had distributed to peasants. In addition, a subplot traces the love between Maximilian and Carlotta (emphasized by a repeated musical motif, "La Paloma"), her frustration at not being able to bear him a male heir, and her descent into madness when she returns to France and Napoleon spurns her requests to aid her husband. The scenes of Carlotta's disintegration are some of the most stylistically expressive of the film. Yet Maximilian is portrayed negatively when he decrees that anyone caught with an unauthorized weapon will be executed within forty-eight hours. This decision—leading to a montage of French soldiers killing rebel citizens—earns Maximilian a death sentence after he is captured. Despite empathizing with Maximilian's plight, Juarez reluctantly chooses the justice of the constitution over the mercy of his sentiments, allowing Maximilian to die.

In setting up the narrative as a struggle between democracy and dictatorship for the soul of Mexico, *Juarez* sidestepped one key issue and exaggerated another. Juarez's anticlerical beliefs—his Liberal party took land from the Catholic Church for redistribution—were ignored; as Vanderwood puts it, "A movie calculated to induce hemispheric cooperation simply had to skirt the Catholic issue" (24). The film also exaggerated Juarez's relationship to Lincoln: although Juarez admired Lincoln, he never expected Lincoln to intervene on his behalf, nor did he have a close friendship with Lincoln, as the letters in the film suggest (Vanderwood 30–31). Both these changes helped the film articulate its contemporary affirmation of democracy and critique of dictatorship. Although American reviewers in general applauded that theme—*Newsweek* praised *Juarez* as a "declaration of faith in the principles of democratic government" ("Review of *Juarez*" 22)—reviewers in Mexico were less generous, despite the endorsement of President Lazaro Cardenas, who had arranged the film's

Mexico City premiere in the prestigious Palace of Fine Arts. One reviewer, referring to the Mexican War, objected to the impression that the United States "felt great love for Mexico sixteen years after it despoiled us of half our territory." Another found it laughable that Juarez carried around Lincoln's picture "like it was his best girl" (Vanderwood 36–37). Although the film was named one of the year's ten best by *Film Daily* and was among the top twenty box office hits of 1938–39, it was something of a disappointment because its high production costs cut into profits. Yet it remains an important example of how the biopic was being employed for the purposes of contemporary allegory during this year.

▬▬▬▬▬ *Confessions of a Nazi Spy, The Wizard of Oz,* and *Mr. Smith Goes to Washington*

Confessions of a Nazi Spy, released by Warner Bros. the same week as *Juarez,* offered Hollywood's first direct denunciation of Nazi ideology. Even though organizations like the Hollywood Anti-Nazi League had found many supporters in the movie community from 1936 on, the Production Code Administration (PCA) had made it almost impossible to make films criticizing foreign powers: one provision of the code, after all, required that "the history, institutions, prominent people and citizenry of other nations shall be represented fairly." Unsurprisingly, Warner Bros. encountered stiff resistance from the PCA over the making of *Confessions*—one PCA official warned that making the film "will be one of . . . the most lamentable mistakes ever made by this industry" (Ross 52)—yet the film, after some revising, was eventually approved for release.

Given this resistance, how and why did the project ever get approved? First of all, Warner Bros. had been the first Hollywood company to close its offices in Germany, refusing to do business there after June 1934, and the company was far bolder than other studios in criticizing the Nazis (Birdwell 19). Jack Warner fought hard to get the film made, writing that "we felt it exposed conditions concerning which every American . . . should be informed" (Ross 52, 54). In addition, as Richard Maltby has observed, the government's June 1938 antitrust suit in part questioned the PCA's jurisdiction, pressuring it to accept films with "politically more controversial content" to show that the PCA wasn't unfairly censoring movies ("Production Code" 69–70). Thus the antitrust suit forced the PCA to shift its position, and *Confessions* was a beneficiary. Finally, the film was based on FBI Agent Leon Turrou's autobiographical account, *The Nazi Spy Conspiracy in America,* making it more palatable to the PCA than a purely fictional story.

Scripted by Milton Krims and John Wexley and directed by Anatole Litvak, the film changed the names of the central figures of the spy case to protect the studio from legal action, but it also included many details found in Turrou's account. Two notable features characterize the film. First, the narrative draws on the G-man genre, in which an FBI agent, Ed Renard (Edward G. Robinson, the Turrou character), methodically investigates a Nazi spy network in the United States that is stealing military secrets and sending them to Germany. Second, the film employs a documentary style resembling the "March of Time" newsreels: it is interspersed with a voiceover narrator's commentary and documentary montages that include newspaper headlines, titles of German propaganda tracts, and documentary footage of Nazi rallies in Germany, the German invasion of Czechoslovakia, and so on.[1]

As with *Juarez,* a central narrative conflict contrasts dictatorship (the Nazis) and democracy (the United States). The film's mise-en-scène is saturated with swastikas and other visual evidence of Nazi ideology, and its central spokesman for Nazi values is the intellectual Dr. Karl Kassell (Paul Lukas). Speaking at a Nazi rally in the United States, Kassell urges "racial unity" for all Germans and says that Germans should be "revolted" by the United States, a "basically uncultured" country. He tells his audience that Germans should appear to be patriotic Americans yet should work hard to eliminate the Bill of Rights and the Constitution. When an American Legion member and a German American unsympathetic to Nazism speak up to repudiate Kassell, uniformed thugs start a fight and force the critics from the hall. Fascist ideology is also espoused by Schlager (George Sanders), the Nazi political leader and spy contact. When Schlager gives a speech to German supporters aboard a ship, a sign in the background says "Morgen de ganze Welt": tomorrow the whole world. Later, speaking to Greutzwald (Willy Kaufman), a German American who is uncomfortable with Hitler's authoritarianism, Schlager tells him that the party wants not "criticism, only obedience." (With the aid of two Gestapo, Kassell has Greutzwald forcibly locked into a ship room and returned to Germany for punishment.) Finally, when Kassell is placed in charge of all Nazi operations in the United States, his uniformed superior explains the new German strategy:

> National Socialism must dress itself in the American flag. It must appear to be a defense of Americanism, but at the same time our aim must always be to discredit conditions in the United States and in this way make life in Germany admired and wished for. Racial and religious hatred must be fostered on the basis of American Aryanism. Class hatred must be encouraged in such a way

that labor and the middle classes become confused and antagonistic. In the ensuing chaos, we will be able to take control.

The core of the sinister ideology is clear.

Others criticize Nazism and defend American democracy. The voiceover narrator asserts that the Nazis have created a "new fascist society based on a devout worship of the Aryan superman . . . infused with a glorification of conquest and war," and an economy whose motto is "cannons, not butter." Attorney Kellogg (Henry O'Neill), who prosecutes the spies, articulates the American perspective in his summation to the jury. "America is not simply one of the remaining democracies," he says. "America is . . . a democracy that has a god-given inspiration of free men, determined to defend forever the liberties we have inherited in our Bill of Rights of the Constitution of the United States." After the convicted spies are given sentences lighter than the far "more fearful" sentences they would have received in Nazi courts, Kellogg and the G-man talk over the case in a diner. Renard says that the spies seemed insane, their methods nightmarish and terrifying, to which Kellogg replies: "I don't think that kind of people are going to have much luck in this country. It's true, we are a careless, easygoing, and optimistic nation, but when our basic liberties get threatened, we wake up." In short, democracy trumps dictatorship.

With such a clear political perspective, *Confessions* created a stir upon its release, eliciting high praise in some quarters and denunciation in others. In general, internationalists found it a courageous document, while isolationists rejected it as propaganda. As Joseph Breen predicted, the film was banned wherever German influence was strong enough, and two Polish theater owners were murdered for even showing the film—yet it packed theaters in London (Ross 55, 57). *Confessions* remains notable as the first overtly antifascist critique of Nazi Germany to come from Hollywood, deeply engaged in exploring the "social function of the screen."

That Warner Bros. produced both *Confessions* and *Juarez* is understandable, given Jack Warner's friendship with FDR and Harry Warner's public opposition to Hitler and Nazism. Neither film would have been approved at MGM, the profitable studio advertised as having "more stars than the heavens" and ruled firmly by its sentimental patriarch, Louis B. Mayer. More characteristically, MGM produced the fantasy-centered muscial *The Wizard of Oz*. Compared to the two serious and topical Warner Bros. films, *Oz* leans toward Hollywood's "pure entertainment" portion of the movie spectrum. It was also the success of another fantasy film that prompted its production: once Disney's animated fairy tale *Snow White and the Seven Dwarfs* (1937) had become a big box office success, Mayer optioned the rights to L. Frank Baum's popular children's novel *The Wonderful Wizard of Oz* (1900) from Samuel Goldwyn for $75,000 in late February 1938. Interested in developing a live-action fairy tale with American roots, Mayer assigned Mervyn LeRoy to produce the film and Arthur Freed to assist him. As Aljean Harmetz has noted, MGM made it as a prestige film—budgeting it at well over $2 million and not expecting to make much money (Making 19). A genuinely, almost dizzyingly, collaborative project, the film involved ten screenwriters and four directors, with a young British screenwriter, Noel Langley, and director Victor Fleming contributing more than the others. The musical was unusual for that time: the composer, Harold Arlen, and the lyricist, E. Y. "Yip" Harburg, were involved early in the script-writing stage. Harburg, uncredited, even helped blend various screenplay drafts as the script neared completion (Harmetz 57–58), making the film an early example of the "integrated musical." The film's fantasy elements were emphasized (in the Oz sequences) by the Technicolor film stock; by the elaborate and striking costumes and set design; by the stunning special effects, like the tornado sequence that gets Dorothy from Kansas to Oz; and by the music, lyrics, and choreography during the film's musical numbers. Lacking a single auteur but enjoying the contributions of so many, *Oz* offers a good example of the "genius of the system" at work in 1939 Hollywood.

Interestingly, though, the Technicolor Oz fantasy is framed—some would even say contained—by the opening and closing Kansas sequences, shot in sepia-tinted black and white. Dorothy Gale (Judy Garland) is an orphan being raised on a Kansas farm by her Auntie Em (Clara Blandick) and Uncle Henry (Charley Grapewin). Besides Dorothy and her dog, Toto, a number of characters in the Kansas world—the ill-tempered Miss Gulch, Professor Marvel, and the three farm hands (Hunk, Hickory, and Zeke)—also appear as other characters when the narrative moves to the beautifully Technicolor fantasy world of Oz. These five characters become, respectively, the Wicked Witch of the West (Margaret Hamilton), the Wizard of Oz (Frank Morgan), the Scarecrow (Ray Bolger), the Tin Man (Jack Haley), and the Cowardly Lion (Bert Lahr).

The Oz plot employs a journey structure, punctuated by musical numbers and suspenseful conflicts with the Wicked Witch. After the tornado deposits Dorothy's farmhouse in Oz, crushing to death the Wicked Witch of the East, Dorothy meets the Good Witch Glinda (Billie Burke), the Wicked Witch of the West, and the Munchkins. Heeding their advice, Dorothy follows the yellow brick road that leads from Munchkinland to the Emerald City and the Wizard, encountering along the way the Scarecrow, the Tin

Man, and the Cowardly Lion, each of whom decides to accompany Dorothy to see if the Wizard can provide what he lacks: brains, a heart, or courage. After the group arrives at the Emerald City, the Wizard orders them to get the Wicked Witch's broom if they hope to have their desires fulfilled. In a suspenseful scene at her castle, they achieve their goal after Dorothy melts the Wicked Witch with water. Although Toto exposes him as a charlatan, the Wizard grants the Scarecrow a diploma, the Tin Man a heart-shaped watch, and the Lion a medal of valor, outward signs of the brains, heart, and courage they have possessed all along. Dorothy needs the Good Witch, her ruby slippers, and a "no place like home" mantra to return to Kansas. As she lies on her bed, we realize it has only been a dream. Surrounded by her uncle and aunt, the Professor, and the three farm hands, though, Dorothy insists it wasn't a dream—Oz was a real place and a beautiful one at that. But she also says in the film's final lines, "I'm not going to leave here ever again because I love you. Oh, Auntie Em, there's no place like home." The film thus begins with Dorothy's dream of a wonderful fantasy place over the rainbow "where there isn't any trouble," but ends up containing that dream by assuring Dorothy that home is best. If the dream urges Dorothy to stand up to tyrants in a far-away land, the awakening at home replaces an interventionist perspective with an isolationist one. As if to underline that tension, as the credits roll, we get a reprise of "Over the Rainbow."

Oz was vigorously marketed by MGM as a fantasy, and reviewers—whether they liked it or not—understood it as a fantasy. MGM's press kit assured exhibitors that it had mounted "the biggest and most colorful advertising campaign ever put behind a motion picture," and their posters featured color pictures of the Wizard, Dorothy, and her three Oz companions—close-ups in some posters, long shots in others—accompanied by such phrases as "Gaiety! Glory! Glamour!" and "Magnificent in Its Brilliant Technicolor Splendor" (Scarfone and Stillman 176). Reviewers responded in kind. Frank Nugent called the film a "fairybook tale" told in a "fairybook style," and said that not since *Snow White* had "anything quite so fantastic succeeded half so well" (16). *Newsweek,* also praising the fantasy sets, costumes, and special effects, predicted that most moviegoers "will find it novel and richly satisfying to the eye" ("Fabulous" 24). Even in a more negative review, Otis Ferguson emphasized the fantasy, telling readers that he most liked the design of the Wicked Witch's castle, the flying monkeys, and the Wizard's control room. Despite some "lovely and wild ideas," though, Ferguson felt that "the picture doesn't know what to do with them." In fact, he predicted that "it will be delightful for children mostly to their mothers, and any kid tall enough to reach up to a ticket window will be found at the Tarzan film down the street" (190).

Despite the expensive marketing campaign and a good start, the film was a disappointment at the box office. It opened at the Loew's Capitol in New York, accompanied by a stage show with Garland and Mickey Rooney. It earned $93,000 in its first week at that theater alone, about double the typical amount for a prestige film. But after its fast start, Thomas Schatz notes, it "slowed in the hinterlands and actually ran out of steam in its initial release." Its overall domestic and foreign gross was $3,017,000, and Schatz estimates that because of its heavy production, marketing, and distribution costs, it lost nearly a million dollars. In contrast, the Garland-Rooney *Babes in Arms* had a production budget of $750,000 ($2 million less than *Wizard*!) and grossed $3,335,000 in its initial run (267–68).

Several factors account for the disappointing box office results. First, the high production and distribution costs made it difficult to generate a sizable profit. Second, World War II broke out two weeks after the New York premiere, which immediately closed off some foreign markets but also slowed down domestic moviegoing as people stayed home to listen to the news on radio or read about it in the newspapers and magazines. Finally, the narrative's resolution is troublesome for some viewers, particularly those who identify with Dorothy. At the end of the Oz story, the Wizard doesn't have anything for Dorothy after providing for her three companions, and Dorothy then tells Glinda that after seeking her "heart's desire," she has learned that she "never really lost it to begin with." As Ina Rae Hark has argued, "Dorothy, as woman, must internalize the message that absence of desire ('I never really lost it') is her lot" (33). To end a film that starts with the fantasy of Dorothy's dream of a beautiful and exciting place over the rainbow "where there is never any trouble" with Dorothy's denial of desire and conclusion that "there's no place like home" really lets the air out of the balloon. That may be what the *Time* reviewer meant when he wrote, "As long as *The Wizard of Oz* sticks to whimsy and magic, it floats in the same rare atmosphere of enchantment that distinguished Walt Disney's *Snow White and the Seven Dwarfs*. When it descends to earth, it collapses like a scarecrow in a cloudburst" ("Review of *Wizard of Oz*" 41). The film would have to wait for the television era to raise it into its current standing within the pantheon of American movies.

If *Oz* was a consummate studio collaborative project, *Mr. Smith Goes to Washington* offers a good example of an auteur project contributing to the resurgence of American nationalism. That film, scripted by Sidney Buchman, concerns a patriotic idealist named Jefferson Smith (James Stewart) who is appointed by the governor to the U.S. Senate to fill out the last two months of a term when a senator dies in office. The state is controlled by the political machine of a powerful and sinister newspaper magnate, James Taylor (Edward Arnold), who orders around both the governor (Guy Kibbee) and the state's senior U.S. senator, Joseph Paine (Claude Rains). Taylor has silently bought up some land that he will sell at great profit when it is announced that a dam, buried in a deficiency bill, will be built on that site. Smith, a wide-eyed innocent when he arrives in Washington, is shepherded by Clarissa Saunders (Jean Arthur), a cynical secretary who knows (and despises) the ways of Washington. After newsmen mock Smith as a "paper tiger," he enlists Saunders to help him draft a bill that will establish a national boy's camp, funded by private donations, and built—unbeknownst to Smith—on precisely the same land as Taylor's pork-barrel dam. Paine, who as a young lawyer knew and admired Jeff's father, an idealistic newspaper editor, tries to persuade Jeff to drop the bill. When Jeff learns about Taylor's scheme, tries to expose it, and then refuses to be bought off by Taylor, the machine ratchets into action, falsifying documents to make it look like Jeff silently bought the land to profit from his bill. Paine—the "villain/hero" of the film, in Capra's words (256)—reluctantly plays along with Taylor. A disillusioned Smith nearly leaves Washington, but on the steps of the Lincoln Memorial—yet another film of the year to celebrate Lincoln's image—an empathetic Saunders convinces him to challenge Taylor's corruption by filibustering on the Senate floor. Assisted by Saunders's mastery of Senate protocol and a sympathetic vice president (Harry Carey Sr.), Smith tries to get the message to his state, but Taylor's iron-clad control of the state's media makes Jeff's cause look doomed. At the climactic moment, however, the guilt-ridden Paine cracks on the floor of the Senate, admits his complicity in Taylor's scheme, and Smith is vindicated in an emotional, but partial, victory.

Mr. Smith is a powerful melodrama—in the words of Raymond Carney, "both the most yearningly idealistic and the most shockingly topical and politically realistic of all of Capra's work" (300). The topical political realism emerges from the depiction of Taylor and his machine. The film suggests that representative democracy is threatened by powerful and wealthy men whose disproportionate wealth and power allow them to manipulate the system to their nefarious ends—a perspective widely shared along the political left during the Depression. Capra frequently frames his characters to emphasize Taylor's power: the physically imposing tycoon is often framed in a low angle, while those he is dominating are framed below him within the frame or, in separate shots, from a high angle. In one crucial

Senator Paine (Claude Rains, left) tells Jefferson Smith (James Stewart) in *Mr. Smith Goes to Washington* (Frank Capra, Columbia): "This is a man's world, a brutal world, Jeff, and you've no place in it. You'll only get hurt." A picture of James Taylor (Edward Arnold) above Paine's head suggests the tycoon's power over the senator. Digital frame enlargement.

scene, Paine sits on his desk in his office, trying to convince Smith to drop his plan for the boy's camp. Capra shrewdly frames Paine directly below a picture of Taylor on his office wall, visually emphasizing the power relations between them.

Lincoln's image counters Taylor's ruthless acquisitive pragmatism. "The soul of our film would be anchored in Lincoln," which, Capra wrote, would express "a ringing statement of America's democratic ideals" (260). Two scenes at the Lincoln Memorial are crucial. Smith arrives in Washington as a patriot who can "quote Jefferson and Washington by heart," and his first-day tour of D.C. sites culminates at the monument. There Smith's eyes are drawn to Lincoln's unifying plea in the Second Inaugural Address of "malice toward none and charity for all." The final double-exposed shots of the montage present a close-up of the Lincoln statue's face and a swinging Liberty Bell. The second scene occurs when Smith, after learning of Taylor's corruption and Paine's complicity, decides to pay one more visit to the Lincoln Memorial before leaving Washington in disgrace. In perhaps the film's darkest moment, Smith berates himself for believing "a lot of junk about

American ideals." Apparently, he tells Saunders, the Taylors and Paines carve "fancy words" on monuments "so suckers like me can read them." Yet Saunders refuses to accept his despair and, using Lincoln's example, challenges Jeff to "tear into the Taylors and root them into the open." The last shot of the scene, which leads into Jeff's climactic filibuster, highlights Lincoln's plea that "government of the people, by the people, and for the people shall not perish from the earth."

The film's melodrama appalled Washington but inspired much of the rest of the country. *Mr. Smith* premiered to politicians and newsmen in D.C. just six weeks after World War II broke out, and Capra recalls that a third of the audience walked out in disgust before the film was over. *Variety* reported that senators considered it a "serious smirch on senatorial character"; senators used such terms as "'infamous,' 'treasonable,' 'disgusting,' 'outrageous'" to describe it ("Capra's" 1). Both politicians and some D.C. press members found the film offensive. Elsewhere, however, the film generally garnered good reviews, even in England. In the *London Sunday Graphic* James Hilton called *Mr. Smith* "just about the best American patriotic film every made" (qtd. in McBride, *Capra* 422). In the United States, William Boehnel concurred in the *New York World-Telegram*, arguing that to Capra, "the meaning of democracy is real and vivid and precious—not something to be taken for granted" (qtd. in McBride, *Capra* 422). In addition, the film did very well at the box office, but because of the film's high costs for production and distribution ($1.96 million), studio books indicated only a modest profit of $168,501 (McBride, *Capra* 424). Yet in an era of crisis, the film certainly contributed to the cultural conversation about the essence of American democracy.

Gone with the Wind

Released two months after *Mr. Smith, GWTW* was the year's— and the decade's—greatest box office success. It was also an auteur film; however, here the auteur was not a director but the film's creative producer, David O. Selznick. Although the film boasted the highest budget of any Hollywood film to that time—$4.1 million—it also enjoyed huge advance notice, due partly to the popularity of Margaret Mitchell's 1936 novel: the saga of Scarlett O'Hara had sold 50,000 copies in its first day in the stores and over two million copies by the time the film was released. Selznick had purchased the movie rights in May 1936 for $50,000, and his publicity staff at Selznick International cultivated tremendous advance publicity for the film (Vertrees 23–24). Beginning as early as December 1936 the press had begun speculating about who would play the coveted role of Scarlett, and the discussion was particularly frenzied in the months before Selznick finally announced in January 1939 that he had chosen Vivien Leigh.

Selznick worked with a wide variety of talented collaborators and spared no expense in making the film. In particular, *GWTW* was the first film to use a newly developed, faster Technicolor stock that "put color cinematography somewhat closer to monochrome methods" (Bordwell et al. 356) and resulted in a more sharply defined color image. Selznick also worked closely with William Cameron Menzies in pre-planning the film's "look"; he even invented a new term—production designer—for Menzies's title credit. Part of the film's popularity stems from the fact that—due to the film stock, cinematography, and careful production design—it looks so visually striking. Selznick's active involvement with all his collaborators—which included at various times eleven screenwriters and four directors—demonstrates in practice his belief that a major film should be made "according to the vision of one man" (Vertrees 9).

The $4 million film led to a nearly four-hour movie. The woman's film was an important Hollywood genre in the 1930s, and with its focus on Scarlett, *GWTW* became—in a year of memorable women's films like *Dark Victory, Love Affair,* and *The Old Maid*—"the biggest woman's attraction of them all" (Balio 235). The film's two key plotlines revolve around Scarlett. One is a triangle with her first love, Ashley Wilkes (Leslie Howard), and the charming cad Rhett Butler (Clark Gable). That neat triangle is complicated, however, by Ashley's marriage to Melanie Hamilton (Olivia de Havilland), and Scarlett's own succession of marriages: first to Charles Hamilton, Melanie's brother, who dies in the Civil War, then a marriage of convenience to Frank Kennedy (Carroll Nye), who dies leading a vigilante raid, and finally to Butler. The second plot involves Scarlett's struggle to salvage Tara through the devastation of the Civil War, the death of her father (Thomas Mitchell), and the poverty of Reconstruction, all while trying to heed her father's advice: "Land's the only thing that matters." Scarlett is portrayed as independent, coquettish, passionate, and strong-willed, and increasingly in the second half of the film as a shrewd and sometimes ruthless businesswoman. The firmness of her final line before the intermission—"As God is my witness, I'll never go hungry again"—is balanced with the tempered optimism of the film's final lines, which occur shortly after Rhett has left her following the death of their daughter: "I'll think of some way to get him back. After all, tomorrow is another day." Scarlett's ability to survive—a quality that Mitchell once called "gumption"—surely con-

Bemused Rhett Butler (Clark Gable) smiles when, following his marriage proposal, feisty Scarlett O'Hara (Vivien Leigh) tells him he is "coarse." Moments later, she accepts his proposal in the year's biggest epic, *Gone with the Wind* (Victor Fleming, Selznick International–MGM). Digital frame enlargement.

tributed to her appeal to audiences at the end of the Depression era (Vertrees 9).

The film's conservative social ideology both contributed to its popularity and opened it to critique. *GWTW* portrays the Southern Plantation Myth and the place of African Americans in it from the perspective of the white southern planter class. (Lincoln may figure prominently in *Juarez* and *Mr. Smith*, but he is no mythic hero here.) The film opens with "Dixie" playing softly on the sound track, accompanied by scrolling titles: "There was a land of Cavaliers and Cotton Fields called the Old South. . . . Here in this pretty world Gallantry took its last bow. . . . Look for it only in books, for it is no more than a dream remembered. A Civilization gone with the wind." The "house slaves" Mammy (Hattie McDaniel, the first African American to win an Oscar), Prissy (Butterfly McQueen), and Pork (Oscar Polk) stay with Scarlett and her family throughout the film, and after the war one of their former field hands, Big Sam (Everett Brown), saves Scarlett after she is attacked driving alone through Shantytown. Although in the novel Frank

Kennedy and Ashley Wilkes lead a Klan vengeance raid after the attack on Scarlett, Selznick downplayed this in the film. In a letter to screenwriter Sidney Howard, Selznick wrote: "I personally feel quite strongly that we should cut out the Klan entirely. There is nothing in the story that necessarily needs the Klan" (qtd. in Vertrees 33)—and, indeed, the term never appears in the film. By downplaying the Klan presence, Selznick softened the Plantation Myth and helped broaden the film's popularity.

And popular it was—enormously popular. Seznick used an exclusive release strategy, booking the movie only in cities of 100,000 or more and in theaters seating at least 850 people. Exhibitors charged seventy cents, which was about twice to three times the typical ticket price, and the film's distributor, Loew's, charged those exhibitors 70 percent of box office revenues, twice the normal rate. Loew's and Selznick International split those revenues, leading to enormous profits. When the film finally went into widespread release in the late summer of 1940, *GWTW* had already grossed $20 million. Because of the film, Selznick International generated $10 million in profits in 1940, higher than any of the seven major studios, even though it had only three films in release that year (Schatz, 291–92).

Many reviews were ecstatic—but not all. *Variety,* the industry bellwether, wrote, "In some ways the most herculean film task ever undertaken, *GWTW* appears finally as one of the screen's major achievements, meriting highest respect and plaudits." The box office take, it accurately predicted, "may be second to none in the history of the business" ("Review of *Gone*" 3). The headline on the front page of the *Atlanta Constitution* on 16 December, the day after the Atlanta premiere, read: "*Gone With the Wind* Enthralls Audience with Magnificence." African American commentators were divided between a more accommodationist perspective that praised the film's sweep and the performances of African American actors, particularly McDaniel, and a harshly negative response to the film (Everett 179–80). Of the latter, one of the most forceful was by Melvin B. Tolson, who sharply criticized the film in the *Washington Tribune,* an African American newspaper, for failing to say why the Planter Civilization was "gone with the wind." It died, he said, because it "was built on the rape of Negro women, the hellish exploitation of black men, the brutalities of overseers, and the bloodhounds that tore human beings to pieces" (215). Writing in the context of the war in Europe, as many Americans were seeking to define the essence of American democracy in opposition to European fascism, Tolson felt that *GWTW* was spreading a seductive but troubling myth—the "philosophy of the Big House" that celebrated class and racial hierarchy rather than democracy (223). In Tolson's view, the absorbing narrative of Scarlett's trials and tribulations, along with the film's stylistic brilliance, only made that myth more powerful and pernicious.

In the final analysis, the year was an *annus mirabilis*—one of both wonders and disasters. It and the decade ended with World War II in progress, Americans arguing about their nation's proper response to that war, and the release of *GWTW,* the movie that would rewrite box office records, even as it invited nostalgia for Scarlett's struggle to find love and showcased Hollywood's amazing storytelling and filmmaking skills. Some of the year's movies, like *The Wizard of Oz,* celebrated Hollywood's ethic of "pure entertainment" by addressing itself to the "young at heart" and making use of the studio system's considerable resources to do so. Others directly engaged social and political dynamics with stories set in contemporary America, like *Confessions* and *Mr. Smith,* while still others, like *Stagecoach* and *Juarez,* used stories set in the past to comment metaphorically on pressing current issues in American life. While many in the industry were pleased with the variety and quality of the year's films, they were equally anxious because this output did not lead to greater profits. Uncertainties like the antitrust suit facing the industry and the deepening European crisis made it understandable that many in the movie colony turned toward the new decade with some anxiety and trepidation. Only time would tell where the movies were headed.

NOTE

1. The film was reissued in 1940 with voiceover references to and footage of the 1940 German invasions of various Western European countries added to the print.

1930–1939

Select Academy Awards

1929/1930

Best Picture: *All Quiet on the Western Front,* Universal

Best Actor: George Arliss in *Disraeli,* Warner Bros.

Best Actress: Norma Shearer in *The Divorcee,* MGM

Direction: Lewis Milestone, *All Quiet on the Western Front,* Universal

Writing: Frances Marion, *The Big House,* MGM

Cinematography: Joseph T. Rucker, Willard Van Der Veer, *With Byrd at the South Pole,* Paramount

1930/1931

Best Picture: *Cimarron,* RKO Radio

Best Actor: Lionel Barrymore in *A Free Soul,* MGM

Best Actress: Marie Dressler in *Min and Bill,* MGM

Direction: Norman Taurog, *Skippy,* Paramount

Writing (adaptation): Howard Estabrook, *Cimarron,* RKO Radio

Writing (original story): John Monk Saunders, *The Dawn Patrol,* First National

Cinematography: Floyd Crosby, *Tabu,* Murnau-Flaherty, Paramount

1931/1932

Best Picture: *Grand Hotel,* MGM

Best Actor: (tie) Wallace Beery in *The Champ,* MGM
                    Fredric March in *Dr. Jekyll and Mr. Hyde,* Paramount

Best Actress: Helen Hayes in *The Sin of Madelon Claudet,* MGM

Direction: Frank Borzage, *Bad Girl,* Fox

Writing (adaptation): Edwin Burke, *Bad Girl,* Fox

Writing (original story): Frances Marion, *The Champ,* MGM

Cinematography: Lee Garmes, *Shanghai Express,* Paramount

1932/1933

Best Picture: *Cavalcade,* Fox

Best Actor: Charles Laughton in *The Private Life of Henry VIII,* London Film, United Artists

Best Actress: Katharine Hepburn in *Morning Glory,* RKO Radio

Direction: Frank Lloyd, *Cavalcade,* Fox

Writing (adaptation): Victor Heerman, Sarah Y. Mason, *Little Women,* RKO Radio

Writing (original story): Robert Lord, *One Way Passage,* Warner Bros.

Cinematography: Charles Bryant Lang Jr., *A Farewell to Arms,* Paramount

1934

Best Picture: *It Happened One Night,* Columbia

Best Actor: Clark Gable in *It Happened One Night,* Columbia

Best Actress: Claudette Colbert in *It Happened One Night,* Columbia

Direction: Frank Capra, *It Happened One Night,* Columbia

Writing: Robert Riskin, *It Happened One Night,* Columbia

Cinematography: Victor Milner, *Cleopatra,* Paramount

Film Editing: Conrad Nervig, *Eskimo,* MGM

Music (scoring): Louis Silvers, Victor Schertzinger, Gus Kahn, *One Night of Love,* Columbia

Music (song): Herb Magidson (lyrics), Con Conrad (music), "The Continental," *The Gay Divorcee,* RKO Radio.

1935

Best Picture: *Mutiny on the Bounty,* MGM

Best Actor: Victor McLaglen in *The Informer,* RKO Radio

Best Actress: Bette Davis in *Dangerous,* Warner Bros.

Direction: John Ford, *The Informer,* RKO Radio

Writing: Dudley Nichols, *The Informer,* RKO Radio

Cinematography: Hal Mohr, *A Midsummer Night's Dream,* Warner Bros.

Film Editing: Ralph Dawson, *A Midsummer Night's Dream,* Warner Bros.

Music (scoring): Max Steiner, *The Informer,* RKO Radio

Music (song): Al Dubin (lyrics), Harry Warren (music), "Lullaby of Broadway," *Gold Diggers of 1935,* Warner Bros.

1936

Best Picture: *The Great Ziegfeld,* MGM

Best Actor: Paul Muni in *The Story of Louis Pasteur,* Warner Bros.

Best Actress: Luise Rainer in *The Great Ziegfeld,* MGM

Supporting Actor: Walter Brennan in *Come and Get It,* Goldwyn, United Artists

Supporting Actress: Gale Sondergaard in *Anthony Adverse*, Warner Bros.

Direction: Frank Capra, *Mr. Deeds Goes to Town*, Columbia

Writing (original story): Pierre Collings, Sheridan Gibney, *Anthony Adverse*, Warner Bros.

Cinematography: Gaetano Gaudio, *Anthony Adverse*, Warner Bros.

Film Editing: Ralph Dawson, *Anthony Adverse*, Warner Bros.

Music (best score): Erich Wolfgang Korngold (composer), Leo Forbstein (music department head), *Anthony Adverse*, Warner Bros.

Music (song): Dorothy Fields (lyrics), Jerome Kern (music), "The Way You Look Tonight," *Swing Time*, RKO Radio

■ 1937

Best Picture: *The Life of Emile Zola*, Warner Bros.

Best Actor: Spencer Tracy in *Captains Courageous*, MGM

Best Actress: Luise Rainer in *The Good Earth*, MGM

Supporting Actor: Joseph Schildkraut in *The Life of Emile Zola*, Warner Bros.

Supporting Actress: Alice Brady in *In Old Chicago*, Twentieth Century Fox

Direction: Leo McCarey, *The Awful Truth*, Columbia

Writing (original story): William Wellman, Robert Carson, *A Star Is Born*, Selznick, United Artists

Writing (screenplay): Norman Reilly Raine, Heinz Herald, Greta Herczeg, *The Life of Emile Zola*, Warner Bros.

Cinematography: Karl Freund, *The Good Earth*, MGM

Film Editing: Gene Havlick, Gene Milford, *Lost Horizon*, Columbia

Music (best score): Charles Previn (department head), *One Hundred Men and a Girl*, Universal

Music (song): Harry Owens (lyrics and music), "Sweet Leilani," *Waikiki Wedding*, Paramount

■ 1938

Best Picture: *You Can't Take It With You*, Columbia

Best Actor: Spencer Tracy in *Boys Town*, MGM

Best Actress: Bette Davis in *Jezebel*, Warner Bros.

Supporting Actor: Walter Brennan in *Kentucky*, Twentieth Century Fox

Supporting Actress: Fay Bainter in *Jezebel*, Warner Bros.

Direction: Frank Capra, *You Can't Take It With You*, Columbia

Writing (original story): Dore Schary, Eleanore Griffin, *Boys Town*, MGM

Writing (screenplay): George Bernard Shaw, W. P. Lipscomb, Cecil Lewis, Ian Dalrymple, *Pygmalion*, Pascal, MGM

Cinematography: Joseph Ruttenberg, *The Great Waltz*, MGM

Film Editing: Ralph Dawson, *The Adventures of Robin Hood*, Warner Bros.

Music (best score): Alfred Newman, *Alexander's Ragtime Band*, Twentieth Century Fox

Music (original score): Erich Wolfgang Korngold, *The Adventures of Robin Hood*, Warner Bros.

Music (song): Leo Robin (lyrics), Ralph Rainger (music), "Thanks for the Memory," *The Big Broadcast of 1938*, Paramount

1939

Best Picture: *Gone with the Wind*, Selznick, MGM

Best Actor: Robert Donat in *Goodbye, Mr. Chips*, MGM

Best Actress: Vivien Leigh in *Gone with the Wind*, Selznick, MGM

Supporting Actor: Thomas Mitchell in *Stagecoach*, Walter Wanger, United Artists

Supporting Actress: Hattie McDaniel in *Gone with the Wind*, Selznick, MGM

Direction: Victor Fleming, *Gone with the Wind*, Selznick, MGM

Writing (original story): Lewis R. Foster, *Mr. Smith Goes to Washington*, Columbia

Writing (screenplay): Sidney Howard, *Gone with the Wind*, Selznick, MGM

Cinematography (black-and-white): Gregg Toland, *Wuthering Heights*, Goldwyn, United Artists

Cinematography (color): Ernest Haller, Ray Renahan, *Gone with the Wind*, Selznick, MGM

Film Editing: Hal C. Kern, James E. Newcom, *Gone with the Wind*, Selznick, MGM

Music (best score): Richard Hageman, Frank Harlking, John Leopold, Leo Shuken, *Stagecoach*, Walter Wanger, United Artists

Music (original score): Herbert Stothart, *The Wizard of Oz*, MGM

Music (song): E. Y. Harburg (lyrics), Harold Arlen (music), "Over the Rainbow," *The Wizard of Oz*, MGM

WORKS CITED

AND CONSULTED

"Abyssinia 1935 to 1936." *History Learning Site. http://www.historylearningsite.co.uk/abyssinia. htm.* 23 June 2006.

Alexander, Charles C. *Nationalism in American Thought, 1930–1945.* New York: Rand McNally, 1969.

Allen, Frederick Lewis. *Since Yesterday.* New York: Harper & Row, 1940. Reprint, Bantam, 1961.

"American Masters: Robert Capa." *http://www.pbs.org/wnet/americanmasters/database/capar. html.* 3 Sept. 2006.

"Automobile Trade Looking Forward." *Wall Street Journal* 2 Jan. 1937: 1.

Bach, Steve. *Marlene Dietrich.* New York: William Morrow, 1992.

Balio, Tino. *Grand Design: Hollywood as a Modern Business Enterprise, 1930–1939.* Berkeley: U of California P, 1993.

Barone, Michael. *Our Country: The Shaping of America from Roosevelt to Reagan.* New York: Free Press, 1990.

Barrier, Michael. *Hollywood Cartoons.* New York: Oxford UP, 1999.

Barrios, Richard. *A Song in the Dark: The Birth of the Musical Film.* New York: Oxford UP, 1995.

Barrow, Joe Louis Jr., and Barbara Munder. *Joe Louis: 50 Years an American Hero.* New York: McGraw-Hill, 1988.

Barry, Iris. "The Museum of Modern Art Film Library." *Sight and Sound* 5.18 (Summer 1936): 14–16.

Baulch, Vivian M., and Patricia Zacharias. "The Historical 1936–37 Flint Auto Plant Strikes." *Detroit News. http://info.detnews.com/history/story/index.cfm?id=115&category=business.* 1 Sept. 2006

Baxter, John. *Hollywood in the Thirties.* London: Tantivy, and New York: A. S. Barnes, 1968.

Baxter, Peter. *Just Watch: Sternberg, Paramount and America.* London: British Film Institute, 1994.

Bazin, André. *"La Politique Des Auteurs." The New Wave.* Ed. Peter Graham. Garden City, N.Y.: Doubleday, 1968. 137–55.

Behlmer, Rudy, ed. *Memo from David O. Selznick.* Hollywood: Samuel French, 1989.

Bendiner, Robert. *Just Around the Corner.* New York: Dutton, 1967.

Benshoff, Harry. *Monsters in the Closet: Homosexuality and the Horror Film.* Manchester: Manchester UP, 1997.

Bergman, Andrew. *We're in the Money: Depression America and Its Films.* New York: New York UP, 1971.

Bernstein, Matthew. *Walter Wanger: Hollywood Independent.* Berkeley: U of California P, 1994.

Birchall, Frederick T. "War or Peace in Europe?" *New York Times* 27 Dec. 1936: E3.

Birdwell, Michael E. *Celluloid Soldiers: Warner Bros.'s Campaign against Nazism.* New York: New York UP, 1999.

Bogle, Donald. *Toms, Coons, Mulattoes, Mammies & Bucks: An Interpretative History of Blacks in American Films.* Expanded ed. New York: Continuum, 1989.

Bolino, August C. *From Depression to War: American Society in Transition—1939.* New York: Praeger, 1998.

Bordman, Gerald. "Jerome David Kern: Innovator/Traditionalist." *Musical Quarterly* 71.4 (1985): 468–73.

Bordwell, David, Janet Staiger, and Kristin Thompson. *The Classical Hollywood Cinema: Film Style and Mode of Production to 1960.* New York: Columbia UP, 1985.

Boyle, Kevin. *Arc of Justice: A Saga of Race, Civil Rights, and Murder in the Jazz Age.* New York: Henry Holt, 2004.

"Breaks Again for Veteran Silent Scenarists." *Variety* 18 March 1931: 6.

Breon, Robin. "*Show Boat*: The Revival, the Racism." *Drama Review* 39.2 (Summer 1995): 86–105.

Brodkin, Karen. "How Jews Became White." *Privilege.* Ed. Michael Kimmel and Abby L. Feber. Boulder, Colo.: Westview, 2003. 115–34.

Buhle, Paul, and Dave Wagner. *Radical Hollywood: The Untold Story behind America's Favorite Movies.* New York: New Press, 2002.

Butler, Jeremy. "Imitation of Life (1934 and 1959): Style and the Domestic Melodrama." *Imitation of Life.* Ed. Lucy Fischer. New Brunswick: Rutgers UP, 1991. 289-301.

Campbell, Donna. "'Written with a Hard and Ruthless Purpose': Rose Wilder Lane, Edna Ferber, and Middlebrow Regional Fiction." *Middlebrow Moderns: Popular American Women Writers of the 1920s.* Ed. Lisa Botshon and Meredith Goldsmith. Boston: Northeastern UP, 2003. 25–44.

Capra, Frank. *The Name above the Title.* New York: Macmillan, 1971.

"Capra's 'Mr. Smith' Goes to Washington and Solons, Seemingly, Can't Take It." *Variety* 25 Oct. 1939: 1, 54.

Carney, Raymond. *American Vision: The Films of Frank Capra.* Cambridge UP, 1986.

"Censorship Dangerous." *Billboard* 15 Sept. 1934: 19.

Ceplair, Larry, and Steven Englund. *The Inquisition in Hollywood: Politics in the Film Community, 1930–1960.* Berkeley: U of California P, 1983.

Chaplin, Charles. *My Autobiography.* New York: Simon & Schuster, 1964.

———. "A Rejection of the Talkies." *Focus on Chaplin.* Ed. Donald W. McCaffrey. Englewood Cliffs, N.J.: Prentice-Hall, 1971. 63–65.

Chartier, Roy. "The Year in Pictures." *Variety* 3 Jan. 1940: 5, 32.

———. "The 1939 B.O." *Variety* 3 Jan. 1940: 8.

"Cinema—The New Pictures: *Manhattan Melodrama.*" *Time* 14 Aug. 1934: 33.

"Cinema—The New Pictures: *Our Daily Bread.*" *Time* 8 Oct. 1934: 36.

Clark, Danae. *Negotiating Hollywood: The Cultural Politics of Actors' Labor.* Minneapolis: U of Minnesota P, 1995.

"Commodities in Strong Demand." *Wall Street Journal* 2 Jan. 1937: 37.

Cook, David. *A History of Narrative Film.* 4th ed. New York: W. W. Norton, 2004.

Corey, Melinda, and George Ochoa, eds. *The American Film Institute Desk Reference.* New York: Stonesong P, 2002.

Courtney, Susan. *Hollywood Fantasies of Miscegenation: Spectacular Narratives of Gender and Race, 1903–1967.* Princeton: Princeton UP, 2005.

Cowley, Malcolm. *The Dream of the Golden Mountains: Remembering the 1930s.* New York: Viking Press, 1980.

Crafton, Donald. *The Talkies: American Cinema's Transition to Sound, 1926–1931.* Berkeley: U of California P, 1997.

Cripps, Thomas. *Slow Fade to Black: The Negro in American Film 1900–1942.* New York: Oxford UP, 1977, 1993.

Croce, Arlene. *The Fred Astaire and Ginger Rogers Book*. New York: Vintage, 1972.

———. "Ginger Rogers." *New Yorker* 8 May 1995: 70–71.

Dale, Edgar. "Teaching Motion-Picture Appreciation." *Harvard Teachers Record* 6 (1936): 23–28.

"Dance Conventions." *Motion Picture Herald* 12 Sept. 1936: 12.

Deane, Hamilton, and John L. Balderston. *Dracula: The Vampire Play*. Garden City, N.Y.: Nelson Doubleday, 1971.

Delameter, Jerome. *Dance in the Hollywood Musical*. Ann Arbor: UMI Research Press, 1981.

Deleyto, Celestino. "Self-Consciousness and the Classical Text: An Analysis of *Swing Time*." *Film Criticism* 16.3 (Spring 1992): 17–33.

Dening, Greg. *Mr. Bligh's Bad Language: Passion, Power and Theatre on the Bounty*, Canto Edition. Cambridge: Cambridge UP, 1994.

"Department Store Sales." *Wall Street Journal* 2 Jan. 1937: 29.

DiBattista, Maria. *Fast-Talking Dames*. New Haven: Yale UP, 2001.

Doherty, Thomas. *Pre-Code Hollywood: Sex, Immorality, and Insurrection in American Cinema, 1930–1934*. New York: Columbia UP, 1999.

Dooley, Roger. *From Scarface to Scarlett: American Films in the 1930s*. New York: Harcourt Brace, 1984.

Douglas, Ann. *Terrible Honesty: Mongrel Manhattan in the 1920s*. New York: Farrar, Straus, and Giroux, 1995.

Duberman, Martin. *Paul Robeson: A Biography*. New York: New Press, 1989.

Durgnat, Raymond, and Scott Simmon. *King Vidor, American*. Berkeley: U of California P, 1988.

Dyer, Richard. *Only Entertainment*. London and New York: Routledge, 1992.

———. "White." *Screen* 29.4 (Autumn 1988): 48.

"Economic Recovery Gains." *Wall Street Journal* 28 Dec. 1936: 1.

Ehrlich, Matthew C. *Journalism in the Movies*. Urbana: U of Illinois P, 2004.

Elsaesser, Thomas. "Six Degrees of Nosferatu." *Sight and Sound* (Feb. 2001): http://www.bfi.org.uk/sightandsound/2001_02/nosferatu.htm.

"End of Silent Films." *Variety* 20 Oct. 1931: 1+.

Erb, Cynthia. *Tracking King Kong: A Hollywood Icon in World Culture*. Detroit: Wayne State UP, 1998.

Espy, M. Watt, and John Ortiz Smylka. "Executions in the U.S. 1608-1987: The Espy File." Death Penalty Information Center, 2006. http://www.deathpenaltyinfo.org/article.php?scid=8&did=269.

Everett, Anna. *Returning the Gaze: A Genealogy of Black Film Criticism, 1909–1949*. Durham, N.C.: Duke UP, 2001

Everson, William K. *Classics of the Horror Film*. Secaucus, N.J.: Citadel Press, 1974.

———. *Love in the Film*. Secaucus, N.J.: Citadel Press, 1979.

"An Exhibitor Gives Slant on Damage Done by Picture Smut." *Billboard* 5 May 1934: 18.

"Exhibitors Now Taking to Radio." *Motion Picture Herald* 26 Dec. 1936: 13–16.

"The Fabulous Land of Oz: Dream World via Cyclonic Ride Re-created with Technicolor." *Newsweek* 21 Aug. 1939: 23–24.

"Federal Lien Filed." *New York Times* 25 June 1936: 46.

Ferber, Edna. *Show Boat*. New York: Doubleday, 1926.

Ferguson, Otis. "There are Wizards and Wizards." *New Republic* 20 Sept. 1939: 190.

Feuer, Jane. *The Hollywood Musical*. Bloomington: Indiana UP, 1993.

"Film Executives Costly." *Billboard* 10 May 1934: 20.

"Films vs. Television." *Variety* 9 Sept. 1936: 3 + 20.

Finler, Joel. *The Hollywood Story*. New York: Crown, 1988.

"Foreign News." *Time* 4 Jan. 1937: 13–19.

"Fox Wants $100,000,000." *Billboard* 27 Oct. 1934: 19.

Freud, Sigmund. "Repression" (1915). *The Freud Reader*. Ed. Peter Gay. New York: W. W. Norton, 1989. 568-572.

———. *Civilization and Its Discontents*. Trans. James Strachey. New York: W. W. Norton, 1961.

Fumento, Rocco, ed. *42nd Street*. Madison: U of Wisconsin P, 1980.

Gardaphe, Fred. *From Wiseguys to Wise Men*. New York: Routledge, 2006.

"Get Off the Air." *Variety* 15 July 1936: 1 + 57.

Gorbman, Claudia. *Unheard Melodies: Narrative Film Music*. Bloomington: Indiana UP, 1987.

Gottlieb, Sidney. "From Heroine to Brat: Frank Capra's Adaptation of 'Night Bus' (*It Happened One Night*)." *Literature Film Quarterly* 16.2 (1988): 129-36.

"Govt's Film Salary Questionnaire Permits for No Evasions; Probably Also Utilized for Tax Check-up." *Variety* 16 Jan. 1934: 5.

Hake, Sabine. *Passions and Deceptions: The Early Films of Ernst Lubitsch*. Princeton: Princeton UP, 1992.

Halberstam, Judith. *Skin Shows: Gothic Horror and the Technology of Monsters*. Durham, N.C.: Duke UP, 1995.

Hall, Mordaunt. "Review of *The Champ*." *New York Times* 10 Nov. 1931, late ed.: 29.

Hamilton, Marybeth. *When I'm Bad, I'm Better: Mae West, Sex, and American Entertainment*. Berkeley: U of California P, 1997.

Hark, Ina Rae. "Moviegoing, 'Home-leaving,' and the Problematic Girl Protagonist of The Wizard of Oz." *Sugar, Spice, and Everything Nice: Cinemas of Girlhood*. Ed. Frances Gateward and Murray Pomerance. Detroit: Wayne State UP, 2002. 25–38.

Harmetz, Aljean. *The Making of the Wizard of Oz*. New York: Knopf, 1977.

———. *On the Road to Tara: The Making of Gone with the Wind*. New York: Harry Abrams, 1996.

Hart, Karega, and Sundiata Keita Cha-Jua. "Contemporary Police Brutality and Misconduct: A Continuation of the Legacy of Racial Violence." *Monthly Review* (March 2001): *http://www.monthlyreview.org/301brc.htm*.

Harvey, James. *Romantic Comedy in Hollywood: From Lubitsch to Sturges*. New York: Knopf, 1987.

Haskell, Molly. *From Reverence to Rape: The Treatment of Women in the Movies*. New York: Penguin, 1974.

"Hays' Whipping . . . Films Must Toe the Moral Line." *Variety* 13 March 1934: 5.

Herman, Jan. *A Talent for Trouble: The Life of Hollywood's Most Acclaimed Director, William Wyler*. New York: Putnam, 1996.

Hillenbrand, Laura. *Seabiscuit: An American Legend*. New York: Ballantine, 2001.

Hilton, George W. "Editor's Introduction." *The Front Page: From Theater to Reality* by Ben Hecht and Charles MacArthur. Hanover, N.H.: Smith and Kraus, 2002. 1–32.

Hoberman, J. *Bridge of Light: Yiddish Film between Two Worlds*. Philadelphia: Temple UP, 1995.

———. *42nd Street*. London: British Film Institute, 1993.

"Hold Over on *Swing Time*." *Film Daily* 10 Sept. 1936: 1.

"Hollywood Starts War Cycle." *Motion Picture Herald* 19 Oct. 1935: 18.

Horak, Jan-Christopher. "Avant-Garde Film." In Balio: 387–404.

Hove, Arthur, ed. *Gold Diggers of 1933*. Madison: U of Wisconsin P, 1980.

"*Imitation of Life*." *Time* 3 Dec. 1934: 47.

Inaugural Addresses of the Presidents of the United States: 1789–1985. Atlantic City, N.J.: American Inheritance Press, 1985.

"Indications Point." *Wall Street Journal* 2 Jan. 1937: 21.

"Industry Manpower." *Film Daily* 28 Dec. 1936: 1 + 6–7.

"Italy Ban Hits U.S. Pix." *Hollywood Reporter* 4 Jan. 1936: 1 + 2.

"Italy Penalizes U.S. Pix." *Hollywood Reporter* 8 Aug. 1936: 1 + 2.

"It Happened One Night." *Variety* 27 Feb. 1934: 17.

Izod, John. *Hollywood and the Box Office, 1895–1986*. New York: Columbia UP, 1988.

Jacobs, Lea. *The Wages of Sin: Censorship and the Fallen Woman Film, 1928–1942*. Madison: U of Wisconsin P, 1980. Reprint, Berkeley: U of California P, 1997.

Jenkins, Henry. *What Made Pistachio Nuts? Early Sound Comedy and the Vaudeville Aesthetic*. New York: Columbia UP, 1992.

Jewell, Richard, with Vernon Harbin. *The RKO Story*. London: Arlington House, 1982.

Karney, Robyn ed. *Cinema Year by Year 1894–2004*. London: Dorling Kindersley, 2004.

Kennedy, David M. *Freedom from Fear: The American People in Depression and War, 1929–1945*. New York: Oxford UP, 1999.

Knight, Arthur. *Disintegrating the Musical*. Durham, N.C.: Duke UP, 2002.

Kozloff, Sarah. *Overhearing Film Dialogue*. Berkeley: U of California P, 2000.

Lambert, Gavin. *On Cukor*. New York: G. P. Putnam's Sons, 1972.

Larsen, Robin, and Beth A. Haller. "Public Perception of Real Disability: The Case of *Freaks*." *Journal of Popular Film and Television* 29:4 (Winter 1992): 164–72.

Leider, Emily Wortis. *Becoming Mae West*. New York: Farrar Straus Giroux, 1997.

Lennig, Arthur. *The Immortal Count: The Life and Films of Bela Lugosi*. Lexington: UP of Kentucky, 2003.

"Less Talk Is Bringing Back Vet Film Writers." *Variety* 14 July 1931: 4.

Leuchtenberg, William E. *Franklin D. Roosevelt and the New Deal, 1933–1940*. New York: Harper, 1963.

Levinas, Emmanuel. "The Old and the New." *Time and the Other*. Trans. Richard A. Cohen. Pittsburgh: Duquesne UP, 1987. 121-38.

Lippmann, Walter. *Interpretations: 1931–1932*. New York: Macmillan. 1932.

Lugowski, David. "A Bronx Morning (USA, Jay Leyda, 1931–32)." *Encyclopedia of the Documentary Film*, vol. 1. Ed. Ian Aitken. New York: Routledge, 2006: 147–49.

———. "Queering the (New) Deal: Lesbian and Gay Representation and the Depression-Era Cultural Politics of Hollywood's Production Code." *Cinema Journal* 38: 2 (Winter 1999): 3–35.

"Majors Quit Germany." *Hollywood Reporter* 16 June 1936: 1 + 2.

"Majors to Cut Production." *Billboard* 13 Jan. 1934: 18.

Maland, Charles J. *Frank Capra*. New York: Twayne, 1995.

———. "'Powered by a Ford': Authorship and Cultural Ethos in *Stagecoach*." *John Ford's Stagecoach*. Ed. Barry Keith Grant. New York: Cambridge UP, 2003. 48–81.

Maltby, Richard. "The Production Code and the Hays Office." In Balio: 37–72.

———. "A Short and Dangerous Life: The Gangster Film, 1930–1932." *Prima dei codici 2: Alle Porte di Hays/Before the Codes 2: The Gateway to Hays*. Ed. Giuliana Muscio. Venice: Fabbri Editori, 1991: 159–74.

————. "Why Boys Go Wrong: Gangsters, Hoodlums, and the Natural History of Delinquent Careers." *Mob Culture: Hidden Histories of American Gangster Film*. Ed. Lee Grieveson, Esther Sonnet, and Peter Stanfield. New Brunswick: Rutgers UP, 2005. 41–66.

Martin, Jeffrey Brown. *Ben Hecht: Hollywood Screenwriter*. Ann Arbor: UMI Research P, 1985.

"Mass Industries." *Wall Street Journal* 27 Dec. 1936: E6.

Mast, Gerald. *Can't Help Singin'*. Woodstock, N.Y.: Overlook, 1987.

————. *The Comic Mind*. 2nd ed. Chicago: U of Chicago P, 1979.

Mayne, Judith. "'King Kong' and the Ideology of Spectacle." *Quarterly Review of Film Studies* 1.4 (Nov. 1976): 373–87.

McBride, Joseph. *Frank Capra: The Catastrophe of Success*. New York: Simon & Schuster, 1992.

————. *Searching for John Ford*. New York: St. Martin's, 2001.

McCarthy, Todd. *Howard Hawks: The Grey Fox of Hollywood*. New York: Grove, 1997.

McElvaine, Robert. *The Great Depression: America, 1929–1941*. New York: Three Rivers, 1993.

Mordden, Ethan. *The Hollywood Musical*. New York: St. Martin's, 1981.

Munby, Jonathan. "*Manhattan Melodrama*'s 'Art of the Weak': Telling History from the Other Side in the 1930s Talking Gangster Film." *Journal of American Studies* 30.1 (April 1996): 102.

————. *Public Enemies, Public Heroes*. Chicago: U of Chicago P, 1999.

Musser, Charles. "Ethnicity, Role-Playing, and American Film Comedy: From *Chinese Laundry Scene* to *Whoopee* (1894–1930)." *Unspeakable Images: Ethnicity and the American Cinema*. Ed. Lester Friedman. Champaign: U of Illinois P, 1991. 39–81.

Naremore, James. *Acting in the Cinema*. Berkeley: U of California P, 1988.

"Nazis Go Plumb Loco." *Hollywood Reporter* 10 June 1936: 1 + 2.

"Newsreel Man Held." *Motion Picture Herald* 5 Sept. 1936: 20.

"1936 One of the Most Remarkable Years." *Wall Street Journal* 2 Jan. 1937: 12.

Nugent, Frank. "Review of *The Wizard of Oz*." *New York Times* 18 Aug. 1939: 16.

Ohmer, Susan. *George Gallup in Hollywood*. New York: Columbia UP, 2006.

Ollier, Claude. "Un roi à New York." *Cahiers du Cinéma* 166–67 (May-June 1965): 64–73. Reprinted as "A King in New York." *The Girl in the Hairy Paw: King Kong as Myth, Movie, and Monster*. Ed. Ronald Gottesman and Harry Geduld. New York: Avon Books, 1976. 111–16.

Parish, James Robert, and Michael R. Pitts. *The Great Hollywood Musical Pictures*. Metuchen, N.J.: Scarecrow Press, 1992.

Paul, William. *Ernst Lubitsch's American Comedy*. New York: Columbia UP, 1983.

Peary, Gerald. "A Speculation: The Historicity of KING KONG." *Jump Cut* 4 (Nov.–Dec. 1974): 11–12.

Pells, Richard. *Radical Visions and American Dreams: Culture and Social Thought in the Depression*. New York: Harper and Row, 1973.

Pew, Curtis. "Mutiny on the Bounty (ex-Bethia)." *Journal of Maritime Law & Commerce* 31.4 (Oct. 2000): 609–15.

Phillips, Kendall R. *Projected Fears: Horror Films and American Culture*. Westport, Conn.: Praeger, 2005.

"Popular Front and World War II." *Infoplease*. http://www.infoplease.com/ce6/history/A0857500.html. 23 June 2006

"Practical Television." *Hollywood Reporter* 18 May 1936: 5 + 7.

Ramsaye, Terry. "Hollywood Is Looking to New Business Order with Fewer Pictures." *Motion Picture Herald* 6 Jan. 1934: 9–11.

Ray, Robert B. *A Certain Tendency of the Hollywood Cinema, 1930-1980*. Princeton: Princeton UP, 1985.

"Report." *Newsweek* 23 Jan. 1939: 9.

Rev. of *Gone with the Wind*. *Variety* 13 Dec. 1939: 3, 6.

Rev. of *Juarez*. *Newsweek* 8 May 1939: 22–23.

Rev. of *The Wizard of Oz*. *Time* 21 Aug. 1939: 41.

"RKO Reorg Fight." *Hollywood Reporter* 24 Nov. 1936: 1 + 3.

Robertson, James C. *The Casablanca Man: The Cinema of Michael Curtiz*. London: Routledge, 1993.

Roddick, Nick. *A New Deal in Entertainment: Warner Brothers in the 1930s*. London: British Film Institute, 1983.

Rodgers, Lawrence R. "Introduction." *Roast Beef, Medium* by Edna Ferber. Urbana: U of Illinois P, 2001. ix-xxvii.

Roffman, Peter, and James Purdy. *The Hollywood Social Problem Film*. Bloomington: Indiana UP, 1981.

Rogin, Michael. *Blackface, White Noise*. Berkeley: U of California P, 1996.

Rosow, Eugene. *Born to Lose: The Gangster Film in America*. New York: Oxford UP, 1978.

Ross, Stephen J. "*Confessions of a Nazi Spy*: Warner Bros., Anti-Fascism, and the Politicization of Hollywood." *Warners' War: Politics, Pop Culture, and Propaganda in Wartime Hollywood*. Los Angeles: Lear Center, 2004. 48–59.

Rosten, Leo. *Hollywood: The Movie Colony, The Movie Makers*. New York: Harcourt Brace, 1941.

Rotman, Edgardo. "The Failure of Reform: United States, 1865–1965." *The Oxford History of the Prison*. Ed. Norval Morris and David J. Rothman. New York: Oxford UP, 1995. 169–97.

Saab, A. Joan. *For the Millions: American Art and Culture between the Wars*. Philadelphia: U of Pennsylvania P, 2004.

"Sam Katz in Columbia Deal." *Billboard* 28 April 1934: 18.

Scarfone, Jay and William Stillman. *The Wizardry of Oz: The Artistry and Magic of the 1939 M-G-M Classic*. Rev. ed. New York: Applause, 2004.

Schatz, Thomas. *The Genius of the System: Hollywood Filmmaking in the Studio Era*. New York: Pantheon, 1988.

Schickel, Richard. *The Disney Version: The Life, Times, Art and Commerce of Walt Disney*. Rev. ed. New York: Simon & Schuster, 1985.

"Seek 5,000,000 Boycotters." *Billboard* 23 June 1934: 20.

Sennwald, Andre. "A Newcomer Named Errol Flynn in a Handsome Film Version of 'Captain Blood,' at the Strand." *New York Times* 17 Dec. 1935: 14.

"Simplified Rules." *Washington Post* 9 Sept. 1936: 28.

Sklar, Robert. *City Boys: Cagney, Bogart, Garfield*. Princeton: Princeton UP, 1992.

———. *Movie-Made America: A Cultural History of the Movies*. New York: Random House, 1975.

Slotkin, Richard. *Gunfighter Nation: The Myth of the Frontier in Twentieth-Century America*. New York: HarperCollins, 1992.

Smoodin, Eric. *Regarding Frank Capra: Audience, Celebrity, and American Film Studies, 1930–1960*. Durham, N.C.: Duke UP, 2004.

Spiegel, Ellen. "Fred and Ginger Meet Van Nest Polglase." *Velvet Light Trap* 10 (Fall 1973): 17–22.

Stanfield, Peter. *Hollywood, Westerns, and the 1930s: The Lost Trail*. Exeter: U of Exeter P, 2001.

Stearns, Peter N., et al., eds. *The Encyclopedia of World History*. 6th rev. ed. Boston: Houghton Mifflin, 2001.

"Steel Faces 1937." *Wall Street Journal* 30 Dec. 1936: 3.

Studlar, Gaylyn. *In the Realm of Pleasure: Von Sternberg, Dietrich, and the Masochistic Aesthetic*. Urbana: U of Illinois P, 1988.

Suckow, Ruth. "Hollywood Gods and Goddesses." *Harper's* June-Nov. 1936: 189–200.

Swenson, Karen. *Greta Garbo: A Life Apart*. New York: Scribner's, 1997.

Swindell, Larry. "Nineteen Thirty Nine: A Very Good Year." *American Film* 1.3 (Dec. 1975): 24–31.

"*Swing Time* a N.Y. Riot." *Hollywood Reporter* 28 Aug. 1936: 1 + 2.

Tauranac, John. *The Empire State Building: The Making of a Landmark*. New York: Scribner's, 1995.

Taves, Brian. *The Romance of Adventure: The Genre of Historical Adventure Movies*. Jackson: U of Mississippi P, 1993.

Telotte, J. P. "'A Little Bit Savage': *Stagecoach* and Racial Representation." *John Ford's Stagecoach*. Ed. Barry Keith Grant. New York: Cambridge UP, 2005. 113-31.

"Terkel, Studs." *A Nation Lost and Found*. Ed. Frank and Stanley K. Sheinbaum. Los Angeles: Tallfellow Press, 2002. 72–74.

"Text of Papal Encyclical." *Motion Picture Herald* 11 July 1936: 14–15, 67–68.

Thomas, Bob. *Walt Disney: An American Original*. New York: Pocket Books, 1976.

Thomson, David. *The New Biographical Dictionary of Film*. New York: Knopf, 2002.

Thorp, Margaret. *America at the Movies*. New Haven: Yale UP, 1939.

Thrasher, Frederic M. "The Motion Picture: Its Nature and Scope." *Journal of Educational Sociology* 10.3 (Nov. 1936): 129–42.

Tolson, Melvin B. *Caviar and Cabbages: Selected Columns by Melvin B. Tolson*. Ed. Robert Farnsworth. Columbia: U of Missouri P, 1982.

"*Trail of the Lonesome Pine*." *Hollywood Reporter* 19 Feb. 1936: 3.

"Transcript of the Wagner Act." *Infoplease*. http://www.infoplease.com/ce6/history/A0857500.html. 23 June 2006.

Turrou, Leon G. *The Nazi Spy Conspiracy in America*. Freeport, N.Y.: Books for Library Press, 1939.

Ungar, Arthur. "Nineteen-thirty-nine Hollywood Toppers: Stewart-Rooney in B.O. Standoff." *Variety* 3 Jan. 1940: 1, 28–29.

Valenti, Peter. *Errol Flynn: a Bio-Bibliography*. Westport, Conn.: Greenwood, 1984.

Vanderwood, Paul. "Introduction: A Political Barometer." *Juárez*. Ed. Paul Vanderwood. Madison: U of Wisconsin P, 1983. 9–41.

Vasey, Ruth. *The World According to Hollywood: 1918–1939*. Madison: U of Wisconsin P, 1997.

Vertrees, Alan David. *Selznick's Vision: Gone with the Wind and Hollywood Filmmaking*. Austin: U of Texas P, 1997.

"Waste in Story Preparation Is Studios' Biggest Bugbear." *Variety* 1 April 1931: 7.

Watkins, T. H. *The Great Depression*. Boston: Little, Brown, 1993.

Watts, Jill. *Mae West: An Icon in Black and White*. New York: Oxford UP, 2001.

Weales, Gerald. "Good-bye, Jean." *Reporter* 2 July 1964: 39.

"William Fox's Comeback." *Billboard* 20 Oct. 1934: 19.

Williamson, Joel. "How Black Was Rhett Butler?" *The Evolution of Southern Culture*. Ed. Numan V. Bartley. Athens: U of Georgia P, 1988. 87–107.

Wood, Robin. *Howard Hawks*. London: Martin Secker & Warburg and the British Film Institute, 1968, 1981.

Yapp, Nick, ed. *The Hulton Getty Picture Collection: 1930s*. Cologne, Germany: Könemann, 1998.

Young, William H., and Nancy K. Young. *The 1930s*. Westport, Conn.: Greenwood, 2002.

CONTRIBUTORS

AARON BAKER is an associate professor and the associate director of the Program in Film and Media Studies at Arizona State University. He is the author of *Contesting Identities: Sports in American Film* (2003) and is currently writing a book on Steven Soderbergh.

CYNTHIA ERB teaches film in the English Department at Wayne State University. She is the author of *Tracking King Kong: A Hollywood Icon in World Culture* (1998). She has published articles and reviews in *Cinema Journal, Journal of Film and Video, Film Quarterly,* and elsewhere. She has recently published an article on Hitchcock and Foucault in *Cinema Journal* (2005).

SAM B. GIRGUS is a professor of English at Vanderbilt University. He is the author of, among other books, *America on Film: Modernism, Documentary, and a Changing America* (2002), *Hollywood Renaissance: The Cinema of Democracy in the Era of Ford, Capra, and Kazan* (1998), and *The Films of Woody Allen* (2002). He also has edited several works, including *The American Self: Myth, Ideology, and Popular Culture* (1982), and has written many essays and reviews, including articles on humor and Jewish writers. A recipient of a Rockefeller Humanities Fellowship and other scholarly and teaching awards, he has lectured and taught extensively in universities throughout America and around the world. He is currently working on a new study of the crisis in modernism, the evils of racism, and the "new culturalism" in world cinema.

INA RAE HARK is a professor of English and film studies at the University of South Carolina. She has edited or co-edited *Screening the Male* (1993), *The Road Movie Book* (1997), and *Exhibition, the Film Reader* (2001). Among her forty articles and book chapters are studies of *The Adventures of Robin Hood* starring Errol Flynn, MGM's *The Wizard of Oz,* and Alfred Hitchcock's British films of the 1930s.

ALLEN LARSON is an assistant professor of communications at Penn State University's New Kensington campus. *Alienated Affections,* his book about stardom, social melodrama, and Jacqueline Susann, is forthcoming from Duke University Press. He has also written about the political economy of new and convergent media and public media policy.

DAVID LUGOWSKI holds a Ph.D. in cinema studies from NYU. He is currently an associate professor of English and the director of the interdisciplinary

Communication Studies program at Manhattanville College. He has published in *Cineaste, Cinema Journal, Senses of Cinema, Baseline, Arizona Quarterly, The Encyclopedia of Documentary Film*, and *The International Encyclopedia of Queer Culture*, among others. Forthcoming are essays in such anthologies as *Film and Sexual Politics: A Critical Reader* and *Looking Past the Screen: Case Studies in American Film History and Method*.

CHARLES MALAND teaches film and American studies in the English Department at the University of Tennessee. Among his books are *American Vision: the Films of Chaplin, Ford, Capra, and Welles 1936–1941* (1977), *Frank Capra* (1981), and *Chaplin and American Culture: The Evolution of a Star Image* (1989), which won the Theater Library Association Award. He is currently completing a book on Chaplin's *City Lights* for the BFI Classics series.

SUSAN OHMER teaches film and television history and digital culture in the Department of Film, Television, and Theatre at the University of Notre Dame. Her research focuses on industry and audience studies and has appeared in the *Journal of Film and Video, Film History*, and the anthologies *Identifying Hollywood's Audiences* and *Global Currents*. She is the author of *George Gallup in Hollywood* (2006).

CHARLENE REGESTER is an assistant professor in the Department of African and Afro-American Studies at the University of North Carolina. Her publications include essays on early black film stars and filmmakers, which have appeared in journals such as *Film Literature Quarterly, Popular Culture Review, Western Journal of Black Studies, Studies in American Culture, Film History*, and the *Journal of Film and Video*. She published *Annotated Bibliography of Black Entertainers and Newspaper Coverage in the Pre-1950 Era, Volume I* (2002). She co-edits the *Oscar Micheaux Society Newsletter* and serves as an editorial board member of the *Journal of Film and Video*.

MARTIN RUBIN is an associate director of programming at the Gene Siskel Film Center in Chicago. His books include *Thrillers* (1999) and *Showstoppers: Busby Berkeley and the Tradition of Spectacle* (1993).

INDEX

Page numbers in italics indicate illustrations.